Life After Encephalitis

Encephalitis is a devastating condition whose impact upon people should not be underestimated. It robs people of abilities most of us take for granted, it leaves people without their loved ones, and even in those families where the person affected survives, the person they once knew can be dramatically changed.

Life After Encephalitis provides a unique insight into the experiences of those affected by encephalitis, sharing the rich, perceptive and often powerful narratives of survivors and family members. It shows how listening to patient and family narratives can help us to understand how they make sense of what has happened to them, and also help professionals better understand and engage with them in practice. The book will also be useful for considering narratives associated with brain injuries from other causes, for example traumatic brain injury.

Life After Encephalitis will appeal to a wide range of professionals working in rehabilitation settings, and also to survivors of encephalitis, their families and carers.

Ava Easton is Chief Executive of The Encephalitis Society. Ava has specialised in encephalitis, in particular its consequences for people affected, and family members, for over 15 years. Ava is an accomplished speaker and lecturer on encephalitis and her work has taken her all over the world. Ava has also produced and published several papers on various aspects of encephalitis and its after-effects, and is involved in a number of research studies looking into the processes and outcomes of encephalitis. Ava is an Honorary Fellow at The University of Liverpool, Vice-Chair of the United Kingdom Acquired Brain Injury

Forum (UKABIF), a member of The International Encephalitis Consortium and Auto-immune Encephalitis Association Working Group, and sits on the editorial board of the journal *Brain Injury*. Follow her day-to-day work on Twitter: @encephalitisava.

After Brain Injury: Survivor Stories

Series Editor: Barbara A. Wilson

After Brain Injury: Survivor Stories was launched in 2014 to meet the need for a series of books aimed at those who have suffered a brain injury, and their families and carers. Brain disorders can be life-changing events with far-reaching consequences. However, in the current climate of cuts in funding and service provision for neuropsychological rehabilitation, there is a risk that people whose lives have been transformed by brain injury are left feeling isolated with little support.

So many of the books on brain injury are written for academics and clinicians and filled with technical jargon so are of little help to those directly affected. Instead, this series offers a much-needed personal insight into the experience, as each book is written by a survivor, or group of survivors, or family members who are living with the very real consequences of brain injury. Each book focuses on a different condition, such as face blindness, amnesia and neglect, or diagnosis, such as encephalitis and locked-in syndrome, resulting from brain injury. Readers will learn about life before the brain injury, the early days of diagnosis, the effects of the brain injury, the process of rehabilitation and life now.

Alongside this personal perspective, professional commentary is also provided by specialists in neurology, intensive care and neuropsychological rehabilitation. The historical context, neurological state of the art and data on the condition, including the treatment, outcome and follow-up will also make these books appealing for professionals working in rehabilitation such as psychologists, speech and language therapists, occupational therapists, social workers and rehabilitation doctors. They will also be of interest to clinical psychology trainees and undergraduate and graduate students in neuropsychology, rehabilitation science and related courses who value the case study approach as a complement to the more academic books on brain injury.

With this series, we also hope to help expand awareness of brain injury and its consequences. The World Health Organization has recently acknowledged the need to raise the profile of mental health issues (with the WHO Mental Health Action Plan 2013–20) and we believe there needs to be a similar focus on psychological, neurological and behavioural issues caused by brain disorder, and a deeper understanding of the importance of rehabilitation support. Giving a voice to these survivors of brain injury is a step in the right direction.

Published titles:

Life After Brain Injury
Survivors' stories
Barbara A. Wilson, Jill Winegardner, Fiona Ashworth

Identity Unknown
How acute brain disease can destroy knowledge of oneself and others
Barbara A. Wilson, Claire Robertson, Joe Mole

Surviving Brain Damage After Assault
From vegetative state to meaningful life
Barbara A. Wilson, Samira Kashinath Dhamapurkar, and Anita Rose

Life After Encephalitis
A narrative approach
Ava Easton

Life After Encephalitis

A narrative approach

Ava Easton

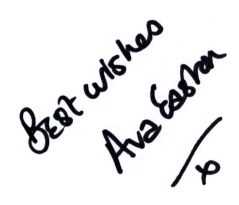

Best wishes
Ava Easton

Routledge
Taylor & Francis Group

LONDON AND NEW YORK

First published 2016
by Routledge
2 Park Square, Milton Park, Abingdon, Oxon OX14 4RN

and by Routledge
711 Third Avenue, New York, NY 10017

Routledge is an imprint of the Taylor & Francis Group, an informa business

British Library Cataloguing in Publication Data
A catalogue record for this book is available from the British
Library

Library of Congress Cataloging in Publication Data
Names: Easton, Ava, author.
Title: Life after encephalitis : a narrative approach / Ava Easton.
Description: Milton Park, Abingdon, Oxon ; New York, NY :
Routledge, 2016. | Includes bibliographical references and index.
Identifiers: LCCN 2015036540| ISBN 9781138847200 (hardback) |
ISBN 9781138847217 (softcover) | ISBN 9781315726922 (ebook)
Subjects: LCSH: Encephalitis.
Classification: LCC RC390 .E27 2016 | DDC 616.8/32–dc23
LC record available at http://lccn.loc.gov/2015036540

ISBN: 978-1-138-84720-0 (hbk)
ISBN: 978-1-138-84721-7 (pbk)
ISBN: 978-1-315-72692-2 (ebk)

Typeset in Times New Roman
by Wearset Ltd, Boldon, Tyne and Wear

Printed and bound in Great Britain by
Ashford Colour Press Ltd, Gosport, Hampshire

MIX
Paper from
responsible sources
FSC
www.fsc.org   FSC® C011748

This book is dedicated to all people whose lives have been touched by encephalitis.

Contents

After Brain Injury: Survivor Stories iii
List of illustrations xi
Foreword – Simon Hattenstone xii
Preface xvi
Acknowledgements xviii

1 Introduction 1

2 Encephalitis: what it is and what it does 4

3 Medicine and the history of narratives 24

4 The survivors 36

5 The spouse 67

6 The parents and their children 90

7 The one who didn't make it 119

8 Neuro-narratives: authors and readers 137

9 Narratives in professional practice 173

10 Concluding remarks   189

    Index   191
    Charity contact page   199

Illustrations

Figures

0.1	Ava Easton	xvii
2.1	The consequences of encephalitis	11
4.1	Roy Axon	37
4.2	Sophie Baughan	43
4.3	Professor Tom Solomon	50
4.4	Ross Buggins	55
4.5	Dr Sarosh Irani	61
5.1	Jean Evans	67
5.2	Phillip, Jean and their family	79
5.3	Janet Hodgson	80
6.1	Kay Adlington	90
6.2	Laura, Rebecca, Chloe and Kay Adlington	95
6.3	David Birtwisle	96
6.4	David, Richard and Marion	102
6.5	Thomas Tarlton	104
6.6	Thomas and his mum, Rachel	107
6.7	Dr Audrey Daisley	108
7.1	Tiggy Sutton	120
7.2	Robert, Johnny, Tiggy, Patrick and Joanna	122
7.3	Dr Michelle Hayes	134

Tables

2.1	Encephalitis sub-sets	5
2.2	Symptoms of encephalitis	6

Foreword

Simon Hattenstone
Journalist and features writer, The Guardian

If only *Life After Encephalitis* had been around when I was a kid. Between the ages of nine and 11 I was bedridden with encephalitis, living behind permanently closed curtains without light, music, television and friends. My parents assumed I would die, and my mum still regards it as a miracle that I didn't. I remember the shock of being asked by an insensitive doctor I was being rude to (I was rude to everyone back then) "Do you want to die?" After that whenever I woke in the middle of the night or morning, the first thing I did was test my pulse to check I was still alive.

Eventually I did come out of it, and three years after encephalitis first struck I returned to mainstream school. I divided my life into BE and AE: before encephalitis and after encephalitis. Not simply because it was so significant for me, but because I had emerged from the illness a different person. One day in my early twenties a woman I barely knew read my palm, and looked shocked at what she saw, "That is so weird," she said, "about a third of the way through your life line stops, and a new one starts." It made perfect sense to me.

I always thought I was a one-off; unique. Ava Easton makes it clear that there is nothing unique about encephalitis.

Back then I had no one to share my experience with, except my mother who had fought through those years which saw me labelled a 'malingerer' and said her neurosis resulted in 'Munchausen by Proxy'.

If this book had been available then, I would have realised others had gone, and were going through, similar things to me. So many people affected are (still) misdiagnosed, so many are labelled cranks or hypochondriacs, so many sufferers think their brain is on fire (*Brain*

On Fire is the name of the brilliant encephalitis memoir by Susannah Cahalan, an Ambassador of The Encephalitis Society), and nearly all of those who contract encephalitis and are lucky enough to survive divide their lives into two – before and after.

This book is equally relevant to survivors, family members, carers, neurologists, psychiatrists, nurses, relatives and even disinterested readers. Ava Easton has brought the same demotic wisdom to this book that she exercises as the inspirational CEO of The Encephalitis Society. Over the years she has taken what was a deadly but obscure illness out to the world, and explained it simply and cogently to people who had no reason to have thought about it before, and to experts who had almost certainly never thought about it in those terms before.

The Encephalitis Society has brought together top professionals such as neurologist Professor Tom Solomon with survivors such as me, bereaved family members, and those unfortunate enough to still be living with the after-effects of encephalitis to create a wonderful, and strangely uplifting extended family. There is no hierarchy in The Society – but if Easton had to choose my guess is that she'd rather hear first from the survivors, then the experts.

She has brought the same philosophy to *Life After Encephalitis*. There is a useful explanation of the different forms of encephalitis, prevention measures, experts have their say, but at the heart of the book is a series of beautifully written, desperately moving first-hand accounts from those who have lived with the illness.

High-achieving Roy Axon alienates his loved ones because he becomes "unpredictable and dangerous". Sophie Baughan has innumerable epileptic seizures in the first 12 months following diagnosis, and has no recollection of the six months leading up to contracting encephalitis. Ross Buggins wraps a belt around his neck and tries to kill himself with it after doctors discharge him, telling him there is nothing physically wrong with him. Kay Adlington, mother of Laura (and of Olympic swimming gold medallist Rebecca, another Encephalitis Society Ambassador) writes about realising something was seriously wrong when her daughter placed her mobile phone in a glass of water and said "I've just parked my car on the motorway". Jean writes beautifully about her husband Phillip who tells her he has a "cement mixer in head" (encephalitis might damage the brain irreversibly, but it doesn't dampen the imagination!) and ends up infantilised, sliding around on his bottom with a carrier bag putting anything he finds into it ("Today I found a stethoscope, a toilet deodorant block and a nurse's coffee mug amongst other things"). David Birtwisle, 72-year-old father of Richard who can do hardly anything for himself, fights battle after battle with benefits bureaucrats convinced the family is trying to defraud them. Meanwhile 13-year-old Thomas Tarlton, who supports his mother, is older and wiser than his years ("If I was to give health professionals any advice I think one of the main things I would tell them is not to be patronising").

Finally, we have the heart-wrenching testimony of Tiggy Sutton who watched 17-year-old son Johnny die from an illness she had never even heard of.

> Our beautiful boy lying there covered in tubes and wires. This was something you saw on television; this couldn't be happening to us. We were still in this vacuum of a twilight world, just existing and not thinking backwards or forwards.

The stories are as humane as they are brutal. Everybody manages to take what few positives there are from the tough hand life has dealt them. For a book dealing in such bleakness, there is astonishing optimism. Laura Adlington marries, has a baby and becomes a teacher; Phillip's hopes are summed up in two words "Stay alive!". Nearly all say that their experience has changed them for the better, not in spite of, but because of what they have faced. The death of Johnny has challenged what faith Tiggy had, but she concludes poignantly: "We have tried to be kinder and more thoughtful, and by helping others, we endeavour to heal ourselves. We have been loved by all around us. If there is a god it is love."

Life After Encephalitis is the perfect antidote to those who say leave it to the professionals alone. Professional input is vital (and is given great weight here), but in the end nobody can explain encephalitis quite like those who have lived with it. Talking or writing about the illness is a coping mechanism, a way of transcending the illness, an educational tool and a means of giving voice to those who too often go unheard. The people we hear from in this book bear witness to the terrible illness they have suffered, nursed people through and lost loved ones to. Easton stresses that just because a narrator might be angry or unreliable does not make their story any less worth hearing. She makes it clear where she stands with members of a medical establishment that might believe patients should be seen and not heard. In the preface she quotes feedback given by a delegate at a brain injury conference in 2014: "I am not sure of the value of having survivors with brain injury [as presenters]. Many survivors cannot communicate so I suggest that you consider this for next time. I would prefer case studies/presentations with clinical evidence." *Life After Encephalitis* is Easton's riposte to any remaining outdated attitudes.

Preface

It is hoped that this book gives voice to survivors of encephalitis and provides unique insight into the experiences of those affected – be they survivors, family members or those left bereaved. Encephalitis is a devastating condition whose impact upon people should not be underestimated. We call it a thief. Their stories are heartfelt, at times distressing to witness, but also full of hope and inspiration.

Despite its focus on encephalitis, the book deals with many issues that can be applied across the board in relation to neurological ill-health and disability, in particular brain injury, regardless of its cause. The contributors to these chapters were not chosen on the basis of their story. They were engaged with the book before their stories were seen in an attempt to deliver a genuine picture of what it is like to live with encephalitis, and to avoid any inclination to choose 'extraordinary' accounts. These are the stories of the 'common' face of encephalitis. Their stories were edited only to render some people and places anonymous, to create a sense of flow, or for grammatical corrections. The 'essence' of their stories were untouched by the editing process.

Their stories are 'extraordinary' however, and provide a rich insight into what it is to live with encephalitis, and to be left bereaved by it.

Often people ask me 'What is your connection with encephalitis?'. The honest answer is I don't have a direct one. My life took a turn just over 15 years ago when I secured a position with The Encephalitis Society, to set up their support service. Initially I was engaged for 30 hours a week and was working from home as they had no office space. Fast forward six months and I was working many more hours. The stories of the people I met both horrified and inspired me – I had come home ...

I want to thank my husband Tony who champions me and my work, tolerates my absences and my moods, and encourages me when I doubt myself or worry. I could not do any of it without you. I want to thank Earl The Dog who brings much joy to not only my home, but also to the staff and The Encephalitis Society offices.

I want to thank our President and series editor of this book Professor Barbara Wilson, OBE for giving me this opportunity and for being such a believer in all that we do in our work for survivors of this devastating condition.

I want to thank Professor Karl Atkin at the University of York who supervised my PhD which was the inspiration for this book, and to all the members of The Encephalitis Society who shared their experiences with me as part of that study, some of whom are contained in this work.

Thanks also go to Lucy Kennedy and Michael Fenton (and the team behind them) at Psychology Press and Routledge for gently guiding me through this journey and helping bring this book to a successful conclusion.

Especial thanks must go to Simon Hattenstone for agreeing to write the Foreword. Simon is a journalist for *The Guardian* and also a loyal and committed Ambassador of The Encephalitis Society. Simon knows first-hand what it is to survive encephalitis and the impact it can have.

Special recognition goes to Bill Ward (better known to many of you as an actor from *Coronation Street* and more recently *Emmerdale*) who is an amazing photographer and who kindly donated the front cover imagery. Bill judged one of our Society competitions in 2012 and has remained humbled by the experiences of our members. Bill's image is from the Antony Gormley installation on Crosby Beach, Liverpool, entitled 'Another Place'. How fitting a title: is brain injury after encephalitis 'another place', one no-one expected, nor would ever have chosen to be in? Are those who die from encephalitis in 'another place'? Or does 'another place' represent the isolation so often felt by those affected by brain injury? Does the slightly haunted, lonely image, looking out to sea, represent the unknown and uncertain future following encephalitis? Thank you Bill for sharing with us what you see (www.billwardphotography.co.uk).

My thanks also to the peer-reviewers who reviewed and supported the idea for this book.

A substantial amount of the work contained in this book is from the doctoral thesis of the author: Easton, A. 2012. *The Role of Written Narratives in the Recovery of People Affected by Encephalitis.* PhD, University of York. Elements of Chapters 3, 8 and 9 contain work originally published in: *Narrative Approaches to Brain Injury*, edited by Stephen Weatherhead and David Todd (published by Karnac Books in 2014), and is reprinted with kind permission of Karnac Books; and in 'Medicine and Patient Narratives', by Ava Easton and Karl Atkin (published in *Social Care and Neurodisability* (2011): Vol. 2, Issue 1: 33–41, www.emeraldinsight.com/doi/abs/10.5042/scn.2011.0082).

Figure 0.1 Ava Easton.

I had found my vocation. I connected with their experiences in a way I had never expected to. As the years went on I threw myself into a PhD and spent a gruelling eight years running The Encephalitis Society full-time, and at night and on weekends studying the narratives of survivors and family members. This book is, in part, a culmination of that work.

Shortly before beginning to write this book I had two experiences which both surprised and disappointed me. There is much wonderful work being done in brain injury across the world so imagine my disappointment when I read the following quote after a conference where the audience had heard eloquent accounts from a brain injury survivor, and a family member:

> I am not sure of the value of having survivors with brain injury [as presenters]. Many survivors cannot communicate so I suggest that you consider this for next time. I would prefer case studies/ presentations with clinical evidence.
>
> (Brain injury conference (2014) delegate feedback)

A few weeks prior, I had been writing a book review which was a wife's account of her husband's brain injury. In my review I stated the book was "a great addition to the brain injury literature". I was asked to change this because I was informed that the term 'brain injury literature' was reserved for 'academic and research-related' publications.

Fortunately they don't represent the majority but nevertheless it remains disappointing to still witness such reactions.

This book is in part a response to these sceptics, and a conduit I hope, in getting survivor and family member experiences more widely and better understood by those best placed to help them; and for survivors – to let them know they are not alone.

Acknowledgements

My first thanks go to the eight survivor and family member contributors without whom this book would be an inferior work: Roy, Sophie, Ross, Jean (and Phillip), David (and Richard and Marion), Kay (and Laura, Rebecca, Chloe and Steve), Thomas (and Rachel) and finally to Tiggy (and Robert, Patrick and Joanna) in memory of Johnny. It is not simply the eight direct contributors to whom my heartfelt thanks is owed but also to those around them who allowed the stories of their sons, daughters, mums, dads, brothers and sisters to be told. I will be forever indebted to you and I am humbled by you.

I want to thank all the members of The Encephalitis Society worldwide – this book is about you, and for you.

Sincere thanks also to the professionals who committed to this book – Professor Tom Solomon, Dr Sarosh Irani, Janet Hodgson, Dr Audrey Daisley and Dr Michelle Hughes – for taking the time to read the stories and share their expertise, helping us understand people's experiences in the context of their respective professions.

I want to thank all The Encephalitis Society staff team for being so tolerant of my absences in getting this book completed, and in particular Phillippa Chapman, our Director of Operations, who shoulders additional burden when I am not there, but in whom I see the same spark I had, when I first began with The Society. All of the team at The Encephalitis Society are exceptional and I am proud to work with each and every one, but I do feel it would be remiss of me not to also send a particular thank you to Jon Ainley. Jon has worked with me for many, many years now. It is his voice you will often hear if you call us in need of support and it is Jon who hears a kaleidoscope of people's stories every day. He is indeed a special chap!

Chapter 1

Introduction

A search of the broader, brain injury narrative literature suggests it to be an area dominated by personal accounts often biographical in origin (see Chapter 3 for more on neuro-narratives). In contrast published journal articles and papers are often single case studies or individual accounts, by people who are in medicine, or professions allied to medicine (who in some cases have themselves experienced neurological ill-health or brain injury). Generally however there is a lack of medical and academic literature by or about people with an acquired brain injury (Jones and Turkstra, 2011; Lorenz, 2010), and there is certainly a dearth of literature concerning encephalitis and people's experiences following this acute illness (Easton, 2012).

In a co-authored paper (both authors having been affected by neurological trauma or disease) Smith and Squire (2007) consider how mentoring, narrative inquiry and reflection have influenced their academic work. It is interesting to see two authors writing research papers explicitly documenting how their changing selves are influencing their narratives and their work, and how through the cyclical nature of reflection their narratives continue to change. In it Squire acknowledges that using narratives provides a new component to psychosocial research which facilitates people's experiences in being understood from more than one perspective. She does however go on to caution about the difficulties in getting this type of research accepted, because of a biomedical dominance in the field. The difficulty of narrative research being accepted as a process with intrinsic scientific value was also one alluded to by Kreiswirth (2000) and illustrated by Lorenz (2010: p. 163) who recounts a conversation with a director of research at a renowned rehabilitation hospital in the US. Lorenz asked if he had room on his staff for a qualitative researcher. He responded by saying qualitative research with brain injury survivors was pointless because: "you just keep hearing the same story over again"! Some authors suggest that the contributions of people with neuro-disabilities are not considered reliable, valuable or important (Cloute *et al.*, 2008; Lorenz, 2010; Segal, 2010), whilst others caution that the temporal nature of narratives mean that some people question their "authenticity, integrity, and believability" (Shapiro, 2011: p. 68).

This book is written in response to the sceptics, and the lack of literature around brain injury survivor experiences, in particular those who have been affected by encephalitis. The book takes you on a journey that explores what encephalitis is and how people experience the consequences of the condition (Chapter 2); why people's stories of their experiences have been important throughout history and how they change over time (Chapter 3); survivor and family member experiences of encephalitis along with professional reflections on them (Chapters 4–7); the impact of people's stories on those who engage with them (Chapter 8); how professionals engage with patient narratives and how they might be used to improve practice and the patient experience (Chapter 9); and a short final chapter containing concluding remarks (Chapter 10). Each chapter that follows this one ends with a useful box of 'Key Messages' in order to provide at-a-glance insights for learning.

Although encephalitis is the condition of focus for this book it does not mean the content is only appropriate in relation to this condition to the exclusion of all others. Whilst the book will spend some time identifying and illustrating the unique attributes of this population, much of the commentary can be applied to those affected by other neurological illnesses and disabilities, in particular by acquired brain injury from other causes, be they illness or accident.

Although the emotional and social impacts of encephalitis and any subsequent brain injury might become more clear after survivors are discharged from hospital and thus beyond their relationships with the medical and therapeutic professionals who treat them, their experiences after treatment – and our understanding of them – are areas that remain poorly understood and rarely given space for discourse.

This book argues that it is important to witness people's narratives and stories, to understand their reasons for reading and writing them, and the impact they have for those who use them. For some, they may reflect a way of coming to terms with their experience of illness, while for others they may be renegotiating a new sense of identity following ill-health. Narratives might, at certain times and in certain contexts, offer a means of support and comfort. Others might not see them as helpful or relevant to their experience. It is hoped greater understanding of people's experiences following encephalitis will help in addressing the gaps around a condition and in an area of work that has received little attention to date.

To begin the journey the next chapter (Chapter 2) examines the nature of encephalitis and discusses its consequences for those affected and their families; it looks at experiences common to brain injury more broadly; and considers implications for people's narratives (for example its hidden nature and issues affecting identity); and concludes by discussing why the stories of survivors, and those indirectly affected, such as family members, are important.

References

Cloute, K., Mitchell, A. and Yates, P. 2008. Traumatic brain injury and the construction of identity: a discursive approach. *Neuropsychological Rehabilitation*, 18, 651–670.

Easton, A. 2012. *The Role of Written Narratives in the Recovery of People Affected by Encephalitis.* PhD, University of York.

Jones, C. A. and Turkstra, L. S. 2011. Selling the story: narratives and charisma in adults with TBI. *Brain Injury*, 25, 844–857.

Kreiswirth, M. 2000. Merely telling stories? Narrative and knowledge in the human sciences. *Poetics Today*, 21, 293–318.

Lorenz, L. 2010. *Brain Injury Survivors: Narratives of Rehabilitation and Healing*, London, Lynne Rienner Publishers.

Segal, D. 2010. Exploring the importance of identity following acquired brain injury: a review of the literature. *International Journal of Child, Youth and Family Studies*, 1, 293–314.

Shapiro, J. 2011. Illness narratives: reliability, authenticity and the empathic witness. *Medical Humanities*, 37, 68–72.

Smith, C. and Squire, F. 2007. Narrative perspectives: two reflections from a continuum of experience. *Reflective Practice*, 8, 375–386.

Chapter 2

Encephalitis: what it is and what it does

I was discharged home and had to believe that my husband was the right person, but I had no sense of certainty about him. Although I could not recognize our children I did have the belief that they were mine. I have memories of that time which are very frightening and upsetting. I had no sense of belonging to this family who I was told was mine. I remember feeling very frightened about the identity of my husband in particular and very separate from a unit of individuals who seemed so intense and confident together.

Encephalitis survivor: Rytina, 2007: pp. 18–19

Introduction

Encephalitis is a thief. In the same way that we have watched in recent months Ebola rob people of their lives and those they care about, encephalitis has quietly been at work for hundreds of years, robbing families of their loved ones, and even in those families where the person survives, it robs them of the person they once knew. Encephalitis steals survivors' capacity to remember as well as their personalities and the types of abilities we generally take for granted: memory, concentration, attention, thinking, judgement, inhibition. For many there are additional outcomes such as epilepsy and levels of fatigue so great that returning to work or education will remain elusive. This is, of course, where the person survives; many don't.

This chapter describes what encephalitis is; considers its global presence; and the outcomes for survivors and their families. We look in brief at diagnosis, treatment and management of the condition. In particular this chapter considers the psychosocial implications for people affected and issues around quality of life. As this chapter draws to a conclusion we will have begun to develop an understanding of encephalitis and why people's narratives may be important. In order to give this a broader context Chapter 3 will look in more detail at narratives and their role in medicine more generally.

What is encephalitis?

Encephalitis is a complex illness in its presentation, diagnosis, prognosis and long-term consequences (Solomon *et al.*, 2012). Encephalitis is inflammation of the brain tissue and is a syndrome with hundreds of potential causes. It can occur at any age, in any part of the world and is caused either by infection, usually viral, or by autoimmune disease. It is useful to think about encephalitis as having two primary causes: infection and autoimmune malfunction. There are two primary sub-causes of autoimmune encephalitis (post-infectious and other non-post-infectious causes) and finally there is a fourth type where people are progressively ill and sadly, in many cases, die. These descriptions can be a little more understandable if you think of them as four sub-sets (see Table 2.1):

Table 2.1 Encephalitis sub-sets

Infectious encephalitis	Post-infectious (autoimmune) encephalitis
This type of encephalitis is caused when someone has an infection which breaches the blood-brain barrier, mounting a direct infectious attack on the brain tissue.	This type of encephalitis is caused when someone has had an infection or vaccine and their own immune system overreacts and launches an attack on the tissue of the brain.
Autoimmune encephalitis	*Sub-acute, chronic and slow*
This type of encephalitis is caused when a person's own immune system overreacts to something in the body it considers is alien. For example in response to a tumour or anti-neuronal antibodies.	These types of encephalitis are often terminal and can result for a variety of reasons. Examples include being unable to identify the cause of an autoimmune reaction or as the result of a persistent infection (for example a mutated measles virus resulting in sub-acute sclerosing pan-encephalitis (SSPE)).

Damage to the brain is caused by the direct protagonist (for example an infection) and also by the resultant inflammation and swelling of the brain.

Infectious and autoimmune encephalitides can present in quite dramatically different ways. Table 2.2 illustrates the symptoms that might present in the two different types:

Table 2.2 Symptoms of encephalitis

Infectious encephalitis	Autoimmune encephalitis
Infectious encephalitis often has a rapid onset.	Autoimmune types of encephalitis can have a longer onset than infectious causes.

Flu-like symptoms
   Dizziness
   Malaise
   Headache
   Vomiting/gastro-intestinal upset
   Fever
	Symptoms will vary depending on the cause but may include:
	   Confusion
	   Altered personality or behaviour
	   Psychosis

Later stages indicating a more serious illness involve lowered consciousness which may include:
   Confusion/Drowsiness/
   Seizures/Coma
Other symptoms may include:
   Photosensitivity/Sensory Change/
     Inability to speak or control
     movement
   Uncharacteristic Behaviour
	Movement disorders
	Repetitive, involuntary motor or
	   vocal tics
	Seizures
	Hallucinations
	Memory loss
	Sleep disturbance

If you begin to think about all the sources of infection that exist (viruses, bacteria, parasites, fungi) the complexity and extent of this condition, and the problems it poses for diagnosis and treatment begin to become clear.

The numbers

For many years statistics around incidence and prevalence were scarce to non-existent. Global incidence figures are difficult to ascertain due to variations such as geographic distribution of causative agents, immunisation policies of different countries and methodological issues such as how cases are defined, diagnosed and recorded. A paper by Jmor *et al.* (2008) is probably the best attempt at global incidence figures: a minimum of 10 per 100,000 in children, 2 per 100,000 in adults and a minimum incidence of 6 per 100,000 for all age groups. If we assume a global population of 7.125 billion (www.google.co.uk/publicdata/explore?ds=d5bnc ppjof8f9_&met_y=sp_pop_totl&hl=en&dl=en, accessed 9 July 2015) then we can estimate a minimum of 4.25 million cases of encephalitis (for all age groups) a year globally.

In 2013 the first realistic figures for incidence were released for England. A study conducted by Public Health England estimates (based on capture–recapture models) an incidence of 5.23 cases/100,000/year, although the authors state the models' indicated incidence could be as high as 8.66 cases/100,000/year (Granerod *et al.*, 2013). This means there are likely to be in the region of 6000 people diagnosed with encephalitis in the United Kingdom each year. That's 16 people every day. This, it is suggested, is also considered an underestimate. Not only that but the study suggests (again considering it an underestimate), that encephalitis is costing the NHS around £40 million a year. This figure does not include the costs of rehabilitation, long-term care and the loss to the economy from those of working-age unable to return to work (Granerod *et al.*, 2013).

This means that encephalitis has a higher incidence than motor neurone disease (Hoppitt *et al.*, 2011) and certain forms of meningitis (www.meningitis.org/facts, accessed 9 July 2015). Yet, despite these conditions being less common, they receive a much higher clinical and public profile than encephalitis. People have often not heard of encephalitis unless it has happened to them or they are caring for a survivor.

Mortality is higher than many other neurological diseases (Chaudhuri and Kennedy, 2002; Raschilas *et al.*, 2002), and may be even higher than necessary in resource-poor countries which lack vaccination programmes for preventable forms (see section below on prevention). Rates of recovery following encephalitis for those who survive are less than for some other forms of acquired brain injury (Moorthi *et al.*, 1999; Pewter *et al.*, 2007). The consequences of encephalitis and its impact upon the people it affects (directly and indirectly) are more often than not social in nature and poorly understood (Easton *et al.*, 2006; Stapley *et al.*, 2008). What follows is a brief and broad account of these consequences, providing context in which the use of narratives of those affected by encephalitis can be explored in more detail in the chapters that follow.

Diagnosis

Diagnosis includes a number of tests and is often considered a diagnosis of exclusion (other conditions are ruled out one by one). Generally a full patient history will be important: what is their health status (do they have any conditions that might affect their immunity – for example HIV; do they have a history of mental health problems, drug or alcohol use)?; have they been exposed to any infections recently (for example measles, mumps or chickenpox)?; have they been abroad recently (for example could they have been bitten by ticks or mosquitoes that may have been carrying infection)?; what is their occupation (for example have they been exposed to any toxins or chemicals)? As a matter of course, blood will be taken and patients are (or should be) tested for HIV (Nightingale *et al.*, 2013). Patients will often be sent for brain imaging (CT or MRI) to ascertain if there is any inflammation of the brain and its extent. Electro-encephalograms (EEG) are used to establish patterns of brain activity. Finally, and perhaps crucially, a lumbar puncture (or spinal tap) will be conducted where it is safe to do so. This involves inserting a needle in the base of the spine and extracting some of the fluid that bathes the brain and spinal cord (cerebro-spinal fluid). This can then be tested to identify if infection is, or has been, present. Some types of autoimmune encephalitis can be diagnosed through specific tests measuring the presence of antibodies (for example anti-NMDA receptor encephalitis) or through identifying the presence of a tumour. In some cases where diagnosis is proving more difficult, a biopsy of some tissue of the brain will be performed in order to conduct further testing in an attempt to identify the cause. There is no single diagnostic test for encephalitis so all of these methods are used to help create a picture that will contribute toward diagnosis.

Researchers across the world are working hard to develop methods to better diagnose encephalitis in all its various forms and excellent progress has, and continues to be made, toward producing guidelines (Britton *et al.*, 2015; Kneen *et al.*, 2012; Solomon *et al.*, 2012). See also the biographies and narratives of Professor Tom Solomon and Dr Sarosh Irani in Chapter 4, for details of some of the latest and ongoing work.

Treatment

Treatment will vary dependent upon the cause. Where infectious types of encephalitis are suspected a drug called Aciclovir is administered. This is really only useful where the herpes virus is the cause (the herpes simplex virus which causes cold sores is a key protagonist in encephalitis); however, it is generally given as a precaution as soon as encephalitis is suspected. Other viral infectious causes generally have to run their course and depend on the person's own immune system being strong. Other infectious causes such as bacterial or fungal are much rarer but would be treated with antibiotics or anti-fungal treatments as appropriate. In autoimmune types patients are treated with a range of immune-modulatory therapies such as high-dose steroids, immunoglobulin and plasma exchange. Where there is an underlying cause such as a tumour then it will need to be removed or treated to help stop the autoimmune response.

Outside of this, treatment is symptomatic and usually involves the type of nursing care used in very poorly patients (for example ventilation, monitoring of consciousness and respiration, sedation, anticonvulsants and treatments to address secondary infections along with keeping the patient hydrated).

Professor Solomon and Dr Irani discuss in more detail the diagnosis and treatment of infectious and autoimmune types of encephalitis (see Chapter 4).

Prevention

Some forms of encephalitis are preventable. For example tick-borne encephalitis and Japanese encephalitis are vaccine-preventable. Travellers, in particular those from many Western countries, have access to vaccinations via their health services or travel clinics, if they are travelling to areas where these types of encephalitis may be endemic, particularly rural areas. Despite this an increasing number of people are travelling to what they consider 'harmless' locations such as Austria, Sweden and Switzerland for walking holidays without considering vaccination against tick-borne encephalitis (www.encephalitis.info/files/8813/8694/8907/Putting_Tick-borne_Diseases_on_the_Map.pdf, accessed 9 July 2015). Vaccination programmes can dramatically drive down incidence in endemic countries. However, in resource-poor countries where, for example, Japanese encephalitis is prevalent, delivering vaccination programmes to indigenous populations can prove challenging (Michael and Solomon, 2012). In addition many environmental prevention measures can be taken such as using sprays to deter vectors (ticks and mosquitoes), using mosquito nets and full clothing protection, and in other instances such as rabies encephalitis, avoiding engagement with animals such as dogs and bats.

The consequences of encephalitis

Whilst some people may make a good recovery, the long-term consequence of encephalitis for many is injury to the brain. Brain injury may manifest in a number of ways, in particular cognitive, physical, behavioural, emotional and psychosocial problems are all umbrella terms under which a vast array of difficulties may occur (Williams and Evans, 2003; Wilson *et al.*, 2015). These are illustrated in Figure 2.1 below. As well as issues with fatigue and epilepsy, people who are affected by encephalitis may experience changes in their view of themselves (or their relatives): they are not the person they were before (Atkin *et al.*, 2010; Segal, 2010). Memory problems may result in a lack of continuity and order to their lives, in particular for those with loss of memory. Changes in personality, a sense of feeling different, as well as loss of control over emotions, thoughts or actions, can be upsetting. People may initially regard these changes as temporary, and are sometimes mistakenly confident of a good recovery (Easton *et al.*, 2006).

Encephalitis and its subsequent brain injury are, however, a hidden disability (Wilson *et al.* 2014). You cannot see a 'broken brain': a concept considered briefly in the next section.

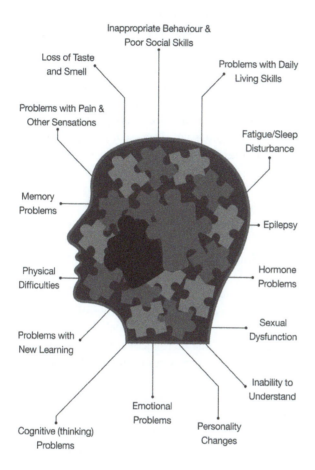

Figure 2.1 The consequences of encephalitis (reprinted with kind permission: The Encephalitis Society).

Brain injury: a hidden disability

If a person presents with a broken leg, everyone can see it as well as the related medical interventions and treatments, and people are also, over time, able to witness progress and recovery (Ponsford and Fleminger, 2005; Stone, 2005). Understandably, during the acute illness, physicians are focused upon saving life and limiting damage. The patient is usually too ill at this point to be capable of, or interested in, engaging in any meaningful way with their treatment or medical team (Rier, 2000). However, once the acute phase of encephalitis has subsided then the time following this is an important but often neglected feature of encephalitis. People are often discharged from hospital once they appear to have made functional progress: for example they can walk and talk. The possibility of acquired brain injury being a consequence of encephalitis is often not discussed, and so when people return to their communities and find they are no longer able to do everyday tasks and participate in their usual social relationships and activities, they have little understanding of what they are coping with and are left frightened and confused.

The primary brain injury can also be combined with secondary psychological difficulties, and Webb (1998) suggests the lack of an obvious physical impairment is "poor compensation for the sequestration of the mind" (p. 543), suggesting "those who are mind-impaired are consigned to the wastelands of social exclusion" (p. 549). A gradual and painful process of adjustment may follow, when the person realises the full extent of their residual disabilities and an appreciation that they may be unable to recover former skills and lifestyle. This process of recognition may result in periods of anger, grief and depression, characterised by mood swings, confusion, frustration and uncertainty. Such reactions are delayed for some people who understandably find it hard to accept their limitations. They may respond with a renewed determination to make a full recovery, and may set themselves unrealistic targets, leading to repeated disappointment and despair (Easton et al., 2006).

Complicating people's experiences further, there is commonly an oft-quoted 'story' of how a person's brain injury occurred, for example a road traffic accident, a sporting injury or as the result of an assault. This is not so for encephalitis. In addition in these early days of recovery the person affected may have no memory of their illness onset and families are often confused and lacking in the information required to understand and recount what has happened to their loved one. This results in a degree of uncertainty that shakes people's foundations, and the impact and devastation people experience when they can no longer rely upon their own minds or memories should not be underestimated.

This lack of an event or accident, along with no memory of their illness onset, is significant and results in a lack of a 'story'. Understandably, descriptions of brains and infections are not attractive, and can be frightening for audiences, particularly where fears around contamination or contagion might exist. Resultantly people have fears not only about the future but also about the responses of other people if they explain what has happened to them. Encephalitis strikes at the core of who people are, creating uncertainties, self-doubt and biographical disruption (Atkin *et al.*, 2010). This, in turn, along with the hidden nature of brain injury all has an impact upon people's social experience and their identity, a concept considered in this next section.

Identity and social consequences

Illness is, as I have already suggested, negotiated within a wide social context that includes relationships, family dynamics, the wider community and environment. Our identity is mixed up within a social context – identity is not just about who we think we are, but also who others think we are, and who we think others think we are (Jenkins, 2006). Our identity then is negotiated within a social context: people have to make sense of what is happening to them in relation to others. Their illness experience therefore is socially negotiated. Particularly in encephalitis it is important to remember that the condition is variable both in its clinical consequences and also in relation to how those affected make sense of their condition (Stapley *et al.*, 2008). In other words, some people are severely affected by the condition and this is reflected in how they describe themselves and the outcomes they experience, while some people report little impact. In addition to this, a person may cope well and distance themselves from the significance of the illness, while at other times they are the illness. These, however, are two separate processes, which will often change over time. The array of problems following encephalitis may be responsible in some cases for people withdrawing from their usual networks and communities, due either to changes in mood and behaviour or because people no longer trust themselves or their abilities when interacting with others (Williams and Evans, 2003). It is also of course important to consider the impact upon the family. Brain injury is a very direct and personal thing, however, it is also interpreted by, and has consequences for, the family and often the wider community (Lezak, 1988). As well as difficulties with memory, mood and behaviour, changes in social interaction may also be seen (Dewar and Gracey, 2007). Therefore people may experience less understanding from family, friends, professionals and the wider society leaving them to feel disrespected and powerless (Lorenz, 2010).

The family of a person with encephalitis often struggle to offer them support, while at the same time coming to terms with changes in their loved one. Family members and carers provide practical, social and emotional support and this can have important implications for their own lives. They are doing things for a relative which they were not doing before. This can include anything from personal care to assuming moral responsibility for another person. Research by Man (2002: p. 1026) on family caregivers' reactions and coping, confirmed that "families' psychological reactions, such as depression and irritability, have been reported to be intense, particularly in relation to the presence of behavioural problems and physical impairment in the injured individual". Ponsford *et al.* (2003) established that anxiety and depression were more likely to be present in those responsible for the care of a brain injured relative. Webb (1998) observed what he termed the "bankruptcy of identity" (p. 550) – a loss of sense of self, or a loss of self-identity that family members often bear witness to in respect of their brain injured family member. A family member's illness can mean a carer might also have to renegotiate their own sense of identity. This may include re-evaluating values and assumptions associated with their relationships (that they previously took for granted). This means a person has to reconstruct some sense of purpose or meaning within their life, all complicated and at the same time realised within the context of their personal and social relationships. Many individuals and their family members do make progress in recovering and subsequently understanding what has happened to them. This is, however, often not done in isolation but with the support and help of those around them (Haslam *et al.*, 2009).

In this next section we consider outcomes and quality of life post-encephalitis in more detail.

Outcomes and quality of life

As mentioned in Chapter 1 there is a dearth of literature on the longer-term implications of encephalitis generally; however, a small but growing literature is beginning to establish that the outcomes and quality of life for a post-encephalitis population may be lower than other similar populations such as those who experience traumatic brain injury and stroke.

In 1999 a study by Moorthi *et al.* discovered that although rates of recovery vary for encephalitis survivors, it is generally less than for those affected by stroke or traumatic brain injury. More recently in a study using a measure called the European Brain Injury Questionnaire (EBIQ – Teasdale *et al.*, 1997), Easton (2012) established that the depth of problems across nine domains (Somatic, Cognitive, Motivation, Impulsivity, Depression, Isolation, Physical, Communication and Core) for people affected by encephalitis are greater in nearly every case than for some other forms of acquired brain injury (traumatic brain injury, cardio-vascular accident (stroke) and other miscellaneous causes). Severe cognitive deficits were noted by Pewter *et al.* (2007) along with abnormally high levels of distress among participants with significant levels of depression, obsessive compulsive behaviours and anxiety.

Similarly when quality of life has been considered in this population it has been found that it can be not only lower than the general population but also lower than for other comparable neurological conditions, for example stroke and traumatic brain injury (Stapley *et al.*, 2008). More recently a similar study conducted by Ramanuj *et al.* (2014: p. 6) provided "compelling evidence that in addition to the significant mortality and morbidity associated with encephalitis, the illness has long-term adverse effects on quality of life for the majority of survivors".

This growing literature is beginning to provide evidence that might suggest outcomes and quality of life for people in a post-encephalitic population can have a depth and gravity not experienced in the same way as other brain injury population groups.

In addition encephalitis is a complex condition that most people have not heard of prior to it affecting their life. This means there is little collective understanding about the condition in the general public and indeed in professional circles, in the same way that there is for other conditions, for example motor neurone disease, meningitis, cancer, and so on. In turn people may experience a lack of understanding of, and empathy for, their difficulties.

Patients recovering from other brain injury-related conditions such as traumatic brain injury and stroke are often in hospital longer due to orthopaedic and other physical deficits. Resultantly their more 'hidden' disabilities such as memory, executive functioning and pain for example, are identified during this time and referrals to other services such as neuropsychology and pain clinics are made. Not so for the encephalitis patient, who rarely experiences physical problems and who is often discharged as soon as the acute phase is over. In some cases referral criteria for statutory services may be biased, catering for more commonly occurring conditions such as traumatic brain injury and stroke.

What we have, therefore, is a condition which is complex, about which there is little understanding and patients who are often discharged quickly and without follow-up. In many cases it is an acute illness, which if the patient survives, is often superseded by acquired brain injury. In particular the acute illness is not in itself the start of what is expected to be a chronic condition. It is only as the injury to the brain emerges in some people over time, and as their awareness and acceptance of it begins, that having had encephalitis can be said to have resulted in a chronic condition. Where people die it is likely to be quick and unexpected for the families. In more rare forms of encephalitis people may experience a long and lingering death, which may have some similarities to other chronic (but unrelated) terminal conditions (for example CJD – Creutzfeldt-Jakob Disease).

Whether these variables contribute to experiencing a poorer quality of life remains unknown. Taken altogether and with the experience of a sudden-onset, life-threatening condition, it could explain why people turn to stories in order to understand and make sense of their condition.

Patient narratives have been a feature of medicine throughout history. Although this is explored in more details in the next chapter (Chapter 3) it is useful to briefly consider here the historical context in which encephalitis narratives exist.

Encephalitis and people's stories

Frank (1997: p. 21) suggests: "Published stories also have a particular influence: they affect how others tell their stories, creating a social rhetoric of illness". In other words the way people tell their stories may be influenced by their reading of stories and this in turn may influence how people perceive themselves, their loved ones and the impact their condition has upon their daily life. The Encephalitis Society staff observe a steady stream of people (those affected or family members and friends) who send in their 'stories' with the intention they be shared with others, perhaps in newsletters or on the website. In many cases the stories follow a familiar pattern: who they were before they became ill, what happened to them (often this section requires the observations of family and friends) and who they are now (post-encephalitis/brain injury). The content of these stories can be moving and heart-rending; confusing and chaotic; bleak and desperate; at other times triumphant, hopeful and inspiring.

Research into chronic and long-standing illness has suggested that narratives play a potentially important role in enabling (some) people to make sense of what has happened to them. Frank (1997: p. xi) states that "The ill person who turns illness into story transforms fate into experience". Frank (1997: p. 13) also raises the issue that "pressures on clinical practice, including the cost of physicians' time and ever greater use of technologies, means less time for the patients to speak. People then speak elsewhere". This combined with other social phenomena such as our increasing geographical dislocation from extended kin, rising use of televisions, computers, gaming devices and other technologies, may all have resulted in reduced opportunities where people once would have spoken and been heard. It must also not be forgotten that the social circles of those affected by encephalitis often decrease dramatically as a result of the limitations they are left with. As already described, relationships may break down, friendships are lost, and employment and colleagues may become a distant memory for some. Personal narratives may therefore play an increasingly important role for those who read and write them.

Understanding narratives in their historical context is important in order to appreciate their meanings for different audiences (for example patient versus physician) and how these have changed over time, and the next chapter looks at this in more detail. During the eighteenth century the patient's story was seen as central to the consultation because this was a time before the development of many medical tests and equipment: the patient's story was often all the evidence the diagnosing physician had. Emerging industrialisation and technologies were, however, in part, responsible for moves away from the importance of the patient's narrative to a biomedical model where the ability to measure physical capacities and strengths were considered the 'gold standard' in terms of diagnosis and treatment: the body became separated from the mind; socio-economic and environmental causes of disease and ill-health were disregarded, and a person's experience of ill-health and disease, along with the meanings they attached to them, were superfluous (Bury, 2001). Disease therefore was considered to be located solely in the body, independent of experience, and patients' accounts of their symptoms were considered to confuse diagnostic processes (Porter, 2003).

A broader interest in patients' narratives has however been re-emerging in recent years because of a shift in acute, life-threatening (often infectious) diseases to more complex chronic states resulting in changes in how they are understood, greater awareness of the wider implications of living with long-term disability and a cultural shift towards self-care and self-management of long-term conditions (Cooper, 2004; Nettleton, 2006). What patients think and say therefore has become more important.

This is mirrored in our experiences of encephalitis over the last four decades. The mortality rate of herpes simplex encephalitis (one sub-type of encephalitis) was in the region of 80 per cent; however, with the introduction of Aciclovir (an antiviral agent introduced to the market in 1984), mortality has reduced to 10–30 per cent (Chaudhuri and Kennedy, 2002). Consequently, more people are surviving. Not only are they surviving but they also have to live with the consequences of the damage to their brain. As reported earlier people often report a sense of loss in terms of their skills or capacity, and relationships, as well as describing a "loss of sense of self" following their illness. It is perhaps these losses that contribute to the need to better understand and make sense of their experience or those of a family member. Narratives are one way of achieving this, and are therefore not only a tool which can be utilised by those affected by ill-health, but which can also be useful in supporting healthcare professionals to better understand how people experience their condition.

Conclusion

Encephalitis is, as I have shown, a complex syndrome with variable outcomes and severity. It is a disease considered acute but which, in fact, has long-term consequences and implications for those who sustain injury to the brain as a result. This is further complicated by the hidden nature of brain injury and the lack of a collective understanding for a condition most people have never heard of. These factors often result in a state of confusion for those involved and those supporting them, as well as changes to how people see themselves and feelings around who they once were and who they are now.

Narratives have had a long history and may offer those affected by encephalitis one way of making sense of, and coping with, their condition. In the next chapter (Chapter 3) we look in more detail at the history of medicine and narratives as this provides a framework for understanding people's use of narratives today, professionals' responses to them and the personal, social and environmental influences that contribute to their changing use over time. Chapter 3 therefore sets the historical scene before the book continues by looking in more detail at some of the stories people write post-encephalitis.

Key messages

- Encephalitis is often an acute illness, and a medical emergency.
- Encephalitis may be caused by infection or by the person's own immune system.
- Brain scanning and lumbar puncture are key investigative procedures in diagnosing encephalitis and determining its cause.
- Acquired Brain Injury (ABI) can be a consequence of encephalitis.
- Epilepsy can be a consequence of encephalitis, along with fatigue, memory problems and differences in personality, behaviour and emotion.

- There are in the region of 6000 cases of encephalitis in the UK, and an estimated 4.25 million worldwide, each year.
- Some forms of encephalitis are vaccine-preventable.
- Brain injury is a hidden disability.
- Outcomes and quality of life post-encephalitis may have a depth and gravity not experienced by some other brain injury populations.
- Narratives are one way people might better understand, and make sense of, what has happened to them post-illness.

References

Atkin, K., Stapley, S. and Easton, A. 2010. No one listens to me, nobody believes me: self management and the experience of living with encephalitis. *Social Science and Medicine*, 71, 386–393.

Britton, P. N., Eastwood, K., Paterson, B., Durrheim, D. N., Dale, R. C., Cheng, A. C., Kenedi, C., Brew, B. J., Burrow, J., Nagree, Y., Leman, P., Smith, D. W., Read, K., Booy, R., Jones, C. A., Australasian Society of Infectious Diseases, Australasian College of Emergency Medicine, Australian, New Zealand Association of Neurologists & The Public Health Association of Australia. 2015. Consensus guidelines for the investigation and management of encephalitis in adults and children in Australia and New Zealand. *Internal Medicine Journal*, 45, 563–576.

Bury, M. 2001. Illness narratives: fact or fiction. *Sociology of Health and Illness*, 23, 263–285.

Chaudhuri, A. and Kennedy P. G. E. 2002. Diagnosis and treatment of viral encephalitis. *Postgraduate Medical Journal*, 78, 575–583.

Cooper, J. 2004. *From Patient to Person: The Living Well Report*, London, The Long-term Medical Conditions Alliance.

Dewar, B.-K. and Gracey, F. 2007. 'Am not was': cognitive-behavioural therapy for adjustment and identity change following herpes simplex encephalitis. *Neuropsychological Rehabilitation*, 17, 602–620.

Easton, A. 2012. *The Role of Written Narratives in the Recovery of People Affected by Encephalitis.* PhD, University of York.

Easton, A., Atkin, K. and Dowell, E. 2006. Encephalitis, a service orphan: the need for more research and access to neuropsychology. *British Journal of Neuroscience Nursing*, 2, 488–492.

Frank, A. W. 1997. *The Wounded Storyteller: Body, Illness and Ethics*, Chicago, University of Chicago Press.

Granerod, J., Cousens, S., Davies, N. W. S., Crowcroft, N. S. and Thomas, S. L. 2013. New estimates of incidence of encephalitis in England. *Emerging Infectious Diseases*, 19, 1455–1462.

Haslam, A., Jetten, J., Postmes, T. and Haslam, C. 2009. Social identity, health and well-being: an emerging agenda for applied psychology. *Applied Psychology*, 58, 1–23.

Hoppitt, T., Pall, H., Calvert, M., Gill, P., Yao, L., Ramsay, J., James, G., Conduit, J. and Sackley, C. 2011. A systematic review of the incidence and prevalence of long-term neurological conditions in the UK. *Neuroepidemiology*, 36, 19–28.

Jenkins, R. 2006. *Social Identity*, Abingdon, Oxon, Routledge.

Jmor, F., Emsley, H., Fischer, M., Solomon, T. and Lewthwaite, P. 2008. The incidence of acute encephalitis syndrome in Western industrialised and tropical countries. *Virology Journal*, 5, 1–13.

Kneen, R., Michael, B. D., Menson, E., Mehta, B., Easton, A., Hemingway, C., Klapper, P. E., Vincent, A., Lim, M., Carrol, E. and Solomon, T. 2012. Management of suspected viral encephalitis in children – Association of British Neurologists and British Paediatric Allergy, Immunology and Infection Group National Guidelines. *Journal of Infection*, 64, 449–477.

Lezak, M. D. 1988. Brain damage is a family affair. *Journal of Clinical and Experimental Psychology*, 10, 11–23.

Lorenz, L. 2010. *Brain Injury Survivors: Narratives of Rehabilitation and Healing*, London, Lynne Rienner Publishers.

Man, D. W. K. 2002. Family caregivers' reactions and coping for persons with brain injury. *Brain Injury*, 16, 1025–1037.

Michael, B. D. and Solomon, T. 2012. Seizures and encephalitis: clinical features, management, and potential pathophysiologic mechanisms. *Epilepsia*, 53, 63–71.

Moorthi, S., Schneider, W. N. and Dombovy, M. L. 1999. Rehabilitation outcomes in encephalitis – a retrospective study 1990–1997. *Brain Injury*, 13, 139–146.

Nettleton, S. 2006. *The Sociology of Health and Illness*, Cambridge, UK, Polity Press.

Nightingale, S., Michael, B., Defres, S., Benjamin, L. and Solomon, T. 2013. Test them all: an easily diagnosed and readily treatable cause of dementia with life-threatening consequences if missed. *Practical Neurology*, 13, 354–356.

Pewter, S. M., Williams, W. H., Haslam, C. and Kay, J. M. 2007. Neuropsychological and psychiatric profiles of acute encephalitis in adults. *In:* Dewar, B.-K. and Williams, W. H. (eds) *Encephalitis: Assessment and Rehabilitation Across the Lifespan*, Hove, Psychology Press.

Ponsford, J. and Fleminger, S. 2005. Long term outcome after traumatic brain injury. *British Medical Journal*, 331, 1419–1420.

Ponsford, J., Olver, J., Ponsford, M. and Nelms, R. 2003. Long-term adjustment of families following traumatic brain injury where comprehensive rehabilitation has been provided. *Brain Injury*, 17, 453–468.

Porter, R. 2003. *Blood & Guts: A Short History of Medicine*, London, Penguin Books.

Ramanuj, P. P., Granerød, J., Brown, D. W. G., Davies, N. W. S., Conti, S. and Crowcroft, N. S. 2014. Quality of life and associated socio-clinical factors after encephalitis in children and adults in England: a population-based, prospective cohort study. *PLoS ONE*, 9.

Raschilas, F., Wolff, M., Delatour, F., Chauffaut, C., de Broucker, T., Chevret, S., Lebon, P., Canton, P. and Rozenberg, F. 2002. Outcome of and prognostic factors for herpes simplex encephalitis in adult patients: results of a multicenter study. *Communicable Infectious Diseases*, 35, 254–260.

Rier, D. A. 2000. The missing voice of the critically ill: a medical sociologist's first-person account. *Sociology of Health and Illness*, 22, 68–93.

Rytina, C. 2007. My life post HSE. *ACNR*, 6 (6), January–February. www. acnr.co.uk/JF07/ACNR_JF07_mylife.pdf (accessed 29 October 2015).

Segal, D. 2010. Exploring the importance of identity following acquired brain injury: a review of the literature. *International Journal of Child, Youth and Family Studies*, 1, 293–314.

Solomon, T., Michael, B. D., Smith, P. E., Sanderson, F., Davies, N. W. S., Hart, I. J., Holland, M., Easton, A., Buckley, C., Kneen, R. and Beeching, N. J. 2012. Management of suspected viral encephalitis in adults – Association of British Neurologists and British Infection Association National Guidelines. *Journal of Infection*, 64, 347–373.

Stapley, S., Atkin, K. and Easton, A. 2008. *Making Sense of Chronic Pain Among People Who Have Had Encephalitis and Developing Service Support that Meets Their Needs*, York: University of York and the Encephalitis Society.

Stone, S. D. 2005. Reactions to invisible disability: the experiences of young women survivors of hemorrhagic stroke. *Disability and Rehabilitation*, 27, 293–304.

Teasdale, T. W., Christensen, A. L., Willmes, K., Deloche, G., Braga, L., Stachowiak, F. Vendrell, J. M., Castro-Caldas, A., Laaksonen, R. K. and Leclercq, M. 1997. Subjective experience in brain-injured patients and their close relatives: a European Brain Injury Questionnaire Study. *Brain Injury*, 11 (8), 543–563.

Webb, D. 1998. A 'revenge' on modern times: notes on traumatic brain injury. *Sociology*, 32, 541–555.

Williams, H. W. and Evans, J. 2003. Brain injury and emotion: an overview to a special issue on biopsychosocial approaches in neurorehabilitation. *In:* Williams, H. W. and Evans, J. (eds) *Biopsychosocial Approaches in Neuro-rehabilitation*, Hove, Psychology Press.

Wilson, B. A., Robertson, C. and Mole, J. 2015. *Identity Unknown: How Acute Brain Disease Can Destroy Knowledge of Oneself and Others*, Hove, Psychology Press.

Wilson, B. A., Winegardner, J. and Ashworth, F. 2014. *Life After Brain Injury: Survivors' Stories*, Hove, Psychology Press.

Chapter 3

Medicine and the history of narratives

Narratives are an integral and important element in modern society. Their use in medicine reflects a changing relationship between patient and doctor...

Introduction

Chapter 1 provided a broad overview and context for this book highlighting in particular its rationale, importance and intention to address not only the importance of narratives post-encephalitis, but also some of the gaps in the existing literature. Chapter 2 presented in detail what encephalitis is, its outcomes and that narratives play a part in both history, and for people post-illness. This chapter aims to provide a context that is broader than simply the condition itself. Narratives have become increasingly popular as a way of understanding the experience of illness. This interest, especially among healthcare professionals, does not occur in a vacuum. In order to understand the narratives of people affected by encephalitis today, a broad understanding of narratives historically helps set the scene and explain how people's narratives of illness and recovery have evolved; some of the key influences upon them; society's changing approach to them; and how they have changed over time. In particular we consider a relatively recent phenomenon: the neuro-narrative, its impact and the public's curiosity and interest in this growing genre. This chapter, along with Chapter 2 which considered encephalitis in detail, provide the foundations for the rest of the book, which looks at people's narratives in more detail (Chapters 4–7), their use by both authors and readers (Chapter 8) and their use and usefulness in professional practice (Chapter 9).

Medicine and narratives

Narratives are an important and central part of how we communicate and engage with each other as social beings as well as being a legitimation of who we are, and more broadly how we make sense of what is happening to us (Bury, 2001; Murray, 2000). People following encephalitis are sometimes drawn to, and in certain cases compelled, to document their story, as well as read the stories of others. These actions may, as Barthes (1992: pp. 251–252) suggests in the quote below, be intrinsic to the human condition:

> [N]arrative is present in every age, in every place, in every society; it begins with the very history of mankind [*sic*] and there nowhere is nor has been a people without narrative. All classes, all human groups, have their narratives, enjoyment of which is very often shared by men with different, even opposing, cultural backgrounds. Caring nothing for the division between good and bad literature, narrative is international, transhistorical, transcultural: it is simply there, like life itself.

The use (and perhaps usefulness) of narratives in medical contexts has changed noticeably during the last two centuries (Easton and Atkin, 2011). The eighteenth century saw physicians concentrating less on the physical examination of a patient and more on what their patients had to say about their condition and its history (Bury, 2001; Hogarth and Marks, 1998; Porter, 2003). This was one of few therapeutic interventions available to the physician at that time but, nonetheless, it was the standard by which 'good' physicians were judged (Wotton, 2006). By the mid-nineteenth century, however, developing technologies, used to objectify health and disease (such as the stethoscope, microscope and X-rays), alongside the rise of the hospital, altered the balance of power in the doctor-patient relationship (Bell, 2000; Carroll, 1998; Jewson, 2009; Kalitzkus and Matthiessen 2009; Porter, 2003). This reflected changing ideas about the body and the role of medicine in treating disease (located in the body), which could be scientifically identified, treated and cured with active input from an expert practitioner (Bury, 2001; Carroll, 1998; Porter, 2003). Illness on the other hand reflects more how people and those around them respond to ill-health (Carroll, 1998).

This reliance upon quantitative evidence (measuring bodily disease) over its qualitative counterpart (the patient's illness narrative), and the more general embodiment of disease saw the beginning of a divergence, which placed opposing significance on the value of the patient's narrative: what people thought about their illness became largely irrelevant (Atkin, 1991). Their narratives moved from the centre of the consultation to its peripheries: transforming into the doctor's case study. Medical practitioners began to engage with vast numbers of patients, many of whom were not personally known to them, which was in direct contrast to family doctors who knew their patients by name and had often treated generations of the same family (Porter, 2003).

During the nineteenth and twentieth centuries medicine saw large-scale expansion and access for the masses continued to grow. The resultant demand for services, along with calls upon precious resources, also meant time pressures, with health professionals having less time to hear their patients' stories. Despite this the latter half of the twentieth century and the beginning of the twenty-first century saw a theoretical return to the importance of the patient's story (Charon, 2001). This resulted from a shift in seeing patients as complex beings made up of many varying factors: their childhood, their environment, their physical self and their emotional and mental self (Nettleton, 2006), and the recognition that modern medicine has its limitations (Carroll, 1998).

There are many conditions for which medicine can offer very little except support. The rise of long-standing illness and a shift from curative to more palliative forms of medicine, along with greater consideration of alternative treatments illustrate this and aim to place the patient at the centre of their health/illness experience (Bury, 2001; Charon, 2001; Nettleton, 2006). The patient is increasingly being seen both as a participant-consumer with rights and responsibilities (self-care) and therefore someone who should be engaged with and who can participate both in the decision-making around their health status and management of their condition and recovery (Department of Health, 2005). Self-management and expert patient programmes see individuals encouraged to engage with, and take greater responsibility for their 'illness experience' (Kendall *et al.*, 2007; Scholz *et al.*, 2006; Tattersall, 2002); cognitive behaviour therapy (CBT) encourages the individual to use their own insight, skills and resources to cope better with, and in some cases reframe, the consequences of their illness.

These significant shifts can, in part, be explained as a response to the changing nature of health and illness: infections are less prevalent, our increased capacity to save and sustain life, and disease that is more chronic, and less life-threatening (Carroll, 1998). This combined with increased life expectancy has resulted in medicine's changing response, from hospital-based interventions to community-based preventions, and where ill-health does exist, to a joint management approach between physician and patient. Health becomes the focus as opposed to disease, with the emphasis upon the person and prevention of ill-health as opposed to cure. These paradigmatic shifts in healthcare are neatly illustrated in Box 3.1:

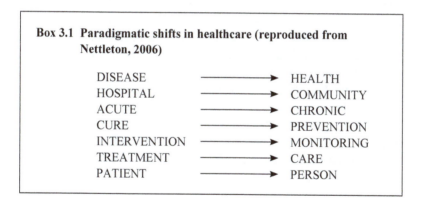

Box 3.1 **Paradigmatic shifts in healthcare (reproduced from Nettleton, 2006)**

DISEASE	HEALTH
HOSPITAL	COMMUNITY
ACUTE	CHRONIC
CURE	PREVENTION
INTERVENTION	MONITORING
TREATMENT	CARE
PATIENT	PERSON

As a result of the limitations of modern medicine, a focus on how a person engages with and manages their condition becomes in many cases more important, with patient narratives offering solutions to long-term and chronic conditions (Easton and Atkin, 2011). Society has, in response, turned to joint ways of managing patients' conditions because it finds it increasingly difficult to afford the continuing care costs of conditions that can absorb substantial sums of money over long periods of time. What goes on therefore at a local level, i.e. between the patient and the clinician, is key to being time-efficient and cost-effective as opposed to promoting a 'one size fits all' approach which is dismissive of the patient's experience of illness (Easton and Atkin, 2011).

The emerging importance of the patient's narrative is evident in some contemporary US medical schools, which contain programmes on narratives, set up to reduce death and suffering of patients as a result of physicians' lack of attention to their patients' stories (Charon, 2007). Even a cursory glance at people's stories suggests that the common complaint of patients or family members is that the hospital or doctors *just don't listen*. Promotion of the 'lost tradition of narrative' is being revived in the teaching and practice of medicine around the world. Supporters believe that narratives offer the treating physicians a more holistic (and therefore more valuable) insight into their patients. It is also envisaged that patient narratives will provide education which enriches the health professionals' understanding, and expands their treatment 'toolkit'. In addition patients' sharing of stories will result in outcomes such as empathy and lower levels of isolation (Greenhalgh and Hurwitz, 1999). Each in turn will have a positive impact on their emotional state, likely to result in less demand for physician or therapeutic intervention. The use of narratives in medical education and its impact on professional practice is discussed in more detail in Chapter 9.

Understanding the role of narratives and medicine has provided a brief but broad foundation, which sets the scene for understanding encephalitis and its consequences for those affected, provided in the next four chapters. It is not, however, only the medical profession in whom narratives have provoked interest and this next section looks at rising public interest.

The public and neuro-narratives

Recent decades have seen a significant rise in public interest in what have been termed 'neuro-narratives' (Harrington, 2005; Kreiswirth, 2000): stories written by or about people who have neurological illness, disease, injury or disorder. A generation ago, little awareness existed around neuro-narratives. This is not to say that documented cases of brain disorder do not exist, just that none existed in the format we have seen develop over the last four or five decades (Kreiswirth, 2000).

The ancestor to the neuro-narrative was of course the single case history of a brain disorder in the early nineteenth century, written by physicians for the science of understanding the brain, not the experience of the patient. This, however, all changed with narrative pioneers such as Alexander Luria (1987) and Oliver Sacks (1986, 1991, 2009). They created a new genre of literature, transforming a 'clinical genre' – the case history – into a literary one (Cassuto, 2000; Couser, 2001) describing people who had extraordinary abilities or deficits, yet to all intents and purposes appeared in many other ways completely normal. These observers/authors didn't conform to the usual medical case history: they probed, illustrated and commented on what it must be like for the people concerned, taking us on personal, literary journeys where readers could almost experience the implications for both themselves, their families and, in some cases, society at large (see also Broks, 2003; Kapur, 1997; Ramachandran and Blakeslee, 1999).

They were texts that broke all the rules of conventional case history writing with readers being asked to "bear witness to the tragedy of illness, with all of its lost life and potential" (Harrington, 2005: p. 32), reinforcing the fragility of human nature and often making us thankful for the normality of our own lives.

These authors were not without their critics, however. Their books create a tension. It could be argued on the one hand they are making a public spectacle of people – creating a 'freak' show – and on the other that they are responsible for increasing public awareness and understanding of little-known and little-understood conditions (Cassuto, 2000; Couser, 2001). Nevertheless they remain popular and receive a substantial amount of public support. Sacks' work appeals to the natural human desire to be curious and directs it so that the outcome is not a salacious ridiculing of another person but one of understanding and empathy (Cassuto, 2000). Whatever the criticisms of them, Sacks and writers like him developed a new literary genre without which it is possible that patients would not have begun to publish their own biographies and illness-stories. The unique nature of neurologic illness makes these neuro-narratives "both fascinating and challenging ... and most in need of being listened to and understood" (Alcauskas and Charon, 2008: p. 893).

The physicians who championed this new genre of writing are responsible for expanding public understanding and it is argued are responsible for bringing together minority groups and de-pathologising them as individuals and communities (Couser, 2001). The implication for neurological conditions and acquired brain injury is that an increased understanding and acceptance of people's difficulties as a result of reading neuro-narratives may occur.

The rise in neuro-narratives and the public's burgeoning interest has also resulted in many people affected by neurological illness and injury writing and publishing their own narratives (see Bauby, 2002; Cracknell and Turner, 2012; Durham, 2005; Hammond, 2007; Johansen, 2002; Kemp, 2000; Lapotaire, 2003; Richmond, 2002). A contemporary neuro-narrative of an autoimmune encephalitis is provided by Cahalan (2013). Her book *Brain on Fire* weaves the personal and dramatic narrative of its author with her journalistic integrity and gritty desire for the facts. Following Sacks' *Awakenings* (1991) about encephalitis lethargica patients, it is perhaps one of the most comprehensive post-encephalitic narratives existing to date. These books may have shared some of the goals of doctor-authors but they also set their own agendas: creating understanding; political activism; and records of last testaments for those with degenerative or incurable disorders. Through these texts physicians and health professionals can explore and engage with the experiences of people affected by neurological conditions and injuries in ways that it would not be ethically appropriate to do in conventional consultations (Alcauskas and Charon, 2008).

The general population has embraced these narratives confirming that these people's experiences are not simply of interest to doctors and health professionals. Through this medium their humanity is recaptured and readers are fascinated as well as humbled by the fragility of the human condition. Readers connect at a human and personal level, raising in awareness our own mortality and that of those we love, along with a genuine empathy for the unexpected devastation that neurological illness and injury can have for those affected and their families.

In addition to text, neuro-narratives are now presented in diverse media such as documentaries, film, photography, performing arts (Hurwitz and Charon, 2013) and of course television: the infamous and fictional *House* was lauded as the most watched television series in the world in 2008 (www.examiner.com/article/house-watching-doctor-uses-show-to-save-dying-man-s-life, accessed 11 September 2015).

The diversity and gripping nature of their content along with a public fascination around neuro-illness and disability are the reasons why medical professionals and the public at large continue to be both focused upon and enthralled by neurological case studies (Thomas and Thomas, 2009). They identified that more than a quarter of all *Lancet* reports and nearly one-fifth of all *British Medical Journal* (*BMJ*) case reports are neurological, despite the fact this in no way reflects the actual burden of disease in the UK population, with the top three being psychiatric (22.3 per cent), cardiovascular (14.5 per cent) and oncological (14.2 per cent).

Of course not all neuro-narratives are high profile. In modern times, opportunities for the layperson to express and share their narratives have expanded beyond the practitioner-patient consultation and beyond the traditional written narrative, log or diary (Easton and Atkin, 2011). The rise of the internet has given millions of people access to new ways of not just exploring their health conditions, but also recording and sharing their own experiences with other people. Examples include patient forums, blogs, chatrooms, message-boards and databases documenting people's experience of health and illness (Bennet, 2007). These emerging and popular social mediums are important, although it must be remembered that they may constitute a trend and are therefore subject to shifts in popularity as new ways of recording narratives come and go. Additionally some authors argue they are a middle-class phenomenon and can create inequalities (Bennet, 2007) as their use can be subject to age, gender and cultural bias for example. Another more established environment for sharing stories includes patient organisations. They have become highly regarded, providing a forum in which people can come together, exchange their stories and continue supporting one another (Easton and Atkin, 2011; Farris Kurtz, 1997; Solomon *et al.*, 2007; Solomon *et al.*, 2012).

Whatever the medium, and as Barthes stated toward the beginning of this chapter, everybody has a narrative. This is something that can easily be forgotten in the day-to-day blur of people, emails, reports, half-eaten sandwiches, cold coffee and parking tickets that can make up our working day. Despite highs and lows in the popularity of narratives over the centuries, there is no denying their prominence and attraction, nor in the suggestion that they are, as Barthes suggests, here to stay.

Conclusion

Narratives are an integral and important element in modern society. Their use in medicine reflects a changing relationship between patient and doctor, and an awareness about the limitations of purely biomedical interventions. An ageing population, a rise in chronic and long-standing conditions and a shift from cure to the palliative, means patients have come to have a greater role in the management of their illness and that narratives play an important part in this, for both the patient and the professional. Neuro-narratives are one element of this and there has been increasing public interest in them during the last five decades, resulting in greater understanding and a welcome addition to the literature from a variety of 'practitioner' and 'patient' authors.

Chapters 1 and 2 have spent some time laying the foundations for the rest of this book. This chapter has considered patient narratives in the broader context of medicine and history more generally. In summary, narrative is a natural human resource and one that has a special place in history and medicine where people have experienced illness. Survivors of encephalitis and families left bereaved by it are no exception. In the next chapter we begin the first three of eight survivor and family member narratives, accompanied by comment from professionals in the field, or those who were directly involved in their care.

Key messages

- Narratives have been, and remain central, to humanity and have a specific role in medicine.
- The patient is returning to a central role in their healthcare as a result of many conditions unique to the twenty-first century, e.g. life-saving advances, ageing populations and ever-reducing resources.
- The 'neuro-narrative' is a relatively recent phenomenon and one that has been embraced by both the medical professional and the general public alike.
- More people than ever record their illness-narratives and increasing technological developments mean they are available to more people than ever before.

References

Alcauskas, M. and Charon, R. 2008. Right brain: reading, writing, and reflecting: making a case for narrative medicine in neurology. *Neurology*, 70, 891–894.

Atkin, K. 1991. Health, illness, disability and black minorities: a speculative critique of present day discourse. *Disability, Handicap & Society*, 6, 37–47.

Barthes, R. 1982. Introduction to the structural analysis of narratives. *In:* Sontag, S. (ed.) *A Barthes Reader* (pp. 251–295), New York, Hill and Wang.

Bauby, J.-D. 2002. *The Diving-Bell and the Butterfly*, London, Fourth Estate.

Bell, S. 2000. Experiencing illness in/and narrative. *In:* Bird, C., Conrad, P., Fremont, A. and Levine, S. (eds) *Handbook of Medical Sociology* (pp. 184–199), Upper Saddle River, NJ, Prentice-Hall.

Bennet, B. 2007. Gaining understanding from patients' stories to inform neuroscience nursing practice. *British Journal of Neuroscience Nursing*, 3, 308–312.

Broks, P. 2003. *Into the Silent Land*, London, Atlantic Books.

Bury, M. 2001. Illness narratives: fact or fiction. *Sociology of Health and Illness*, 23 (3), 263–285.

Cahalan, S. 2013. *Brain on Fire: My Month of Madness*, London, Penguin.

Carroll, L. W. 1998. Understanding chronic illness from the patient's perspective. *Radiologic Technology*, 70, 37–41.

Cassuto, L. 2000. Oliver Sacks: the P T Barnum of the postmodern world? *American Quarterly*, 52, 326–333.

Charon, R. 2001. Narrative medicine: a model for empathy, reflection, profession, and trust. *Journal of the American Medical Association*, 286, 1897–1902.

Charon, R. 2007. What to do with stories. *Canadian Family Physician*, 53, 1265–1267.

Couser, T., G. 2001. The cases of Oliver Sacks: the ethics of neuroanthropology. Indiana University. http://poynter.indiana.edu/files/4213/4513/2230/m-couser.pdf (accessed 4 November 2015).

Cracknell, J. and Turner, B. 2012. *Touching Distance*, London, Century.

Department of Health. 2005. Supporting people with long term conditions: an NHS and social care model to support local innovation and integration. Department of Health.

Durham, C. 2005. *Doing up Buttons*, Camberwell, Australia, Penguin Books.

Easton, A. and Atkin, K. 2011. Medicine and patient narratives. *Social Care and Neurodisability*, 2, 33–41.

Farris Kurtz, L. 1997. *Self-Help and Support Groups: A Handbook for Practitioners*, London, Sage Publications.

Greenhalgh, T. and Hurwitz, B. 1999. Why study narrative? *British Medical Journal*, 318, 48–50.

Hammond, R. 2007. *On The Edge: My Story*, London, Orion Publishing Group Ltd.

Harrington, A. 2005. The inner lives of disordered brains. *Cerebrum*, 7 (2), 23–36.

Hogarth, S. and Marks, L. 1998. The golden narrative in British medicine. *In:* Greenhalgh, T. and Hurwitz, B. (eds) *Narrative Based Medicine* (pp. 140–148), London, BMJ Books.

Hurwitz, B. and Charon, R. 2013. A narrative future for health care. *The Lancet*, 381, 1886–1887.

Jewson, N. D. 2009. The disappearance of the sick man from medical cosmology, 1770–1870. *International Journal of Epidemiology*, 38, 622–633.

Johansen, R. K. 2002. *Listening in the Silence, Seeing in the Dark: Reconstructing Life after Brain Injury*, London, University of California Press.

Kalitzkus, V. and Matthiessen, P. 2009. Narrative-based medicine: potential, pitfalls, and practice. *The Permanente Journal*, 13, 80–86.

Kapur, N. 1997. *Injured Brains of Medical Minds*, Oxford, Oxford University Press.

Kemp, M. 2000. *True: The Autobiography of Martin Kemp*, London, Orion Books Ltd.

Kendall, E., Catalano, T., Kuipers, P., Posner, N., Buys, N. and Charker, J. 2007. Recovering following stroke: the role of self-management education. *Social Science and Medicine*, 64, 735–746.

Kreiswirth, M. 2000. Merely telling stories? Narrative and knowledge in the human sciences. *Poetics Today*, 21, 293–218.

Lapotaire, J. 2003. *Time out of Mind*, London, Virago Press.

Luria, A. R. 1987. *The Man with a Shattered World: The History of a Brain Wound*, Cambridge, MA, Harvard University Press.

Murray, M. 2000. Levels of narrative analysis in health psychology. *Journal of Health Psychology*, 3, 337–347.

Nettleton, S. 2006. *The Sociology of Health and Illness*, Cambridge, UK, Polity Press.

Porter, R. 2003. *Blood & Guts: A Short History of Medicine*, London, Penguin Books.

Ramachandran, V. S. and Blakeslee, S. 1999. *Phantoms in the Brain*, London, Fourth Estate Ltd.

Richmond, L. 2002. *Healing Lazarus*, New York, Pocket books.

Sacks, O. 1986. *The Man Who Mistook His Wife for a Hat*, London, Picador.

Sacks, O. 1991. *Awakenings*, London, Picador.

Sacks, O. 2009. *An Anthropologist on Mars*, London, Picador.

Scholz, U., Knoll, N., Sniehotta, F. F. and Schwarzer, R. 2006. Physical activity and depressive symptoms in cardiac rehabilitation: long-term effects of a self-management intervention. *Social Science & Medicine*, 62, 3109–3120.

Solomon, T., Hart, I. and Beeching, N. 2007. Viral encephalitis: a clinician's guide. *Practical Neurology*, 7, 288–305.

Solomon, T., Michael, B. D., Smith, P. E., Sanderson, F., Davies, N. W. S., Hart, I. J., Holland, M., Easton, A., Buckley, C., Kneen, R. and Beeching, N. J. 2012. Management of suspected viral encephalitis in adults – Association of British Neurologists and British Infection Association National Guidelines. *Journal of Infection*, 64, 347–373.

Tattersall, R. 2002. The expert patient: a new approach to chronic disease management for the twenty-first century. *Clinical Medicine*, 2, 227–229.

Thomas, R. H. and Thomas, N. J. P. 2009. House calls. *British Medical Journal*, 339, 1416–1417.

Wotton, D. 2006. *Bad Medicine: Doctors Doing Harm since Hippocrates*, Oxford, Oxford University Press.

Chapter 4

The survivors

Roy Axon, Sophie Baughan, Ross Buggins,
Tom Solomon, Sarosh Irani, Ava Easton

> I fought with anybody, anywhere. I was arrested many times, beaten up, hospitalised. I suffered, amongst other injuries, a broken cheekbone, broken nose, split lips and black eyes. I verbally abused my family, my girlfriend and before long I had alienated most of those close to me, purely because I was so unpredictable and dangerous.
>
> Roy, encephalitis survivor

Introduction

This is the first of four chapters dedicated to the stories of people who survived encephalitis and their families. Each chapter contains one or more stories and also provides commentary from experts in the fields of neurology, intensive care and neuropsychology. In this chapter we hear from Roy, Sophie and Ross: survivors of encephalitis. Professor Tom Solomon and Dr Sarosh Irani provide neurological perspectives which includes more detail on their types of encephalitis, commentary on Roy, Sophie and Ross's experiences, as well as additional insights from other patients with encephalitis they have treated.

Roy's story

Roy is 36 years old and currently living in Leeds with his partner Lauren. He was born in Merseyside and grew up in Neston and then Runcorn. He attended Frodsham High School and Sir John Deanes Sixth Form College. Roy moved to Leeds in 1998 to study law at university, graduating in 2002 and subsequently studying postgraduate law in York. He graduated in 2008. Roy has worked in the legal profession since 2003 in various areas includ-

Figure 4.1 **Roy Axon.**

ing Real Estate, Landlord and Tenant, and Property and Debt Recovery. Roy changed careers in late 2014 and now works for the Government as a civil servant. His main sporting interest is football and anything to do with Liverpool Football Club. He has been going to the matches since 1983, as regularly as possible and he was at the game in Istanbul for the Champions League Final in 2005. Roy played football at a decent level for many years and captained his school team throughout his secondary school years. He is also an avid boxing fan as well as a follower of rugby league. Other interests are cooking, eating pizzas, reading real-life crime literature and seeing as many of his friends as much as possible. He has an older sister called Emma and he visits his mother Lorraine back in Runcorn as much as he possibly can. Roy's father passed away in 2011. He plans to progress as a civil servant, maybe have children and hopefully see Liverpool win the league again soon.

As I sat in the ambulance on my way to a psychiatric hospital, hand-cuffed and restrained with nothing on but a pair of lime green hospital standard pyjama bottoms, having just been sectioned under the Mental Health Act, I filled with absolute rage and uncontrollable anger. Rage and anger at everyone and everything around me. How did I get here? Why were they doing this to me? I am right, they are wrong. There is nothing wrong with me!

The specific dates I cannot remember, it was sometime around February 1997. My latest episode of inexplicable volatility and irrational behaviour occurred at the hospital where I was currently being treated for either a severe seizure or injuries sustained in another street fight or bar brawl. Both had become regular occurrences. Hospitalisation had also become a regular occurrence and accepted aspect of my life since about one year prior (April 1996). That's when I collapsed at my parents' house, my first evident and physical exposure to viral encephalitis.

I was born in September 1978 and was 17 years old in April 1996. I had developed into a formidable young man. I was highly intelligent and in my first year of A-levels. I was good-looking, confident, strong, fit, popular and seemingly on my way to a brilliant life. I liked a beer at the weekend just like any teenager, but I didn't smoke or do drugs. I had the best-looking girl in the school and we were in love, as much as you could be at that age. I was a leader in the cool group, was captain of the school football team and played at amateur level to high standard. I worked part-time, had a little money and enjoyed life. Everyone loved me. Life was good.

Then everything changed.

For approximately three months I would be a patient, first in hospital where I resided in a coma for about a week, then subsequently at a specialist neurology hospital where the extent of my illness was diagnosed. In total I spent about six or seven weeks comatose.

I initially collapsed at my parents' house on a Saturday morning. My mother found me on the floor of her living room. I died briefly after suffering a major seizure and was resuscitated by the ambulance and hospital staff. I awoke a week later in a somewhat delirious state, hyperactive and speaking complete nonsense. The majority of this period and the many months after, I have no recollection of. I can only go on what those close to me told me in the years afterwards.

Soon after waking, I began to have extreme seizures, similar to the initial one. My mother was insistent that I was not an epileptic, which was the initial thought. These seizures became so regular and so close to one another that the only choice was to transfer me to a specialist neurology hospital where I was swiftly diagnosed with viral encephalitis.

I was quickly placed into an induced coma on a life support machine, to avoid the very real prospect of heart failure and certain death if the seizures continued. This lasted for a very lengthy period and the majority of my stay I cannot actually recall.

My first recollection is a very vague memory of being moved from the Intensive Care Unit (ICU) onto a small ward shared with three elderly, terminally ill male patients, two of whom died in the coming weeks on the same ward. I was a physical wreck. I had multiple tubes, lines and drips; my hair had grown into a long scraggy mess and I had a beard. What shocked me the most was that I had lost about three stone in weight. When I first tried to stand up, I collapsed. The first person I remember speaking to was my mother who calmly explained what had happened. The coming weeks were a period of monitoring, medication and sedation.

I was not prepared for the dramatic alteration in my entire persona that would follow after I was allowed home. After about four weeks I was allowed back to my parents' house to continue my rehabilitation. It was now July and I had missed around three months of my first year A-levels. Clearly I was going to be unable to complete the year and agreed to repeat my first year in September. This was a huge blow as it meant I would now be an academic year behind: the first implication of my encephalitis. I also felt very uncomfortable around people and did not like leaving the house. My physical condition was not good: my muscles had wasted and I was tired after minimal physical movement.

My family, friends and girlfriend were about to bear the brunt of the new entity that was Roy. My brain had been damaged causing 10 per cent front temporal lobe injury affecting my intelligence levels, concentration, memory, attention span and, most importantly, my temper. I also developed new personality traits: I was no longer afraid of spiders; I no longer liked chocolate; I started to drink a pint of milk in the mornings. Most strangely, I developed a severe compulsive-nature disorder: if I turned a light switch on or off I would have to touch it with both hands and all my fingers; I could only leave a room by the same door I came in from, even in cars; I would count to four when doing certain things such as closing a door, a drawer or a lid, shutting it four times and holding it there each time for four seconds. Very weird!

This was nothing compared to the impact that my new identity would have on social aspects of my life. I eventually began to socialise with friends but for some reason I had taken to drinking extreme amounts of alcohol. I would consume eight cans of lager before I even went out. Of course my family and close friends tried to intervene but I would simply go out and drink in the park. My state of mind resulted in numerous occasions of inexplicable bouts of anger. I would react to the mildest of annoyances with violence. I attacked those who I felt had crossed me with physical damage. More often than not I would come off worse due to my alcohol-induced state. When drunk I fought with anybody, anywhere. I was arrested many times, beaten up, hospitalised. I suffered amongst other injuries, a broken cheekbone, broken nose, split lips and black eyes. I verbally abused my family, my girlfriend and before long I had alienated most of those close to me, purely because I was so unpredictable and dangerous.

Before long I graduated from alcohol to drugs, namely ecstasy and cocaine. I would use drugs recreationally for a number of years, and throughout university, but thankfully I was never dependent on them: I just did them because I felt like it. This is a clear example of how my attitude had changed. Prior to my illness I didn't even smoke, let alone take drugs. I think subconsciously I believed that I was bulletproof: I had survived my illness so I could therefore do what I wanted.

My seizures began again very soon after I left hospital. I had extreme seizures whilst fully conscious, something I had not experienced before. The ones previously I cannot remember, but I can certainly remember the following ones. I would get sensations consisting of pins and needles in my arms, gradually in one arm then the other, building up in its intensity, prior to having a full-blown seizure. My jaw would lock, I would dribble uncontrollably, and then the physical and very violent attack would occur. The worst thing about them was that I was conscious. What lasted for only a few minutes would seem like an eternity, as though the pain would never end. My brain would go through a period of indescribable agony and emotion, I would be longing to be put out of the misery and simply die. They were that bad.

Those witnessing my seizures found them upsetting but relatively brief. I would, at times, require hospitalisation for a few days, at other times I would simply lie in bed and try and let my body recuperate from the physical battering that it had endured. These seizures would be a part of my life for about 12 years, controlled or not so controlled by endless medication. They would lessen in severity over the years and I am now seizure-free for about four years. Their main impact is that I have never actually learned to drive.

My seizures coincided with the lowest point that I can recall: after a number of arrests and understanding from the police and medical staff, they'd had enough. I was in hospital, either as a result of a seizure or an injury when I once again went berserk. I had some sort of altercation with some of the hospital staff, and the next thing I know I was in an ambulance, hand-cuffed and on my way to a psychiatric hospital. I was a patient there for around four weeks but I would also return a few months later for a second stint. I was housed with all sorts of mental patients, from murderers, rapists, criminals, to those who had suffered for other reasons. Some had seen colleagues blown up in wars, some were drug addicts and some were there for the same reason as me. We were fed medication, sent to group chats and basically assessed. It was pretty relaxed: there was a TV, a pool table and gardens to walk around in. But it was still like a prison and we were all still mental, even though we all denied that there was anything wrong with us. After my second stay, I began to realise that I needed to change.

I left my secondary school in October 1996 following my release from hospital because everyone knew me and knew what had happened. On top of that I had split up from my girlfriend and alienated most of my friends. About one year after my initial collapse (April 1997) I began at a new college, starting my A-levels again. A clean start was needed. I did the best I could and I managed to pass my exams in June 1997.

My idea of a new start didn't really work out as I had hoped. My seizures were constant throughout my repeat year and I regularly had the embarrassment of suffering them in seminars at college in front of my fellow students. As a result I felt obliged to explain to everyone just what had actually happened.

I completed my A-levels in 1998 and went on to university to study Law in Leeds. My academic grades were good but nowhere near the level prior to my illness. The same applied to my Law degree and subsequent postgraduate qualification completed at York College of Law in 2008.

My temper, concentration and mental problems would continue to be an issue but I gradually learned to deal with them over time. Thankfully my family remained loyal despite my deplorable behaviour toward them, of which I am ashamed. My family knew it was because of my illness, that I had damage to my brain, and it needed time to recover. I know for certain if I had not been sectioned I would have been dead or in prison, without a doubt.

My attitude in life is to try and never look back: to have no regrets. That is not always easy to do. I do wonder at times where I would be had I not fallen ill. Would I be happily married with children, living in a big house with a top job? I am convinced my life would have been entirely different. But then I take stock … I should be dead, many times over … so my story is not one of complete devastation. I completed my Law degree in 2002, followed by the Law Practice Course in 2008 and I have worked as a paralegal in various areas of law since 2002. I recently changed careers and am now a civil servant. I have a lovely long-term girlfriend and aim to plan our future in the next few years.

I still live with the impacts of the illness. I still have bouts of anger and I find it hard to explain why that is. My dad also died a few years ago very suddenly, and at the young age of just 58. I believe that he never quite recovered from having to witness the worst stages of my illness, where he and the rest of the family were repeatedly told that I was unlikely to live through the night.

Encephalitis is a deadly, devastating and horrendous illness. I would not wish it on anyone. But it doesn't mean life has to be over. You can survive and you can still live a relatively normal life. One thing is for sure, my life has certainly been interesting because of it! Do I wish I had never had the illness – of course. But I am a better person for having it. I hope that by reading my words, if even one person can take some sort of comfort from them, then perhaps I will have dealt a blow to encephalitis.

Sophie's story

Sophie Baughan is 30 years old and grew up in Walthamstow, East London. She recently moved into her first home, a cottage in Old Harlow, with her boyfriend of ten years, Luke. She currently works for the NHS at their main head-quarters in London as a Commissioning Officer for dental practices and opticians. She began work at 18 after finishing college but is currently studying part-time with the Open University for a BA/BSc

Figure 4.2 Sophie Baughan.

(Honours) in Criminology and Psychological Studies. Criminology is a big area of interest for her and she should complete this in 2015. When not at work or studying – if she isn't asleep – she can normally be found cooking (particularly baking), reading, doing cross stitch or falling in love with puppies online in her search to buy one. At the moment a lot of time is being spent with her family in their campaign to raise money and awareness for The Encephalitis Society (www.encephalitis.info).

I contracted viral encephalitis on 26th November 2013. At this time, I was 28 years old and living in East London with my mum, stepdad and brother. I was house hunting with my boyfriend of ten years, Luke, and I was confident and happy in my job of seven years working for the NHS as a Commissioning Officer. I was also undertaking a degree in Criminology part-time with the Open University which was nearing completion.

On the 26th I felt unwell like I was coming down with a cold. I then remember nothing until I woke up in hospital in late December 2013. Not long after going to sleep on the 26th I began to have tonic-clonic seizures so an ambulance was called. My seizures continued and I was taken to my local hospital and given anti-seizure medication. Doctors initially couldn't determine a diagnosis and I was moved to a ward with the belief that I would be released the following day. However, once on the ward my seizures continued and I was unresponsive. I had a lumbar puncture to rule out the possibility of a brain infection but the results were inconclusive. My seizures remained uncontrollable and my oxygen levels dropped so I was placed into intensive care. I had every kind of test possible. The results were inconclusive, so whilst doctors believed encephalitis to be the cause, they decided to treat all options. When I also began to have absence seizures my medication was increased. I was sedated and a second lumbar puncture was carried out. After a week, I was transferred to a specialist Intensive Care Unit so that I could have an MRI whilst sedated. My seizures remained uncontrolled and I developed a chest infection so was placed onto a ventilator.

I remained in intensive care for another week. During this time I was taken off of the ventilator a few times before I was considered well enough to remain conscious. Progress was slow initially: I was weak, confused, couldn't talk and already problems with my memory were becoming apparent. In the following days, my recovery sped up and hints of my personality were beginning to show. After a further week, I was transferred back to my local hospital where I underwent more tests, scans and x-rays. My medication was changed but my seizures remained calm so I was considered stable enough to be discharged at 11.30pm on Christmas Eve.

To date, doctors have been unable to confirm a cause for my contracting encephalitis.

January was spent at home recuperating and I was offered short-term neurological rehabilitation as an in-patient. I agreed for this to take place through February and spent three days a week at a local specialist unit. Whilst there I underwent physiotherapy, occupational therapy, psychology, met with neurologists and visited my workplace. I was surrounded by patients with a range of brain conditions and neurological specialists. I learned so much during my time there and think that every brain injury patient should be offered some form of neurological rehabilitation. It was really helpful to have all of the relevant experience in one place with 24/7 access rather than entering time-consuming referral systems.

On the surface as I write this over a year later, my life looks the same, however surviving encephalitis has changed me completely.

I have numerous side-effects that I will struggle with for the rest of my life.

First, I have 'symptomatic epilepsy due to acquired brain damage from encephalitis'. I have three different types of seizures: tonic-clonic, absence and partial. My tonic-clonic seizures last a few minutes, during which:

- *I lose consciousness;*
- *my body convulses and tenses;*
- *my face goes blue;*
- *I moan and drool;*
- *I infrequently vomit or urinate.*

The majority of these seizures start whilst I am asleep which is positive as it minimises the risk of falling. From time to time however, this is not always the case which is worrying as I am very vulnerable if alone, outside the house and unconscious for any period of time. Recovery is slow and complex. For the first 15 minutes I am confused, disorientated, find it difficult to breathe, my speech is jumbled and I am unable to respond to questions. For the next few hours and sometimes up to a day I am tearful, tired, have a severe headache and aching muscles.

During my absence seizures I mentally and physically switch off as though I am day-dreaming but I cannot be roused and do not realise they have happened. The recovery is faster and for a few hours consists of a headache and confusion.

I have partial seizures most frequently and each lasts for a couple of minutes. I have them so regularly that my family can tell within seconds just by the change in my breathing pattern. Partials are difficult to describe. Although I remain conscious I:

- *feel faint and like I am watching everything from a distance;*
- *get hot and everything starts to spin;*
- *get dots in front of my eyes and my hands start to go numb;*
- *get déjà vu;*
- *feel panicky and woozy.*

On occasion they have transformed into tonic-clonic seizures so I have to ensure that I am in a safe place just in case. I often have to sit down on the pavement or knock at a stranger's house.

Epilepsy is a terrifying and life-consuming condition to have. In the first 12 months I had over 300 seizures. It makes me feel so vulnerable however I have no choice but to carry on unless I want to become housebound. I have had to change every part of my life to accommodate it and it is never out of my mind.

Previous anti-convulsant medication was stopped due to extreme reactions. I am now on three types and take 17 tablets a day. In the future I hope that my medication continues to improve my seizures so that they become something I only have to occasionally experience. I am realistic in that I don't believe my medication would be able to entirely stop them. My doctors are aiming for them to occur just a few times a year.

I also have memory problems. This is for three reasons: a consequence of the encephalitis scarring on my brain; the epilepsy; and epilepsy medication side-effects. For me, my memory loss is the most significant and life-changing difference.

I have completely lost the six months leading up to contracting encephalitis. This includes day-to-day life as well as more significant events such as holidays. It is very surreal to see yourself in photographs when you have no memory at all of that event. On top of this missing timescale, I also now experience significant short-term memory problems. When we moved house I got lost on the walk home from the train station every day for a month. I even drew a map, wrote down the route and tried to pick out memorable aspects, but could not commit it to memory.

My workplace moved office a couple of months before I contracted encephalitis so returning to work was like starting a new job. As well as difficulty in remembering how to do the job itself, I also could not remember the office. I have been back at work for a year now but still do not know my way around the building.

My memory loss also makes day-to-day life very frustrating and I find myself in conversations that include a comment about an event or experience that I was party to, but cannot remember. This is upsetting and means that I have to remind others about my memory loss continuously.

I also experience word-finding difficulties which have affected my confidence greatly. I feel embarrassed speaking in a group of people as I lose my way throughout the conversation.

Having memory problems makes every aspect of my life so difficult. It is very frustrating and I have lost all trust in anything that I think that I 'can' remember. It is also upsetting to have lost memories of important times in my life. It is very difficult for others to understand, particularly if we have a conversation and I have forgotten it within a few minutes. I understand this but it is impossible to explain to them as I do not understand it myself. People can be very insensitive sometimes, intentionally or not, and I am often told not to feel bad as they have a bad memory themselves. Whilst their intention is to make me feel less alone, it has the opposite effect and is distressing as it only highlights how different their day-to-day memory hiccups are versus my major issues.

I also experience fatigue which is all consuming; physically, mentally and emotionally. For the first eight or nine months, I was unable to make it through the day without having several naps, despite sleeping for 10+ hours the previous night. I was unable to concentrate for more than a few minutes at a time or put a sentence together properly; I couldn't walk for more than a few minutes without becoming exhausted. I now always look lifeless with dull skin and large bags under my eyes. Although the fatigue is an issue in all aspects of my life, it affected me most during my return to work.

Initially my neurologists were not sure I would be able to return to work at all and only later in my rehabilitation did this become an option they were willing to consider. However, despite their advice to return slowly I listened to my occupational rehabilitation therapist and went back after only a few months. This was a mistake that I have regretted since. I was keen to return to normality but was not ready. Although I am grateful that I have been able to return to work because many don't, it has been hard and there have been many days where I have been overwhelmed and considered quitting. Despite working in my team for seven years, I am suddenly unsure of how to do my job. My confidence is slowly returning but I know I'll never be the same person at work as I was when I went home that fateful evening, which is difficult to come to terms with.

Following encephalitis it is also hard to manage the expectations of those around you. As it is an invisible disability it must be difficult for my colleagues to understand why I get tired, have forgotten how to do my role or require so much time out of the office. I have been lucky with supportive colleagues who have not made me feel rushed in my recovery or shown their frustration.

If I get too tired, my seizures increase so this is something I try to avoid as much as possible. I have therefore begun part-time working hours which I hope will support this. Obviously this has financial implications but has become unavoidable for me. Even now, a year and a half after contracting encephalitis, I am still unable to manage a day without at least one nap. This also results in a slight difference in my mental alertness which helps with my confidence levels both at work and in general life.

I have noticed several other changes over the past few months. Prior to contracting encephalitis I suffered from anxiety but have found that, despite having more reasons to be anxious now, I am actually more relaxed and calm! This has also been noted by others so the change must be significant. Of course this may be due to sedative aspects of my medication but I am grateful for it and hope that it continues.

I am now classed as disabled. I found this difficult at first. Due to the invisible nature of brain injury I can find people make their opinions known and their reactions can be insensitive. I understand their confusion, I look physically fine but they do not understand how weak, tired and confused I may be.

The only slight physical clue is that I have 'Horner's Syndrome' in my right eye – a minor defect whereby my eyelid droops. It was caused during the insertion of a cannula into my neck and one of the main nerves leading up to my eye was accidentally disrupted. It hasn't affected my vision and isn't too noticeable in day-to-day life but is obvious in photographs. I have been advised by doctors that I am acceptable for an eye lift but this isn't something I want to pursue at this time.

Prior to encephalitis I was renowned for my obsessive levels of organisation, particularly my to-do lists, and since leaving hospital, I have found myself unable to cope without them! I have tried many systems and am currently happy with the one that I have in place. It enables me to monitor every aspect of my life on a very detailed basis. Without consulting my lists I am unable to remember what I need to do and whether I have already done a task. I have had to make a reference book for work including passwords, all crucial reference information, as well as detailed step-by-step instructions on how I undertake each task.

I understand that the encephalitis scarring means that these will be lifelong issues but I hope that I continue to develop processes which make these less obvious and my life easier. It is still early days in my recovery but I suspect that in particular I will need to rethink my career path in order to find one which is easier for me to cope with. I have re-started university studies and hope to complete these: if not I feel that I will have let encephalitis win.

Going through an experience like this has changed every single aspect of me, my life and relationships. I am still trying to learn the new me and my new limits but I have found that determination and humour have been my main strengths. It has been hard and still feels surreal. I'm living a different life: one I have no control over and one that no-one else understands. I spent months feeling overwhelmed and alone but can now see that I am actually lucky when compared to many others.

I now consciously put myself first and do everything I can to make me and those I care about happy regardless of the opinion of others. It has shown me what is important and I am almost desperate to spend time with my loved ones. Luke and I bought a house a few months after I was discharged from hospital. Although the stress was difficult, I have never been happier since we moved in together.

A year and a half later, things are starting to get better. Encephalitis completely took over my life but I survived and I refuse to let it beat me. If my aspirations are not possible, then I can only wish that awareness of encephalitis increases so that others understand the difficulties faced by those of us with acquired brain injuries.

Professor Tom Solomon

Tom Solomon is the Director of the Institute of Infection and Global Health; Head of The Brain Infections Group; Chair of Neurological Science; Honorary Consultant Neurologist, Walton Centre NHS Foundation Trust and Royal Liverpool University Hospital. Tom studied Medicine at Wadham College, Oxford, before undertaking a PhD on central nervous system infections in Vietnam, with a Wellcome Trust Advanced Training Fellowship.

Figure 4.3 Professor Tom Solomon.

He then became a Clinical Lecturer in Neurology, Medical Microbiology and Tropical Medicine at the University of Liverpool, and was awarded a Wellcome Trust Career Development Fellowship. This included two years as a visiting scientist at the University of Texas Medical Branch, Galveston, Texas. Tom was made a Senior Lecturer in Neurology in Liverpool in 2005, and awarded a Medical Research Council Senior Clinical Fellowship the same year. He became Chair of Neurological Science in 2007, and Head of the newly formed Institute of Infection and Global Health in 2010. Tom heads up The Brain Infections Group, which, with millions of pounds in funding in recent years, works to reduce the burden of neurological disease in the UK and globally. Tom has a particular interest in infectious encephalitis and is the Chair of The Encephalitis Society Professional Advisory Panel.

A neurological perspective of Roy and Sophie's experiences

These two accounts of encephalitis, by Sophie who developed encephalitis a year ago, and Roy who developed it more than 15 years ago, provide fascinating reading. They demonstrate some of the many challenges that people who have had encephalitis face.

Although I have probably seen more patients with encephalitis than anyone else in the UK, I still find it moving testimony. In both cases the disease came completely out of the blue, as encephalitis so often does.

Here were two young people, leading normal lives, with an exciting future ahead of them when for no obvious reason they were struck down by a disease which would change their lives forever. In the case of Sophie, who was 29 at the time, she had a simple cold; she remembers going to sleep, and then the next thing she woke in hospital, having had a seizure. Roy was 17 when he became unwell. He also collapsed with a seizure, at his parents' house. These accounts are typical of how encephalitis can present. Someone will have a fever or flu-like illness for a few days, and then develop a seizure. Seizures occur as part of the initial illness in up to half the patients with encephalitis, depending on the underlying cause; they are even more frequent in children (Michael and Solomon, 2012). The other common presentation is a fever, and then abnormal behaviour, or altered consciousness. This is often accompanied by a terrible headache. In both the cases described here, because of the seizure, the patient was brought to hospital quite quickly. However, when patients are just behaving strangely it is much harder for people to work out what is going on. Sometimes it is thought the patient is drunk, has taken drugs or that they have a psychiatric illness.

For these reasons we have been doing research at the University of Liverpool over the last few years looking at this. This is part of a major UK National Institute for Health Research Programme Grant on Understanding and Improving Outcomes in Encephalitis (www. encephuk.org, accessed 3 March 2015), which is being conducted with many UK partners, including The Encephalitis Society. We have been looking at some of the reasons for delays in the diagnosis of encephalitis, and challenges in the treatment, and have produced National Guidelines (Solomon et al., 2012).

Sophie then describes the initial investigations. Key among these is the lumbar puncture, or spinal tap. This allows us to examine the cerebrospinal fluid, which is washing around the brain and spinal cord. Studying the fluid allows us to determine, indirectly, what is happening in the brain. By examining the cells in the fluid we can determine whether there is inflammation – i.e. whether the body's immune system is directing extra white blood cells into the brain to try and fight any infection. We can also then try to determine exactly what the infection is, by detecting the viruses, or other pathogens in the spinal fluid. One of the most important is herpes simplex virus. This is detected by a polymerase chain reaction (PCR) test which detects small bits of the virus' DNA. Herpes simplex virus encephalitis is important because it is the most commonly identified viral cause in Western settings, and is treatable with an antiviral drug called Aciclovir. Before Aciclovir came along in the 1980s, about 70 per cent of people with herpes simplex virus encephalitis died. This has now dropped to about 10 per cent, with the use of the drug (Sköldenberg et al., 1984). Because it makes such a difference, we usually start Aciclovir as soon as we suspect encephalitis. We can always stop it later on if we find out it is not encephalitis caused by herpes simplex virus. In Sophie's case the cause of her encephalitis was never determined. Roy doesn't mention whether a cause was found for his. This is not uncommon; we often don't get the cause. A large study conducted with the Health Protection Agency (now Public Health England) showed that even with most thorough attempts at diagnosis, the cause was still not found in about a third of cases (Granerod et al., 2010).

The magnetic resonance imaging (MRI) brain scan is another essential investigation in suspected encephalitis. This allows us a different way to see if there is inflammation in the brain, how much there is and where it is. In herpes encephalitis the changes are usually in the frontal and temporal lobes. An MRI can also rule out other causes of the patient's illness, such as a stroke. When there is a lot of swelling and inflammation, we sometimes use an anti-inflammatory drug, such as dexamethasone. However, we are not really sure whether it helps overall, and so a new study has been recently set up to answer this question (www.brain infectionsuk.org/portfolio/dexenceph, accessed 3 March 2015).

Both Sophie and Roy then had a very stormy course during their first few weeks of illness, with seizures that were difficult to control, and they ended up on intensive care. In Roy's case he was initially at a smaller hospital, and so was transferred to a neurology specialist hospital after review by a neurologist.

Once the initial acute illness is over, and both patients came off intensive care, that is really when the work began. Rehabilitation after encephalitis is a long and slow process. Both Sophie and Roy spent time on rehabilitation units. I think access to physiotherapy, occupational therapy, and most important of all neuropsychology, is really important. Sadly it is not as widely available as it should be, and patients need the support of their neurologist, general practitioner and family, as well as organisations like The Encephalitis Society (www. encephalitis.info) to gently keep nudging away to ensure they get the support they need. Both Sophie and Roy also emphasise the key supporting role of family and friends.

Ongoing seizures (epilepsy) are common after encephalitis, especially in patients who had lots of seizures when they were first unwell, and both Sophie and Roy were affected by this. Even people with encephalitis who had no seizures during the acute illness are more likely to develop later epilepsy than the general population (Michael and Solomon, 2012).

Memory problems are also common, especially in herpes encephalitis, which affects the temporal lobes. People often find large parts of their memory are simply gone. As Sophie described, they look at photos of major family events, but just cannot remember being there. Laying down new memories can also be difficult. This means they can't remember what happened this week, or yesterday, or even five minutes ago.

One of my patients, who is very severely affected, has lost all his memories since the 1970s, and cannot lay down any new ones. He thinks he is still in the army, and doesn't believe the woman sitting next to him in clinic is his wife. Another fascinating case is a young man, who studied French at university. When he recovered from encephalitis he couldn't speak in English, only French (Egdell et al., 2012). His family needed a translator to talk with him. Even now, much recovered, if he can't find a word in English, he will think of the French first, and then translate. We think this is because verbal memory is strongly lateralised in the left medial temporal lobe, where his damage was; in contrast, learning a foreign language is thought to reside in the right hemisphere, which in his case was intact.

There are a variety of practical things people can do to help get round some of the memory problems in encephalitis. Sophie mentions keeping lists and diaries. Others will set alerts on their smart phones, to remind them what needs doing. Photos can also prove useful: some take pictures throughout the day as a reminder of who they have met, and what they have done.

Encephalitis changes people in other ways too. Roy found his fear of spiders and love of chocolate had been reversed, and he had become obsessional about some numbers. I have a patient who was obsessed with the number 7 for a while, and another who changed from being a rather stroppy teenager into a much more pleasant and engaging member of the family. Sophie appears to have been making good progress, despite her considerable fatigue and memory problems. However, she clearly went back to work too quickly. This is a problem I see time and time again, and I really encourage my patients to take it little by little. If someone rushes back to work, and it all falls apart, then it can be really difficult to get established again.

Sadly Roy had a much more difficult time of rehabilitation. It is hard to know how much of the problem was due to the encephalitis itself, and how much the drinking and drugs, which appear to have been a consequence of the encephalitis. It must have been agonising for his family to see this decline from a bright young A-level student to someone in such trouble. Indeed it must have been terrible for Roy himself, and it is quite amazing that he has pulled through it all, and is able to provide such an eloquent account. I am full of admiration for someone who has managed to turn things around from such a desperate situation.

The final message from both Sophie's and Roy's account is one of hope; that however bad things are, they will improve. Sophie and Roy are different people now, compared with before their illness, but they are both determined to make the best of things. Sophie's illness has helped her focus on what is important, spending time with her loved ones and thinking about their happiness. Roy feels, despite the tumultuous time he had, that he is now a better person for the whole experience.

It is amazing stories like these which make working in the area of encephalitis so humbling.

Ross's story

Ross is a 30-year-old IT consultant who lives in Norwich with his incredibly supportive partner Emma. He enjoys road cycling but would really love to be able to get the time to off-road mountain bike more often. Any spare time is taken up with trying to grow food on the allotment – with varying success. Along with an incredible partner, his parents, siblings and other family are very close; they all gave much needed support through the tough times.

Figure 4.4 Ross Buggins.

After a hard year due to anti-NMDA receptor encephalitis, the recovery has been surprisingly quick – although as an impatient person, full recovery could never come too soon. There are some post-traumatic stress symptoms, minor concentration and memory problems – but nothing bad enough to stop day-to-day life.

Ross is looking forward to moving on with the next chapter in his life – but now with the knowledge of how fragile life is, and how not a single day should be taken for granted.

In April 2014 I was incredibly busy with work, with a lot of travelling around the country. I was tired, stressed and generally feeling under the weather. I had mouth ulcers and over the space of two weeks my cheeks, gums and lips all became incredibly sore. It was nearly impossible to eat or drink. However, being busy with work I ignored it and carried on.

Around the middle of May I woke to vomiting and diarrhoea. I felt exhausted. A few days later a rash started to develop on my body: under my arms, behind my knees, my elbows and neck. My hands and feet were also blistering and peeling.

On the 9th June, after a weekend of feeling very unwell, I finally gave in to my girlfriend's insistence and booked a doctor's appointment. The doctor ran tests. On the 11th I visited the emergency GP. I was not in a good way. I had to spend hours lying on a mattress in the doctor's surgery pretty much unable to move. They finally gave me some antibiotics, steroid cream and anti-sickness tablets.

On the 13th I visited the doctor again to get the results of the tests. Everything was back totally clear. The doctor then gave me a leaflet on anxiety management. This was the first time that a mental health problem was hinted at.

I decided at this point that it would be good to get away so I booked a week in a cottage on the Norfolk coast for my girlfriend and myself. On the first day I decided to try going for a run. I spent the entire time paranoid that I was going to have a heart attack, constantly checking my pulse and praying that it wasn't getting too high. When I finally got back to the cottage I sprawled out on the kitchen floor for hours. I then spent the day fluctuating between being absolutely fine to sitting staring out the window into space wondering what the point of life was with almost no hope of getting to the end of the day. Looking back now, it was very surreal.

The next day we went on a bike ride, and I spent the entire ride constantly worrying about us getting hit by cars or getting lost. We ended up taking a few wrong turns, and I didn't even notice that we were riding along a road that we had been on an hour previous. It was totally out of character but we put it down to the fact that I was exhausted from still not sleeping properly.

Sleep at this point was almost non-existent. I would close my eyes and a tidal wave of worry would pour over me. Every problem I could conceive would flood into my mind; I just couldn't switch my brain off.

After a week of constant ups and downs we returned home. I went back to the GP for results of the final blood test: all clear. The GP gave me sleeping tablets. I was apprehensive but hadn't slept in weeks so I was starting to get pretty desperate.

On the Sunday we had tickets to see the Kings of Leon and were planning on visiting friends. Looking back, driving there was not a good idea. That was the last time I drove, and DVLA have only just given me my licence back (July 2015). I was constantly worried about cars hitting us, or breaking down. I had to fight with myself to stay focused on what was actually happening rather than worry about what could happen. After about an hour I was in an absolute panic curled up on the floor of my friend's kitchen. It was the first time I admitted that I felt suicidal. I couldn't explain why I felt like I did – all I could say was that I felt so fed up with life that I wanted it to be over. The next day was not good. I felt like the world was rapidly collapsing around me. We never made it to the gig.

I returned to the GP, and explained I was starting to be really quite depressed. They prescribed anti-depressants. I spent another few days feeling up and down and ended up back at the GP saying I really did not feel good at all. This GP prescribed another type of anti-depressant, which would help with sleeping as well as the depression. It didn't help me sleep at all. All it did was make me very groggy during the day. Things just kept getting worse.

Then I experienced my first full panic attack. I had been feeling quite short of breath for a few hours, my chest was tight and I had a pins and needles on one side of my neck and face. I was lying on the sofa and my mind wouldn't stop racing. I was convinced I was going to die, and that my heart was going to give in. I became more and more distraught, trying not to blink because I thought if I closed my eyes I would never open them again. My friends called 111 and a doctor there said it was a panic attack.

At the start of July I visited my parents for a week. I was hoping the change would do me good and help me 'snap out of it'. After a day or two my dad asked me to go and see his GP. It was probably the tenth visit to a GP in the space of six weeks, but I agreed. This GP pre-scribed beta-blockers and another anti-depressant. This would be the third anti-depressant drug I had been prescribed in six weeks. I had seen four different GPs all whom had different ideas about how to treat me. How did I know who to believe?

At this point we didn't know what could help. My friends booked me to start seeing a private therapist. It started by covering mindfulness and cognitive behavioural therapy (CBT). I couldn't really believe that this is what I needed. I had always been someone who just got on with life – and now I was in a therapist's room trying to find a problem to my issues. It just didn't make sense. After the third or fourth session I stormed out. The therapist was so concerned that he rang my girlfriend to say that I was very ill and that he wasn't sure if he was the right person to be helping me.

The 10th of July was a very bad day; I started feeling worse: I felt like my brain was on fire. I kept telling my family there was something wrong with me; that it couldn't just be depression. I got more and more worked up, and my head was literally burning. I started hitting my head against walls to try and knock the burning out of it, ending up on the floor totally immobilised. My arms had locked and my back was bending back on itself. I was screaming. I was crying. I was in agony. I begged my parents to do something. I was convinced that I was about to die. They called 999 and an ambulance and paramedic car arrived. I was taken to hospital for chest x-rays and CT scans of my head. I spent the night terrified that the lumbar puncture that they were planning to do would go wrong and I would end up disabled after it. That next morning a doctor told me that there was nothing wrong with me physically, they weren't going to do the lumbar puncture, and that I had a mental problem. I was discharged.

I returned to my parent's home, and not long after I started to feel unwell. The tingling started ... it was going to happen again. I lost all sense of what was right in the world. I was determined to end things. My sister hid all of my medication and barricaded me into a bedroom. The screaming started again ... I couldn't think, and worse, now I couldn't remember. I couldn't picture people's faces in my mind. I started shouting out friends and family names as I thought that if I didn't I was going to forget them. I had a sense that something was very wrong in my brain, but all I could think was that it was dementia that had come on incredibly quickly. It literally felt as if memories were draining out of my brain. I was taken back to hospital for the second time in 24 hours. In the early hours of the morning (ironically when I was fast asleep for the first time in weeks!) two members of the mental health team turned up to assess me. I was discharged for a second time, and the local crisis team visited daily.

Things began to feel a little more under control. I was referred to a psychologist, and I was prescribed an antipsychotic medication. This made me very dozy but at least it controlled things.

By now I had spent months convinced that it couldn't be a mental health problem. I had tried everything I could to make myself happy: I had reduced work, taken breaks away, but nothing was helping. Every morning I started the day questioning what the point of the day was;

what the point of existing was. Every day would start with a battle: on one hand I didn't want to move, didn't want to do anything. On the other, I had to get up, I had to make the most of the day, I had to achieve something.

I made it through the next few weeks, then something happened. I started to feel really bad again. Life was turning very dark. On the 26th August I was at home on my own. I don't remember much, but I do remember feeling like there was no point any more. This is pretty much the last memory I have until November. Everything I relate now is from what other people have told me. I took a belt, wrapped it around my neck and wedged the end in the top of a closed door. I let the belt take the weight and I was happy that it would soon be over. Fortunately the belt snapped. That night my girlfriend found out what had happened. She rang the crisis team, who came to the house and were very concerned for my welfare. At this point I think they were close to taking me away with them, but, they didn't.

On the 30th we were due to fly to Crete. The crisis team said even thinking about going was a bad idea. However, I was determined to try, just to keep some normality in my life. We got in the car but didn't get far before the panic started. I was trying to get out of a moving car, and my girlfriend turned the car round and headed home. She was driving so slowly that the police stopped and breathalysed her. She explained what was going on and they escorted us back home. The holiday was officially over. The crisis team were called again. It was clear what needed to happen. I was placed under section two of the mental health act, and taken to hospital.

I don't remember much, but I really didn't want to be there. I managed to find a fire door to the outside. I was coaxed back inside a little later, but decided to leave again. This time they couldn't get me back in. The police were called and they physically took me back to the hospital. I was deemed too high a risk to remain at this hospital and was transferred to a higher security hospital where I remained for seven weeks. My medication was increased to keep me stable and in the October I was transferred to a general hospital, where I was scheduled to see a sleep specialist since my sleep was getting more bizarre and the level of my snoring was so extreme – patients, staff and visitors were all quite alarmed. I could be out walking or eating a meal and I would start falling asleep.

The sleep specialist mentioned checking for obstructive sleep apnoea (OSA). I couldn't be tested at this point as I was in a state of lowered consciousness – family, consultants and hospital porters were having to drag me from a wheelchair onto the bed – they just could not wake me.

The sleep specialist looked at me in a new way – in a way other doctors hadn't. I owe him a lot, probably my life. After being with him for hours, he wrote a letter to the mental health hospital saying I should be reassessed and probably taken off all of the drugs I was on. I was referred to a neurologist, and spent a month in the neurology ward with the consultants searching for an answer.

After nearly a month with no answer, the test for anti-NMDA receptor encephalitis returned positive. My brain was seriously unwell, and I was immediately started on intravenous immunoglobulin (IVIg) treatment.

The 8th of November 2014 is the first day that I remember since the middle of August. I remember lying in a bed thinking where on earth am I? In front of me was a notepad with a note from my mum saying I was in hospital and that it was the middle of November. I'm not sure what concerned me more, being in hospital or that it was three months later than I last remembered.

I completed treatment and was discharged. In February 2015 I was admitted for a second course of IVIg as there was a concern I may be relapsing.

The sleep consultant eventually ran the tests for OSA and it emerged I have an extreme case requiring a machine to help me breathe at night. Consequently I suffer with fatigue at times.

Five months on I continue to improve. I don't appear to have any permanent damage. The main issue has been around how to cope with something so major affecting my, and my family's lives, for which I am receiving neuropsychological support.

Looking back, the biggest clue to there being something wrong were my memory issues. With the depression and anxiety we kept finding possible reasons for them, but the memory loss? That was unexplainable. I started to forget pin numbers, passwords, directions, how to use maps, how to put up a tent, I couldn't remember names or faces. The only explanation anyone provided was I was so stressed that I was just shutting down.

I don't hold a grudge about what I went through, I just wish they had thought about, and looked for, a cause outside of their own discipline earlier on. Mental Health and Neurology both work with the brain – stronger links between the two may have saved me months of misdiagnosis.

Dr Sarosh Irani

Dr Sarosh Irani is a consultant neurologist and clinician-scientist with clinical and laboratory experiences in the field of autoantibody mediated diseases of the nervous system, in particular the central nervous system. Along with colleagues, he has looked after, and visited, multiple patients with these disorders, He also runs a research group to learn more about the diseases.

Figure 4.5 Dr Sarosh Irani.

Dr Irani has studied the antigenic targets of autoantibodies in patients with encephalitis and epilepsies. In particular, his research has focused on LGI1, CASPR2 and the NMDA receptor. In addition, he has been involved with projects examining autoantibodies against the GABA receptor, glycine receptors and aquaporin-4. He is currently exploring new antigenic targets, methods to measure antibody levels, mechanisms of antibody action and novel therapeutic agents as part of a Wellcome Trust Intermediate Fellowship. Dr Irani is a member of The Encephalitis Society Professional Advisory Panel.

A neurological perspective of Ross's experience

Patients who present with 'neurological' symptoms, such as tingling, headaches and weakness, are often referred to a neurologist. Those with psychiatric symptoms, such as depression, delusions and anxiety, are referred to a psychiatrist. Traditionally, the two specialities have had very different modes of engagement with patients, and very different sets of treatments. However, Ross's story, and those of others in similar situations, highlight the need for overlapping working practice in these two specialties.

The diseases known under the umbrella term 'autoimmune encephalitis' (AE) have recently emerged as a set of conditions which may unite the practice of neurologists and psychiatrists, to the benefit of patient diagnosis and management. Patients with autoimmune encephalitis often develop psychiatric and neurological features. The former include delusions, hallucinations, panic and mania; the latter include speech deficits, seizures, movement disorders and disturbances of the sleep cycle (Irani et al., 2014). But when all or many of these appear in a single patient over the course of a few days to weeks, as in AE, neurology and psychiatry input is required for both effective recognition and treatment of the disorder. Indeed a number of other neuropsychiatric diseases would benefit from such an approach (Zeman, 2014).

Many causes of AE can be rapidly identified by detecting autoantibodies which circulate in the blood and/or the spinal fluid. Autoantibodies are generated when the body's immune system reacts to a foreign organism. Usually these antibodies fight off the infection but sometimes when they turn on your own body they cause an autoimmune disease. If this body organ is the brain, an autoimmune encephalitis ensues. The two commonest autoantibodies target LGI1 and the NMDA receptor. More antibody targets are being discovered annually and, pleasingly, each appears to define an immunotherapy responsive condition (Irani et al., 2011).

In the face of increasing numbers of available tests, researchers are finding that these tests can appear positive in patients without the correct diagnosis. This can be a difficult clinical problem as the clinical diagnosis will almost always override the antibody result. For example, if a patient with a stroke has an autoantibody in their blood this should not distract from the fact that the diagnosis is still stroke. Spinal fluid testing for the autoantibodies can, in part, help narrow down the patients in whom antibodies are found in contact with the brain. These patients very often have a correct diagnosis of AE (Armangue et al., 2014).

Indeed, the major importance of AE lies in its, often marked, response to immunotherapies. This response can be observed very quickly, for example in patients with LGI1 antibodies. Alternatively, the response can sometimes take many months or even years. This is seen particularly in patients with NMDA receptor antibodies, and in this scenario a secure clinical diagnosis with antibodies in both blood and spinal fluid should persuade the clinician to persevere with immunotherapies (Irani et al., 2014).

But how do we continue to improve diagnosis and treatments? One way is to continue to develop new diagnostic tests each of which define immunotherapy responsive conditions. And this will continue. However, it is poorly understood which treatments work best and how they work. One way to answer this question is to perform clinical trials. These involve one drug being used in one half of patients, and a comparator drug is used in the other half. The half who do the best, have received the most effective treatment. But these are often difficult to perform in rare diseases, especially when patients may well have received several empirical treatments before the study. So, maybe this approach will never provide us with the answer.

An alternative approach might be to study the biology of currently used medications, to understand if and how they reduce autoantibody levels, or other disease-relevant parts of the immune response. For example, it is not clear how steroids reduce antibody levels. Nor do we understand how plasma exchange, which depletes antibodies in the blood, can affect the brain. Therefore the generous participation of patients to research projects is essential in furthering our understanding of treatments in this area, and helping the next group of patients affected by these diseases.

However, one critical aspect in diagnosis and in measuring the effects of treatment is a detailed understanding of the patient's symptoms. Ross's clear narrative and similar accounts from other patients and relatives, have allowed clinicians to establish a set of features which define the diagnosis of these disorders, and prompt appropriate antibody testing. Such accounts help us understand the details of the patient's journey, the input required by their relatives and carers, the principal concerns of the patient and carer, and the main residual problems which patients notice after the illness. This can identify features which were unexpected from a clinician's viewpoint: in other studies some of these have become the main measures used to judge patient outcomes (Nelson et al., 2015).

The multidisciplinary approach to neuropsychiatric problems has allowed better identification and treatment of patients with AE. In the future, more attention to patient narratives will assist in future clinical research studies to further improve outcomes.

Conclusion

Roy, Sophie and Ross have provided detailed accounts of their experiences, both the acute phase when they were very unwell (the latter with the help of family and friends), their later experiences and reflections on what happened to them, and the impact that has had for life as they now experience it. We also heard from Professor Solomon who reflected on Roy and Sophie's experiences. We saw that they were relatively typical of infectious encephalitis and he also shared some interesting insights from other patients into how the brain can respond to the effects of neurological illness. Dr Sarosh Irani considered Ross's experience of an autoimmune encephalitis and reminded us how sometimes specialties need to come together, along with how patient narratives such as Ross's empower clinicians and researchers when trying to create diagnostic criteria and in better supporting patients and their families.

We do recognise however that not everyone can share their story in the same way that Roy, Sophie and Ross have been able to. In these cases we sometimes have to rely on family and friends to help us understand a person's experience. In the next chapter we explore this in more detail as we hear from Jean, wife of Phillip, and consultant clinical neuropsychologist, Janet Hodgson.

Key messages
- People affected by encephalitis often describe a different sense of self, or loss of identity.
- People often try to return to their former lifestyles and work too quickly.
- In some situations things may not be able to return completely to how they were.

- Family and friends are all affected when a brain injury occurs, and are critical in the support and recovery of people after encephalitis.
- Life may be very different after encephalitis, but it can still be a life worth living.
- Even with intensive diagnostics we still do not know what causes encephalitis in over one-third of cases.
- There may be a growing need for neurology and psychiatry to work together more closely in the future.
- Patient narratives inform and empower researchers and clinicians.

References

Armangue, T., Leypoldt, F. and Dalmau, J. 2014. Autoimmune encephalitis as differential diagnosis of infectious encephalitis. *Current Opinion in Neurology*, 27, 361–368.

Egdell, R., Egdell, D. and Solomon, T. 2012. Herpes simplex virus encephalitis. *The British Medical Journal*, 344.

Granerod, J., Ambrose, H. E., Davies, N. W., Clewley, J. P., Walsh, A. L., Morgan, D., Cunningham, R., Zuckerman, M., Mutton, K. J., Solomon, T., Ward, K. N., Lunn, M. P., Irani, S. R., Vincent, A., Brown, D. W. and Crowcroft, N. S. 2010. Causes of encephalitis and differences in their clinical presentations in England: a multicentre, population-based prospective study. *Lancet Infectious Diseases*, 10, 835–844.

Irani, S. R., Vincent, A. and Schott, J. M. 2011. Autoimmune encephalitis. *The British Medical Journal*, 342.

Irani, S. R., al-Diwani, A. and Vincent, A. 2014. Cell-surface central nervous system autoantibodies: clinical relevance and emerging paradigms. *Annals of Neurology*, 76, 168–184.

Michael, B. D. and Solomon, T. 2012. Seizures and encephalitis: clinical features, management, and potential pathophysiologic mechanisms. *Epilepsia*, 53, 63–71.

Nelson, E. C., Eftimovska, E., Lind, C., Hager, A., Wasson, J. H. and Lindblad, S. 2015. Patient reported outcome measures in practice. *BMJ*, 350, g7818.

Sköldenberg, B., Alestig, K., Burman, L., Forkman, A., Lövgren, K., Norrby, R., Stiernstedt, G., Forsgren, M., Bergström, T., Dahlqvist, E., Frydén, A., Norlin, K., Olding-Stenkvist, I., Uhnoo, I. and de Vahl, K. 1984. Acyclovir versus vidarabine in herpes simplex encephalitis. *The Lancet*, 324, 707–711.

Solomon, T., Michael, B. D., Smith, P. E., Sanderson, F., Davies, N. W. S., Hart, I. J., Holland, M., Easton, A., Buckley, C., Kneen, R. and Beeching, N. J. 2012. National Encephalitis Guidelines Development and Stakeholder Groups. Management of suspected viral encephalitis in adults – Association of British Neurologists and British Infection Association National Guidelines. *Journal of Infection*, 64, 347–373.

Zeman, A. 2014. Neurology is psychiatry – and vice versa. *Pract Neurol*, 14, 136–144.

Chapter 5

The spouse

Jean Evans, Janet Hodgson, Ava Easton

Good news ... his condition has been stabilised ...
Bad news ... he may have permanent brain damage ...

Jean, Phillip's wife

Introduction

In this chapter we hear from Jean whose husband Phillip was affected
by encephalitis. Jean takes us on their journey of the acute phase when
Phillip was very unwell and what the future held for them in the years
that followed. Phillip decided upon the early information he wished to
include but, as his short-term memory is poor, Jean has written about
events leading up to, during and since his illness on his behalf. Jean's
story is accompanied by a parallel perspective from consultant clinical
neuropsychologist Janet Hodgson. Janet helps us understand how
encephalitis affected Phillip's brain and
make sense of the cognitive difficulties
that Phillip went on to experience.

Jean's story

Jean Evans is a freelance educational
consultant and author who specialises in
early years publications for teachers.
Jean has spent many years in the teaching profession, mainly in nursery and
reception classes. She has managed a

Figure 5.1 Jean Evans.

large nursery unit, opened a nursery within her large Victorian home and lectured in further education colleges. Her career culminated in the role of Ofsted Nursery Inspector and advisory teacher. These experiences now underpin her writing projects, including regular articles in the popular magazine, *Nursery World*, and over 40 educational books, published by Scholastic, Folens and Harper Collins. Following her husband's encephalitis in 2005, Jean continues to live in the family home with her Labrador, Sophie. Regular visits to Phillip prompted Jean to use her skills to support those living with multiple disabilities. She is a regular volunteer at the home where her husband is a resident.

Jean regularly enjoys visits to her children and grandchildren in Edinburgh and Suffolk. Jean and her youngest daughter, Charlotte, work as co-authors, sharing their teaching expertise: Charlotte's current knowledge of educational requirements and Jean's writing skills. Jean relaxes by roaming the countryside with Sophie, reading, lunching with friends and enjoying theatre and cinema trips.

Phillip was born in Darlington in May 1951, the only child of Ron and Evelyn. As a child he enjoyed playing football and attending local matches with his dad. He also spent a lot of time playing with his train set and was a member of the Boys' Brigade. After leaving school Phillip trained to be a teacher at Bede College, Durham. Initially he taught geography in a comprehensive school but found this too stressful. Phillip was quiet and shy by nature, preferring to be a listener rather than a talker, a follower rather than a leader. He found teaching in a primary school easier, and especially enjoyed running football teams and taking children on field trips.

Phillip and I met when we were both teaching at the same school. He refers to this moment nowadays as "love at first sight". We married in 1981 and had a daughter, Charlotte, later that same year. I also had two children from my first marriage, Simon and Sally.

The first few years of our marriage were happy, but then Phillip began to show signs of depression and anxiety. He never wanted to get up, especially on work days, and spent increasingly long periods on his own, usually in the garden. He became irritable and quick to shout at us all. As a result we found that we were all doing things that we knew would please him, or deliberately keeping out of his way.

As the years went on, Phillip became increasingly withdrawn and was diagnosed with depression. He began having panic attacks to the extent that he would not go into town or out for a meal, things he had once enjoyed. Eventually, he was referred to a counsellor who concentrated on managing the panic attacks. Phillip would be told to walk for five minutes among the town shoppers before returning to his car. He was never encouraged to share his anxieties with his family, and never asked about his relationships with family members. To me, this would have helped enormously. Instead he used to shout if I tried to help, stating that he wished to be alone to work through each attack. Watching my husband go through this as a helpless onlooker was extremely difficult.

Eventually, Phillip moved into an empty bedroom where no one could ask him how he was feeling. I did not understand what was happening to us, especially when we had been so happy. I tried everything, even putting a mattress on the floor beside him. His mind might have been in turmoil, but equally I missed him dreadfully and wanted to be next to him. When I continued to intrude on his space he shouted loudly:

"You don't understand, there's something wrong with my brain."

Things grew steadily worse despite the fact that Phillip regularly attended sessions with his counsellor. Occasionally, he would try to involve himself in family outings, but he remained an onlooker listening to us chatting with a bemused look on his face. He could not cope with having the whole family at home and would invariably take himself into the garden away from the noise and chatter. Meals to celebrate special occasions, such as Christmas, birthdays and weddings, were a nightmare to him and the panic attacks often returned.

In 2005 our lives were turned upside down. We decided to have a rare weekend away in the Lakes to celebrate our wedding anniversary. Phillip made a big effort, and the long walks and peaceful surroundings helped him to relax. However, our brief glimpse at possible future happiness was snatched away on our return when I learned that I had breast cancer. A mastectomy was organised immediately and Phillip tried his best to be supportive. On my return home we gradually began *to get back to where we were and planned a holiday in Cornwall to speed my recovery.*

At the time I did not think it odd that Phillip tried his best to cancel this holiday, telling me that the journey would be too tiring and that I wouldn't be up to it. I was so determined to overcome cancer that I was oblivious to the severe tiredness and confusion Phillip was suffering. He managed to drive all the way but, once there, he just wanted to sit on the beach or lie in the apartment, telling me constantly that he had a headache and couldn't think properly.

Recalling his past anxieties and depression, and his knack of withdrawing into himself, I could not help thinking that he was using imaginary symptoms to avoid facing the possibility of my cancer worsening. I felt angry at the time as the support I needed just wasn't there. I spent the week walking along the beach alone while he sat with sunglasses on, holding his head. Warning bells should have been ringing then, especially the night that he began to shake violently. He was clearly running a temperature and had a very nasty cold sore on his upper lip, a sure sign that he was overdoing things.

It is easy to look back now on this dreadful introduction to the acute phase of Phillip's illness and to think 'if only', but no 'if only' actions materialised and the holiday came to an end. As Phillip drove home he began to act very strangely. He pulled into a garage and offered to buy me a new car, the model I had always wanted. Nothing I said would deter him. He tried to persuade me to exchange our car for this sparkling new one. Fortunately I persuaded him to wait until we were home before deciding anything. I often wonder why this behaviour did not strike me as strange at the time. I just assumed he was trying to make amends for the way he had ignored me during the holiday. Remarkably, we made it home again but I will never know how Phillip kept on driving for seven hours in the state he was in. Of course, I was under strict instructions not to drive for three months so could offer no help.

Once home, the headaches increased and within a couple of weeks Phillip began to have blank episodes. Once, while he was driving, my daughter suddenly shouted "Dad!". I looked up with sleepy eyes to see the car veering straight into the oncoming traffic. Luckily, Charlotte's shouting had shocked Phillip into realising what he was doing and he swerved onto the hard shoulder.

A few days later in June, Phillip came in with a bag of compost on his shoulder and car keys jangling in his hand. He regularly helped an elderly friend with her garden and was planning to take the compost to her. He looked at me and stammered "Tarnbll, campasht". He was trying to say "I'm just taking this compost to Mrs Turnbull." "Phillip," I said, "you are not making any sense!" He glared and pushed past me to the door. I began to cry and shout so loudly that Charlotte came running downstairs. She was aware of her dad's strange behaviour patterns and took in the situation immediately. "Give me those keys!" she said, snatching them off him. He simply stared around blankly until I persuaded him to go to bed. I rang the doctor who did not seem unduly worried and told me to bring him to the surgery the next day. I spent a very anxious night but Phillip seemed fairly settled with regular painkillers.

The next day the GP examined Phillip, who was gazing around looking confused, and sent him to the Assessment Centre at the local hospital. Once there, he was given an MRI scan, EEG and blood tests. After a while, the consultant told us that, although there was no sign of a stroke, they were keeping him in overnight as his temperature was slightly high. I am ashamed of my reaction at this point. All I could think was that he was making a big fuss over nothing. After all, shutting off from the world was his usual pattern of behaviour. I told him I was going home and left him with our poor daughter. She was really shocked by my unfeeling reaction. By the time she came home she was very distressed. Phillip had stopped speaking and was gradually becoming paralysed down one side.

I kept a diary throughout this acute phase of Phillip's illness and the quotes in the box below relate to his time in hospital (I refer to him by his nickname, Phills):

Dear Diary...
June 6th
Phills had an MRI scan. He hated it and said "cement mixer in head"/"headphones".
I am managing to walk to the hospital without getting too tired after my operation.
Charlotte worries about Phills and me – poor girl.

Phillip's temperature keeps rising. His condition is worsening. He seems to be moving less and less. The nurse has to help him stand.
Staff seem more concerned with Phills' low temperature today. It is fluctuating constantly.

June 15th
Phillip was moved to the High Dependency Unit where he began to be very sick.
Consultant thinks it may be herpes simplex viral encephalitis. On drip with Aciclovir and antibiotics. Very scary place – more nurses than patients. I'm very scared – I'm told Phillip is very ill.
Phillip's temperature went down with this intensive treatment and so he was moved back to the Assessment Centre. He is still very ill and shivering and shaking.

June 18th
Went to another hospital in a blue light ambulance. Phills all wired up with me fastened in seat beside him.

June 23rd
Good news – his condition has been stabilised.
Bad news – he may have permanent brain damage.
Time will tell. Can't say how much of the old Phills will return.
I have to just think of each day and try to get through.
I wonder about our future but try not to.
All I want is Phills home and a simple life again.

June 27th
Phills very down and shedding tears when we visit.
Phills tries to speak but I can't understand him.

June 28th
I wish Phills could go back on anti-depressants.

July 1st
Phills is in a chair today. His neck flops sideways all the time. There is something called a hoist to get him out of bed.

July 3rd
Phills has a bad chest so an oxygen mask and nebuliser help his breathing.
Phills is managing to point his finger. Maybe feeling is coming back!

July 4th
Chest infection going. Easing off on medication as he has reached a 'plateau'.

July 11th
Phills very tired. Makes walking sign with his fingers and waves to tell us to go home.

July 15th
Consultant says no guarantee of recovery. He says the right side of Phillip's brain may begin to work for the damaged left side. His liver and kidneys are affected by the drugs.

July 17th
Phills on a drip at night because he is not drinking enough.
Phills had seizure in night and bit his tongue.

July 19th
Phills moved to room beside nurses for monitoring.
Phills tells me he had six lumbar punctures by putting up all digits on one hand and one on another!

July 28th
Phills very confused. He opens his mouth when the nurse asks him to open his eyes.

August 16th
Phills moves to rehab ward. Much better. He greets us by shouting "lovely wife, lovely daughter, lovely family".
Phills goes to gym for physio every day and can stand and sit down with two helpers.

August 22nd
Phills greets us with a whole sentence, "I've been waiting all day to see you."

August 25th
Humour is returning! I cut Phillip's very dirty nails. "Where is the dirt from Phills?" – "Could be my nostrils!" Speech therapist testing Phills' vocabulary asks for a word beginning with 't'. He laughs and answers "transvestite"!

September 2nd
Phills moves back to Ward 25. Staff pleased to see him again.
Phills makes up stories – he really believes that he is going to build a
bungalow when he gets home. Big ideas!

September 4th
Phills sobbing loudly when we arrive because we are a bit late.

September 9th
Phills can transfer from bed to chair with a 'banana board'. New word
for us, new skill for him.

September 15th
Consultant says Phills is in 'final phase' of recovery now. They are
planning his discharge! Wonderful news!

September 28th
Consultant says it will be months before Phills can come home perman-
ently. He may never have bladder/bowel control again. Roller coaster of
emotions these days.

October 7th
Phills convinced that he goes home today. He shouts and screams when
I say he has to stay a bit longer. Try going back into ward several times
but he swears at me loudly. Oh dear, he was so loving and doing so
well. Staff are so understanding when I cry.

October 9th
I stay away today. Can't face the anger as it brings back past problems.
Friends are asking about Phills. Seems strange talking about him so
calmly yet being so worried inside.

October 25th
Push Phills in wheelchair to hospital shop today. Daren't push him near
shelves as he steals things and hides them under his clothes. In the
queue to pay I notice the wheelchair move. Phills is trundling it with his
good foot. He picks up a huge bunch of red roses from the shelf and
holds them out to me. I want to cry. How can he be so angry one day
and so loving the next?
Phills tells me he has a helicopter and will fly me to Suffolk to see my
new granddaughter who was born yesterday. No need for the train. I
want him to come with me.

November 7th
Phills has a mattress on the floor as he keeps trying to climb out of his bed and falling. He sits on his bottom and slides around with a carrier bag putting anything he finds into it. I suspect he is packing for home. Today I found a stethoscope, a toilet deodorant block and a nurse's coffee mug amongst other things.

November 8th
Consultant asks for a second opinion from a behaviour specialist. Phills pulls his catheter out and clothes off constantly. He is wet, soiled and uncomfortable but he doesn't realise this. This is so difficult to bear!

November 15th
Very sad day! Consultant says Phills' confusion/behaviour is due to encephalitis and he will never be the same again. The best we can hope is for him to be like he was at his best on the rehab ward in July. I must face the future without the husband I knew. I just have no options.

December 6th
Phills moves to another facility for rehab and more behavioural psychology. It seems lovely and there are only six patients. I will only visit once a week and Phills will have intensive therapy.

December 15th
Nurse says Phills is very unpredictable. Sometimes he shouts and swears and throws his dinner on the floor. She says that happens when there is a lot going on and he can't cope.

December 21st
Nurse advises us not to visit on Christmas Day. His dad is cross and we are sad but I can understand her reasons.

December 26th
Visit Phills as a family. He seems to be settling at last.

January 1st 2006
The start of a new year. So glad to see the back of 2005!!!

The New Year began with Phillip making good progress. He was able to walk with a frame and his speech had improved enormously. Sadly, with his newfound ability to voice his thoughts, he greeted every visit with a smile, shouting loudly: "Good news, doctor says go home Phillip, your bed is needed! Bag is packed!". Staff waited behind a mirrored screen, watching and listening for the inevitable, while I tried my best to convince Phillip that he needed to stay a little longer. The nurse always came in then to calmly tell Phillip that the doctor thought he should stay. Phillip would begin screaming and shouting with tears running down his face. It was worse when Charlotte, our daughter, was with me as Phillip thought she had come to carry his bags. This continued for weeks, making every visit a tearful and traumatic occasion for us all. Strangely enough, Phillip was never upset when his father or friends visited. He seemed to think Charlotte and I were the only ones who could take him home.

By April 2006, almost a year after Phillip was admitted to hospital in Darlington, staff told us he had reached another plateau. It was decided that he needed permanent full-time care, but unfortunately there was nowhere in the area able to cater for his complex needs. Several weeks passed while the possibilities of finding somewhere seemed to slowly fade. Then a staff member remembered a patient with a similar condition who had been transferred to a residential care home. Fortunately there was one place available and so the manager travelled to meet with Phillip and staff. Everyone agreed that this facility was ideal for him.

The morning of Phillip's arrival at his new home, I went early to personalise his room with familiar items from home, such as favourite pictures and family photographs. The home's ethos of focusing on the individual was already apparent as Phillip was given a room overlooking the aviary because he had told the manager that he was a keen bird watcher.

The routine of life in a residential home began, and Phillip adapted surprisingly well. However, I soon realised that this was because he thought it was a convalescent home, another step closer to home. He kept asking why he was living with disabled people (he did not believe he was disabled in any way). He refused to join in with activities as he thought there was no point. "I'm leaving soon", he would say.

He could not be persuaded to take part by anyone, however exciting the activity. I discussed this with staff and we decided I should be the one to tell him that he would never be going home. The next time he asked when he was leaving I pushed my emotions right to the back of my mind and told him firmly, "Phillip, you will never come home again because I cannot manage to look after you. We will always be married and we will always love one another, we will just live in two houses instead of one." I expected the screaming and tears I remembered from previous occasions, but instead he smiled and simply said, "Good ... lunch now?" I suspect he already knew this subconsciously and was just waiting for someone to confirm the situation.

From that moment, Phillip has never mentioned coming home again. He takes part in activities he is interested in and particularly loves karaoke. Strangely enough he can read the words of a song and sing them tunefully even though he struggles with speech. Quizzes are another favourite and, although his memory for emotional life events has altered considerably (he only has good memories and seems to have shut away any bad memories), he can remember facts that many a Mastermind contender would find difficult. His number knowledge is unaffected by his illness and so he loves games involving counting and number recognition. However, if asked the time he will say the names of the numbers, for example, "one, two, two, zero" for 12.20pm.

Since Phillip's illness he has developed a desire for order and always wants his possessions to be where he can see them. I asked him to try to explain this new trait to his character and he said, "Phillip blank, blank, alive, not go again" by which I think he means he lost his identity for so long and now he knows who he is but is frightened he will forget again. By seeing his personal belongings daily, and following his orderly routines, he is still Phillip and feels reassured that he has not lost 'himself'. The staff at the home have been outstanding in the way that they have organised things to retain this identity. He has shelves around the walls where he can display his vast collections of photographs, mugs, badges, cars, owls, soft toys and treasured knick knacks. His radiator is full of fridge magnets and his drawer handles adorned with key rings. The mugs are arranged in categories with motifs facing him, the badges are in groups and the fridge magnets organised according to places they represent. There is a table-top train set complete with farm, zoo and seaside. Every day at the same time, Phillip sits for precisely ten minutes and watches the train go around. The teacher inside me has created green paper fields for the animals and a blue paper seaside. However, the positioning is all down to Phillip. The animals are in lines and they all face his chair. If one falls over he becomes agitated until it is put back in exactly the same place. The soft toys lean on one another companionably on the windowsill, all looking at Phillip. If one slips, then Phillip has to explain so that someone can put it back in the allotted space. However, he does not know the difference between words related to senses and so he will shout, for example, "Mickey, no, hear, Mickey!!" meaning "Mickey has fallen and I can't see him". To Phillip, see, hear, smell, taste and touch mean the same. When I asked him to smell the new aftershave I had bought for him, he tasted it.

Phillip keeps order by writing lists and filling in a diary. He lists things he needs or likes and he writes down television programmes he plans to watch and things he needs to do, right down to entries such as '12.30 go to lunch', '3 pad change' in his diary. He challenges himself to write lists, for example, of all the birds he can remember. His writing is now all in wavering capitals, and no longer includes lower case lettering despite the years he spent teaching children to form letters accurately.

Phillip will have been at the home for ten years in April 2015. During that time he has had several short hospital admissions and minor infections, and a major ordeal in 2009 when he was diagnosed with non-Hodgkin's lymphoma. Initially, his GP said he had mumps and he was put into quarantine but, when the swelling on his neck continued to grow, he was admitted to hospital for a biopsy. Six months of chemotherapy followed and Phillip inspired everyone by remaining positive throughout. When asked he would simply smile and say, "Well, alive!". As his main fear is losing his identity again, and the treatment did not do this to him, he dealt with the harrowing procedures well.

Phillip is now in remission and doing well.

Phillip's story has inevitably focused on some sad aspects of encephalitis, but to us the many happy times running alongside have helped us to cope. Thanks to the wonderful care home staff, Phillip has been able to keep his season ticket to his local football club and attend most of the home games, attend art classes at the local college and exercise classes within the community. He has treasured memories of giving away our daughter at her wedding and making a faltering speech that had everyone in tears, and enjoying a huge 60th birthday party shared by residents, staff, family and friends. He has shared holidays with fellow residents, and enjoyed many trips to places he loves, for example, the theatre, cinema, North Yorkshire Moors Railway, The Metrocentre and the Coronation Street Tour. Since his illness, four grandchildren have been born and Phillip is now a proud granddad.

Encephalitis has changed both of our lives, but it hasn't stopped them. We have lived through the tough times and changed for the better. The care home and their staff have been a major influence in shaping our new world, providing us with supportive, caring friends and helping us to remain a close and happy couple.

Phillip's hopes for the future can be summed up in two words, "Stay alive!" and I have to agree with him!

Figure 5.2 Phillip, Jean and their family.

Janet Hodgson, consultant clinical neuropsychologist

Figure 5.3 Janet Hodgson.

Janet Hodgson is a consultant clinical neuropsychologist specialising in working with people with neurological illness and injury. She is involved in providing individually tailored cognitive assessments, cognitive rehabilitation, psychological intervention and advice and consultation in a range of residential and community settings. Janet's work displays a commitment to helping not only the person affected, but also families in adjusting to life after acquired brain injury, taking a systemic approach.

Janet trained at Macquarie University and the University of New South Wales in Australia before relocating to the UK and completing further study at Glasgow University. She took up her first post with the Brain Injury Rehabilitation Trust. This involved working with service-users with moderate to severe brain injuries in an in-patient multidisciplinary setting. She then made the shift to working for various community teams in the now Leeds & York Partnership NHS Foundation Trust (i.e. Young Adult, Brain Injury, Stroke and MS teams) that subsequently restructured to form the Leeds Community Neurology Service. During this process she had an opportunity to take an active role in service redevelopment. She was subsequently employed by the Huntercombe Group before most recently taking up post as the consultant clinical neuropsychologist with The Encephalitis Society (www.encephalitis.info) in October 2014. Janet also undertakes private practice.

In her current role Janet is leading the development of an innovative specialist service for providing neuropsychological support to people affected by encephalitis across the UK. Technologies such as video-conferencing are being used so that a greater number of people and their family members have access to neuropsychological support post-encephalitis. The neuropsychology service (www.encephalitis.

info/support/neuropsychology-service) also has a strong commitment to improving awareness of and undertaking research into psychosocial outcomes following encephalitis both nationally and abroad.

Janet has shared her work through providing teaching and training to colleagues, students and people affected by acquired brain injury. This has included teaching Doctoral students at Leeds University, presenting at conferences, running workshops and facilitating peer support groups. Janet also chaired the Yorkshire & Humber branch of the Division of Clinical Psychology for the British Psychological Society from 2012 to 2013.

A neuropsychological perspective of Jean and Phillip's story

Unfortunately, I have never met Phillip, or his wife Jean. Nevertheless, having read their truly inspirational story, and drawing on experience I have gained working with people who have had encephalitis, I hope I can provide some additional insights into their journey from a neuropsychological perspective.

First, there is some reflection on the difficulties inherent in diagnosing herpes simplex viral encephalitis (HSVE). A neuropsychological context is then provided for the main difficulties that Phillip is experiencing as a consequence of having had HSVE, such as with memory, executive functioning and with regulating his emotions and behaviour. Consideration is given to the impact of HSVE on family members, and finally, there is a brief comment on rehabilitation. It is important to remember that each person's journey through encephalitis is unique and that the spectrum of outcomes is highly variable. Whilst some people largely return to life as it was before others are left with severe lifelong problems. Bearing this in mind, hopefully this account will help others in a similar situation better understand the pattern of difficulties that might be experienced, as well as factors relevant to recovery and adaptation.

HSVE is caused by the herpes simplex virus. A majority of the population have this virus and usually contract it during childhood. After initial infection, the virus lays dormant in the central nervous system and reactivates in some people periodically, usually in response to some kind of stress (e.g. ultraviolet light, fever). In many cases people experience no symptoms and in some people the virus manifests periodically thereafter as the common 'cold sore'. For reasons that are unclear, on rare occasions the virus can cause encephalitis. HSVE tends to affect particular parts of the brain. This includes the 'limbic cortices', sometimes spreading to the temporal and frontal lobes. These brain areas together are involved in making new memories, regulating emotions, and also in controlling responses needed for goal-directed and appropriate social behaviour (Lezak et al., 2004).

The symptoms associated with the onset of HSVE are often hard to make sense of. The first signs are usually behavioural or psychological in nature (Tselis and Booss, 2003). People may become aggressive or display a large array of strange behaviours. They may experience hallucinations (hearing or seeing things that are not present) or delusions (disordered thoughts, such as paranoia) (Tselis and Booss, 2003). The presence of the disease tends to be suspected when the patient exhibits physical symptoms such as headache, fever, drowsiness, seizures and lowered consciousness (Tselis and Booss, 2003).

Phillip's case highlights the difficulties inherent in diagnosing HSVE, and indeed other types of encephalitis. Initially he was running a temperature, and experiencing headaches. He was described as 'shaking violently' one night and had a nasty cold sore on his upper lip. He had 'blank episodes' including one particularly terrifying incident when he veered into the path of oncoming traffic. He impulsively suggested that he and Jean purchase a new car on the way home from a holiday. A few weeks later his speech became unintelligible (hard to understand) and he developed weakness down his right side.

Taking into consideration that Phillip had a long-standing history of anxiety and depression and a tendency to withdraw and display physical signs of stress; and that his symptoms first appeared after Jean had undergone a mastectomy for treating breast cancer, it is unsurprising that Jean thought Phillip was simply 'not coping' with her illness. It is also understandable that when Phillip suggested that they purchase a new car 'at whim', Jean thought he might be trying to make up for being unsupportive.

People can be ill for days, weeks and in rare cases months before they finally obtain a diagnosis of encephalitis. Sometimes they can be misdiagnosed with mental health problems initially (particularly where there has been a history of psychological problems or in some of the autoimmune causes of encephalitis, as we saw with Ross in Chapter 4). As was true for Jean, it is not uncommon for family members to later reflect on how they responded to the initial symptoms and feel guilty about not having sought medical attention sooner. But in reality, how many in the same situation would have thought anything was seriously wrong? Many of us are likely to have drawn the same conclusion as Jean.

Following the acute illness, the resulting damage to brain structures associated with HSVE leads to a characteristic pattern of difficulties with memory, executive functioning and with regulating emotion and behaviour often being experienced in the longer term.

Memory

Damage to the limbic, temporal and frontal lobe structures involved in the retention and retrieval of memories typically leaves the patient with memory problems. People with HSVE often experience 'anterograde amnesia'. This means difficulty creating new memories after encephalitis such that they can't recall information from the recent past. This appears to be the case for Phillip. For example, he finds it hard to remember things he needs or likes and which television programmes he wants to watch. He also has difficulty with remembering to perform an action or intention at a future point in time (i.e. problems with prospective memory). Phillip tries to overcome his difficulties with memory by writing lists and using a diary.

People with HSVE can also experience 'retrograde amnesia'. This means problems recalling information acquired before experiencing the brain injury, such as from recent adult life or even childhood. Sometimes people can't recall important autobiographical events such as their wedding day or the births of their children. Phillip displays difficulties with memory for word meanings (i.e. semantic memory problems). He confuses the meaning of the senses, mistaking 'smell' for 'taste' and 'hear' for 'see'.

Executive functioning

Executive dysfunction is associated with damage to the frontal lobes. 'Executive functioning' is an umbrella term for functions in the brain that enable a person to engage in purposeful actions and carry them out appropriately. Where executive functioning is concerned, Phillip appears to display difficulties with planning, problem solving and with monitoring and self-regulating his behaviour.

In contrast to difficulties experienced with memory and executive functioning Phillip has retained a great deal of his acquired general knowledge. We know this because to this day, he continues to perform well on quizzes. As is often the case following HSVE, it appears that aspects of Phillip's intellectual functioning have been largely preserved.

Emotion and behaviour

Phillip demonstrates a range of emotional and behavioural problems characteristically associated with damage to the limbic, temporal and frontal areas of the brain.

DIFFICULTY REGULATING EMOTION AND BEHAVIOUR

Phillip's emotions were often exaggerated and characterised by rapid shifts. This is termed 'emotional lability'. Phillip appears to have experienced difficulty with managing both anger and anxiety. He also displayed impulsive behaviour.

For example, early in his recovery Phillip would burst into tears when family members were late visiting him, or scream, shout and cry when being told he could not return home with his wife and daughter. Nurses reported that Phillip swore and threw his dinner on the floor. He had also attempted to pull his catheter out and take his clothes off constantly. Phillip tried to steal items during visits to the shop, hiding things under his clothes.

REDUCED SELF-AWARENESS

On initial admission to the home, Phillip kept asking why he was living with disabled people. Jean said that he was unable to see that he was experiencing difficulties of his own. Poor 'self-awareness' following brain injury is characterised by an inability to recognise problems caused by neurological (brain) damage (Crosson et al., 1989). Difficulties with 'self-awareness' tend to be associated with frontal lobe brain injury and executive dysfunction as the individual is unable to use feedback from errors made to modify their behaviour (Stuss, 1991). Reduced awareness tends to be associated with greater brain injury severity (Morton and Barker, 2010).

Two types of self-awareness following brain injury have been identified (Toglia and Kirk, 2000). These include: (1) awareness of difficulties experienced whilst actually completing a task, and (2) awareness of difficulties likely to be experienced before starting the task. The latter is often particularly compromised following brain injury, and makes it difficult for a patient to be aware of the broader implications of their impairments. This appears to be the case for Phillip. From Jean's description he appears to have some awareness of his memory problems but lacks an appreciation of the full extent of his difficulties with simple and complex tasks of everyday living and his associated support needs. Problems with self-awareness can be apparent both in the early stages of recovery following brain injury and in the longer term (Kelly et al., 2014).

When an individual's insight into their difficulties is compromised this can make it hard for them to benefit from strategies introduced to help them overcome their problems as they don't think they need help. However, reduced awareness can go some way to protecting people from experiencing depression as they are less aware of the degree of loss associated with having had encephalitis. Phillip appears to experience fewer problems with low mood now than he had done prior to becoming ill.

LOSS OF IDENTITY

Patients commonly report feeling that they have lost their 'sense of self' or their 'identity' following brain injury including encephalitis (Dewar and Gracey, 2007; Ownsworth, 2014). There are three areas of 'loss of self' experienced by survivors of brain injury (Nochi, 1998). These include: loss of self in relation to a pre- and post-injury comparison of the self; perceived loss of self in the eyes of others; and discontinuity of identity through lost or disrupted memories.

As Jean suggests, there is evidence to suggest that Phillip has had concerns about losing his identity. Phillip likes his possessions to remain where he can see them, and becomes concerned when an item is moved. It is interesting that Phillip explained this behaviour to Jean by saying "Phillip blank, blank, alive not go again". It appears that both Jean and the home have supported Phillip well in adapting the environment to help him preserve his sense of self by ensuring that items and activities that help him define who he is are visually salient.

Encephalitis – a family affair

Jean's diary exemplifies the emotional journey experienced by family members after a loved one experiences encephalitis. During the acute illness the focus is on survival. In the early stages of recovery attention turns to restoring the person as much as possible to how they were before. This is followed by a growing awareness of the likely longer-term difficulties, and finally, acceptance of the resultant pattern of strengths and weaknesses. In Jean's case, this latter stage was initiated with her poignant diary entry on 15 November 2005: 'I must face the future without the husband I knew'.

Whilst some people recover very well from encephalitis with little or no lasting problems, others experience severe, life-long disability. For family members this can mean that roles need to be redefined. For example, wives and daughters may also adopt the role of carer. People cope differently, but for some the journey to acceptance involves grieving for the loss of the person they once knew and embracing a new partner or father (Jacobson and Butler, 2013). This typically involves progressing through five emotional stages characterised by: denial, anger, bargaining (e.g. praying), depression and, finally, acceptance (see Kübler-Ross, 1969). Achieving acceptance often involves finding meaning in the difficult experience.

Rehabilitation

From a neuropsychological perspective, due to the pattern of difficulties frequently experienced after encephalitis, some of the more common interventions aim to minimise the impact of problems with memory and with emotional and behavioural regulation (e.g. aggression, socially inappropriate behaviour) on an individual's ability to engage in everyday tasks, and on relationships. There may also be a focus on helping the survivor achieve a new and coherent 'sense of self'. Where appropriate it is important to involve the person affected and family members as much as possible in identifying aims and goals for rehabilitation. Making progress toward these might involve teaching new skills (e.g. for improving anger management), introducing compensatory aids (such as a diary or daily timetable for improving memory and organisation) and/or modifying the environment. It is not unusual for carers to be involved in supporting interventions (e.g. prompting the person to use a compensatory aid).

However, it is also important to consider the needs of family members, some of whom will be feeling traumatised by the experience. Although emotional support may be provided within the context of formal psychology sessions, it is often the case that people benefit as much or even more from the support provided by social networks around them (Easton et al., 2007). This support may take the form of advice, practical help, or simply a listening ear being provided by someone that understands. It seems that for many of these reasons, Jean has found the care and support provided by the home in which Phillip resides invaluable.

Whatever rehabilitation and support is provided, it is important to recognise that the needs of each individual are different. Some will benefit greatly from rehabilitation and for others there will be limitations in what can be achieved. It is also important to be aware that as was the case for Phillip and Jean, recovery and adaptation often takes place over the course of months and years, as opposed to days and weeks.

Conclusion

In sharing their personal journey Phillip and Jean have helped people understand more about what encephalitis is, how it affects individuals and families, and how to 'cope'. Janet Hodgson provided some additional understanding of their journey and the difficulties Phillip was left with from a neuropsychological perspective. Jean and Phillip's story is one of resilience and thriving in the face of adversity. Phillip and Jean are living proof that even after severe brain injury, in Jean's own words, it is possible to be "changed for the better … and remain a close and happy couple". In the next chapter we consider what it is like to witness your child become seriously ill with encephalitis and we also hear what it is like to live with a parent who has sustained a brain injury as a result of encephalitis.

Key messages

- Brain injury is a family affair.
- Family members sometimes experience guilt associated with feeling they should have spotted signs of illness earlier.
- People can be incredibly resilient and it is possible in some circumstances for relationships to endure, albeit in roles and ways that may not previously have been imagined.
- Good quality person-centred care, that takes into account the feelings and needs of family members, is crucial in ensuring a good quality of life for people, and in helping maintain meaningful family relationships.
- Herpes simplex viral encephalitis (HSVE) can result in difficulties with memory, executive functioning, self-awareness, and emotional and behavioural problems in the long term.

References

Crosson, B., Barco, P. P., Velezo, C. A., Bolesta, M. M., Cooper, P. V., Werts, D. and Brobeck, T. C. 1989. Awareness and compensation in post-acute head injury rehabilitation. *Journal of Head Trauma Rehabilitation*, 4, 46–54.

Dewar, B.-K. and Gracey, F. 2007. 'Am not was': cognitive-behavioural therapy for adjustment and identity change following herpes simplex encephalitis. *Neuropsychological Rehabilitation*, 17 (4/5), 602–620.

Easton, A., Atkin, K. and Hare, P. 2007. 'A light in a very dark place': the role of a voluntary organisation providing support for those affected by encephalitis. *Neuropsychological Rehabilitation*, 17 (4/5), 638–647.

Jacobson, L. and Butler, K. 2013. Grief counseling and crisis intervention in hospital trauma units: counseling families affected by traumatic brain injury. *The Family Journal: Counseling and Therapy for Couples and Families*, 21 (4), 417–424.

Kelly, E., Sullivan, C., Loughlin, J. K., Hutson, L., Dahdah, M. N., Long, M. K., Schwab, K. A. and Poole, J. H. 2014. Self-awareness and neurobehavioural outcome, 5 years or more after moderate to severe brain injury. *The Journal of Head Trauma Rehabilitation*, 29 (2), 147–152.

Kübler-Ross, E. 1969. *On Death and Dying*, New York, Touchstone.

Lezak, M. D., Howieson, D. B. and Loring, D. W. 2004. *Neuropsychological Assessment* (4th edn), New York, Oxford University Press.

Morton, N. and Barker, L. 2010. The contribution of injury severity, executive and implicit functions to awareness of deficits after traumatic brain injury (TBI). *Journal of the International Neuropsychological Society*, 16 (6), 1089–1098.

Nochi, M. 1998. 'Loss of self' in the narratives of people with traumatic brain injury: a qualitative analysis. *Social Science & Medicine*, 46 (7), 869–878.

Ownsworth, T. 2014. *Self-identity After Brain Injury*, London, Psychology Press.

Stuss, D. T. 1991. Disturbance of self-awareness after frontal system damage. *In:* Prigatano, G. and Schacter, D. (eds) *Awareness of Deficit After Brain Injury* (pp. 63–83), New York, Oxford University Press.

Toglia, J. and Kirk, U. 2000. Understanding awareness deficits following brain injury. *Neurorehabilitation*, 15, 57–70.

Tselis, A. and Booss, J. 2003. Behavioural consequences of infections of the central nervous system: with emphasis on viral infections. *The Journal of the American Academy of Psychiatry & the Law*, 31, 289–298.

Chapter 6

The parents and their children

*Kay Adlington, David Birtwisle,
Thomas Tarlton, Audrey Daisley,
Ava Easton*

Laura asked me to pass her mobile phone. I always remember what she did next – as she took the phone from me she placed it into a glass of water saying "I've just parked my car on the motorway".

Kay, Laura's mum

Introduction

This chapter contains three stories: Kay, David and Thomas. Kay and David are both parents of people who experienced encephalitis, with varying outcomes in their ongoing levels of disability. Thomas recounts his experience of having a parent who sustained a brain injury as the result of encephalitis. They each offer varied perspectives in a condition that provides a limitless number of acute presentations, long-term outcomes and experiences for those who are affected, their family and friends.

Kay's story

Kay is passionate about all things 'family' and is often inspired by other family stories. Kay enjoys a rich and happy family life, which is ever expanding, creating new and great moments for her family to share. Kay has a love of travelling and considers herself very fortunate to have seen many different places around the world. Kay is currently learning Spanish as a second language.

Figure 6.1 Kay Adlington.

*In the early hours of 26th January 1987 I nudged my husband, Steve –
"it's time to go to hospital – oh by the way Happy Birthday!". Laura
arrived later that morning – an 8lb beautiful baby. Chloe was thrilled
at almost three years of age to have a 'new sister' – "she won't cry,
will she, Mum?". From birth, Laura settled in being a gentle, content
and beautiful baby. When her youngest sister, Becky, completed the
family two years later Laura enjoyed being an 'older, wiser' sibling.*

*Laura loved nothing more than going to school when the time came
– all through her educational life she was heavily involved with all
activities and often parents' evenings were a constant cry from her
teachers of "Laura organises me, the school; what would I do without
her?; she loves being here!". Mature beyond her years in both attitude
and aptitude. Her aim in life was to become a teacher.*

*As a family unit our 'chosen' hobby was swimming. All three girls
loved the club environment, the challenges of attaining new 'personal
best' times, the social side, the competitive edge and of course the local
swimming galas and bus trips with the obligatory visit to a well-known
eating place on the way back.*

*In 2005, Laura had just turned 18 years old, successfully achieving
good grades in her chosen AS-level subjects – Chemistry, Biology and
Physical Education (PE).*

*Wednesday 20th April 2005 was the start of 'what was to follow'.
Laura fainted while on duty as a lifeguard at the local pool. Within a
few days, the bug we assumed she had wasn't getting any better. Laura
was vomiting and confused and started walking into walls and door-
ways – she had no coordination at all. Exactly one week since she
became ill – Laura asked me to pass her mobile phone. I always
remember what she did next – as she took the phone from me she
placed it into a glass of water saying "I've just parked my car on the
motorway": my warning sign something was clearly very wrong.*

*Within 15 minutes the responding General Practitioner had checked
Laura over, rung for an ambulance and told me to pack her things for
a stay in hospital – he suspected she had a form of meningitis.*

*Thursday 28th April and Laura was on a general assessment ward in
a local hospital – no vomiting and very little confusion. This much
improved state of affairs lasted through to the Saturday. Many friends
and family visited, all looking somewhat puzzled by her 'good health'.*

However by the Saturday, Laura's mental state suddenly changed to full-blown confusion within seconds. Laura grabbed hold of my hand and in a voice riddled with panic said, "Mum don't leave me". She then had a huge fit. Suddenly alarms were ringing, nurses and doctors now in a frantic rush. Steve and I just stood watching – at some point we were asked to move; we clearly didn't want to leave her but they insisted.

Laura was moved to intensive care after a series of fits. Meningitis was ruled out leaving an unknown cause. She was treated with the strongest antivirals and antibiotics. Laura was put on a ventilator and into a medically induced coma. We stayed with her throughout the night talking to her constantly (something she later said she was fully aware of).

Laura was transferred by special ambulance to the Intensive Care Unit of a city hospital 25 miles away the next day. Registration at the new hospital was a bombardment of questions: Had she been abroad? Where? When? Had she been bitten by an insect? They discussed the brain and its functions before telling us that she had, in their opinion, encephalitis, with the front and rear of her brain affected. We both just sat there, stunned, "Encepha what??". We had never heard of it. There was our little girl on a machine helping to keep her alive, and we were completely useless. As parents you spend your whole waking-life loving, protecting, supporting, encouraging and sharing unconditionally. This shook us all to the core. We now had so many of our own questions.

A couple of days later we were told that the rash that was now covering Laura's body was a reaction to the drugs they were giving her and they were going to remove the ventilator and bring her out of the coma. I remember Laura fighting at this point – whilst we held her hands and talked to her she seemed troubled and not in control – the strength she possessed was immense – I remember feeling frightened by that.

The days following her breathing by herself were filled with endless scans – some aborted as Laura couldn't cope with going through the MRI unit at first, lumbar punctures, CT and ultrasound scans, blood tests, and heart traces as her heart was skipping. Scans were repeated as there was an issue with a potential clot in her chest – fortunately she was given the all clear.

Laura was still really agitated, confused, unable to follow conversation for very long. She often complained of double-vision, frequently vomiting, physically drained and extremely weak. Physiotherapy exercises joined her list of 'things to be done'.

There would be times when Laura presented as 'normal' i.e. she would tell us that the doctor had been round and said she may be able to go home tomorrow. When we mentioned this to the staff they said the doctors hadn't done their round yet. Laura was also convinced her doctor was an actor from the TV series 'Born & Bred' – James Bolam! Laura would tell us she had already eaten her lunch, then lunch would appear. Visitors to other patients were called monkeys or orang-utans by Laura – loud enough for them to hear!!! Thankfully everyone was understanding and took it in good humour.

She had no idea she was in hospital often asking "what are we all doing in Debenhams?"; the bedside cabinet was a caravan.

Looking back we laughed about so much with her. I remember my youngest brother visiting her several times, and each time he arrived Laura would say: "what's Lucy doing here again?".

One thing that was apparent right from her coming out of the coma was the lack of diplomacy or tact. She didn't have any at all. Laura was completely and utterly bone-crushingly honest.

Things began to improve very slightly. On Friday 13th May Laura wanted to get out of bed. I remember this reducing Steve and I to tears as she was so weak and frail. Typical Laura-style she didn't want the walking aid or anyone's hand: "I can do it!". I can hear her now; she did do it for all of four or five steps then almost collapsed. She couldn't walk in a straight line, bumped into things, but help was on hand. We took her determination as a good sign.

Laura's improvement continued over the weekend. There were more tests and scans but the doctors were now talking about her going home within that week.

The day finally came when Laura was allowed to go home, earlier than expected (18th May). A meeting was held on her bed with Dr O'Donoghue (aka James Bolam to Laura). I remember him telling Laura about what had happened to her, how things had progressed and that she would be able to go home. "Any questions?" he asked her. "Yes," said Laura, "are you married?". I remember him laughing and saying, yes he was, and he and his wife were expecting a baby soon. When he explained to Laura that she wouldn't be able to drive for a year her reaction was 'a little' less polite!

Once Laura came home we all breathed a sigh of relief, counted our lucky stars, and thought that was that! Two days later Laura had a vasovagal attack (a loss of consciousness). We were back to the local hospital again as she had completely lost her speech and eyesight after being paralysed. The starting point had been a tingling in her hands. Was this the sign of things to come? How different was her life going to be now?

Home life now centred on doing little 'normal' things with Laura again; nothing too strenuous.

Chloe's exam result arrived on the 9th June – 67%, a 2:1. She had worked so hard for a first and looking back, she had held everything together at home while Steve and I were with Laura. Becky too has always attributed Laura's struggle as her main inspiration which drove her to success in her swimming training and subsequent career.

Before encephalitis Laura was a normal teenager: frustrated with things; life didn't always go at her pace; and her parents seemed like dinosaurs at times. She had qualified as a lifeguard as a part-time job: a natural progression for most swimmers. She was accepted for a post at the local pool. Within a short time her work ethic was rewarded by promotion to duty manager. She would often deal with first aid issues in the pool environment. She was not the sort of person who would 'flap' or squirm at such things. She dealt with things logically and practically. Laura tried to go back to school in the autumn of 2005, but it was evident very quickly that she wasn't ready to cope. We enrolled a home tutor and deferred her university place until 2006.

By hook and by crook Laura somehow managed to achieve reasonable grades. Her short-term memory was non-existent. This was such a tough time for her. Photographs were often required to 'jog' her memory to remember something or someone.

For three years, mainly living at home to ensure as much support as was needed was available, Laura travelled to Sheffield on a daily basis. It was tough for her; she loved what she was doing, but really struggled with tiredness and dealing with so many balls that now needed juggling as a student. Sometimes someone had to drive her and fetch her back again; just the little things that would help her; she could then rest or sleep on the journeys. Wherever we could as a family we helped. Chloe was amazing, having been through university she helped Laura deal with so many things.

During this time I was still taking Becky to training every morning and weekday evening. Steve took over for the Saturday morning session while I spent some time with Chloe and Laura doing the necessary house things.

Laura excelled at university. She did have a wonderful support network on hand within the team at Sheffield. One of the lecturers had herself battled a serious illness and fully understood what Laura was going through, but also how to offer that guiding hand and caring shoulder at just the right time.

After finishing her degree in 2009 Laura started work at the local Academy as a Physical Education teacher and has gone from strength to strength.

Figure 6.2 Laura, Rebecca, Chloe and Kay Adlington.

Laura still has 'episodes' as we call them. Every now and then her hands tingle, her early warning sign, then either her sight or her speech is affected for anything from half an hour to several hours. Once this returns she has a monstrous headache and feels completely drained. We have accepted these things happen and put in place a system to provide her with help quickly.

Fortunately these episodes don't happen too often, but each one always acts as a reminder to just how far she has come and just what she has overcome.

Laura and her boyfriend Alex had a magical wedding day in 2013 organised by the happy couple themselves, and this year completed their own family by having their first baby, Henry. They are looking forward to adding to their family in the future.

David's story

David is the 72-year-old parent of Richard. After obtaining a degree in Applied Biology at Brunel University he researched filariasis (a parasitic disease) at The Liverpool School of Tropical Medicine and went on to join the Wellcome Foundation as an information scientist on tropical medicines. His research work led to the award of a PhD from the University of Liverpool. Later he joined the Regulatory Department and was on the Project

Figure 6.3 David Birtwisle.

Groups for Zovirax antiviral (ironically a drug that eventually helped save his son's life) and Retrovir anti-AIDS medication. He played rugby on the wing for his university and lots of squash and badminton. David has been happily married to Marion (a nurse) since the age of 26, and he is the father of two sons, Peter and Richard.

At 19.00 on Sunday 17th January 2004 our lives were changed suddenly, terrifyingly, horrendously, completely and forever.

Richard is 38 years old and the younger sibling of Peter. He gained a postgraduate diploma at the prestigious Northern School of TV and Film Studies in Leeds then joined BBC Bristol as a sound engineer. He was well liked and industrious. The BBC researched new techniques using Richard's special talents. He worked on the Antiques Roadshow and was especially pleased with his work, and credits, on The Life of Mammals with David Attenborough. For this work he won the award of Best Young Sound Engineer in the United Kingdom in October 2003. He was also an accomplished dinghy sailor, high diver, scuba diver, rugby player, football goalkeeper, etc. In Bristol he lived with his partner Karen on a narrowboat in the harbour and later in a starter home in the suburbs. He had known Karen since the age of 16 from their time together at college.

Life seemed good for our children, and us in retirement in a cottage in the Peak District. In the January after the award Richard and Karen went on holiday to visit relatives in South Africa. He sent back photos of them on Table Mountain and swimming with cousins in Johannesburg.

On Sunday the 17th January Karen rang from South Africa. My first thoughts were "why Karen? Richard speaks to us first". Her opening words sent a chill through me: "Dave, I don't know how to say this – but Richard is in hospital. It looks bad. They don't know whether it is dehydration or something worse. He is really bad and delirious. I'll call you again when I know more."

On the 18th Richard had improved slightly, was off a ventilator and was talking. On the 19th Richard was back on the ventilator and deteriorating. Marion and I travelled to South Africa not knowing whether Richard was alive or dead. We arrived in Durban on Wednesday and Richard was obviously extremely ill in a hospital side-room with tubes and leads all over his body, lights blinking and instruments beeping every few seconds. His temperature was spiking and he had a herpes virus infection which caused severe encephalitis. He was given massive doses of intravenous Aciclovir to kill the infection along with other drugs in an attempt to arrest the swelling of his brain. On Sunday night Richard looked dreadful with a purple face and bulging eyes as his brain swelled more. We were told to have as much time with him as possible that night and the next day.

Richard's brother arrived on Monday morning but the situation had deteriorated overnight. Life support was about to be turned off. Peter shouted and swore at his brother not to leave him then noticed an eyebrow twitch, and alerted the medical staff, who thankfully believed him and affirmed it. At the time, we were talking to a coordinator to harvest Richard's organs, who also told us of a good embalmer in Umhlanga! Over the next days Richard's temperature continued to spike but he slowly improved and by the 18th February was breathing unaided for limited periods. The staff at Umhlanga Hospital had been brilliant and kept us in the loop all the time. They were considerate and very caring at the worst possible time in our lives. We had known the terrible feeling of losing a loved son and then been given some hope. I will never forget my wife and Karen wailing outside the hospital on a lovely summer's evening in total despair, and my insides churning away in knots. We saw the beautiful sunsets on the Indian Ocean but we did not enjoy them. We just had to get through each day. We had the knowledge that Richard would never be the same again but hoped it would not be as bad as we feared. We would give anything for him to live – but at the same time wondered whether we were being very selfish wanting this. In those days we forged a close, unbreakable bond between Karen, Peter and ourselves.

On the 3rd March Richard was airlifted out of South Africa by private jet to a regional neurological hospital in the UK. He was back on a ventilator in the Intensive Care Unit (ICU) and had the first of many lumbar punctures and deep lung suctions. The staff were very good.

Richard had severe brain damage caused by herpes simplex virus encephalitis (HSVE) and was virtually totally paralysed. He was transferred from ICU to the High Dependency Ward after ten days. The nursing and medical staff were so kind to us and took time out to explain things, even though they were extremely busy. He was transferred to the neurological ward ten days later. We now seemed to be ignored somewhat and started to feel 'outside the loop'. All the leads, tubes, bells and whistles had gone. We told a staff member we were so worried that Richard would be vulnerable and she took time to tell us that he would be OK.

The next day we felt much better as he had a good night and was obviously looking well. The physiotherapy team were on his case.

Richard had a PEG tube (a feeding tube), a tracheostomy (a tube that supports breathing) and was having deep suction into his lungs which was horrendous to watch; it made his whole body writhe and his fingers extend backwards in a way I could not begin to imitate. One day while we were in the hospital garden Richard had a respiratory arrest and the crash team were called. About 20 people were around the bed and we could not see him for a few hours. It reminded us just how vulnerable he still was, and that anything could be around the corner in the next minutes, hours, days. Scary!

We thought only of Richard's survival; we were only going through the motions of eating and sleeping. Now it was time to look to the future and we really felt at a total loss. No help seemed available but thankfully we were told about a local charity dedicated to supporting people with brain injuries and their families. I went to an evening meeting and (embarrassingly, tearfully and emotionally) told Richard's story to a group of about 15 other relatives. Although they were sympathetic it became clear that they were more interested in recounting their own stories than listening to mine, so I shut up. However, one of them explained how to get help from the Social Services and benefits offices. At this time I was struck by the total trust we had in the staff at the hospital and the lack of understanding we had of what would happen next. If only someone could have sat us down and mapped out a possible future. Broken promises loomed large in our emotional state. A speech therapist promised to see Richard at a certain time but never arrived. She gave us further promises that never materialised. We were deeply hurt by this. We have since learned the hard way: not to believe everything we are told.

Every time Richard was progressed to a new unit we were worried (unnecessarily) that he did not seem to be receiving enough attention. But the big day arrived when the hospital announced that he was being transferred to another hospital for rehabilitation. We now had to begin to trust a completely new set of people of whom we knew nothing. And they had to meet and learn how to deal with us as well as Richard. We travelled every day to be with him, even though he still did not know us and was unable to talk.

Before we left the neurological hospital the consultant had advised us that Richard would always be a complicated case and that he might not improve. "He may never get any more than a small movement in the fingers of one hand", she said. She "hoped he would prove her wrong". It was good that she did not give us false hope, but Richard did thankfully prove her wrong. He gradually began to breathe better, abandoned his tracheostomy, and began to eat via his mouth. We were told he might be able to make noises and then gradually say a few words. However, straight away he said "ah that's better" and could eat any food. Use of his hands improved and they gave him a computer keyboard. I've still got the words he wrote "Richard iiis bbaaaaaackkkkkk". We travelled every day to see Richard while Karen was at work. She came in the evening whenever she could. Our families, brothers, sisters never saw us during this time and we were completely different people from previously. My sister-in-law commented that we had lost the son we once knew, but she had lost her sister too. Richard's illness was like a pebble dropped in a pool. The ramifications reached outward a long way to friends and family.

Eventually Richard moved to an Assessment and Rehabilitation Centre. We still travelled daily and it was taking its toll. We had used up so much emotional energy worrying and caring for Richard that we had nothing left for each other. We were drifting apart. So we discussed it and promised each other and ourselves that we would make time and reverse this trend. Luckily it worked. Now there were more new people and different working practices to get used to. However, again we were lucky and the staff were magnificent with Richard. His physiotherapy continued, including standing upright on a tilting platform – we had forgotten how tall he was!

Richard's care was still being funded by the local Primary Care Trust (PCT) but he now had annual reviews at which we were told to start thinking of the future when his rehabilitation was ended. But nobody actually explained how we were to do this and we just continued visiting as before. Eventually the PCT decided that Richard would not benefit from further rehabilitation and they would recommend Social Services. The manageress and therapists from the centre where Richard was did not demur, so we assumed everyone was working in Richard's best interest and we accepted the verdict. We then got a letter announcing the change and that we had four weeks to contest this decision. As we believed everyone was working in

Richard's interest we did not question it. Nothing happened so eventually I phoned Social Services in the area where Richard's newly bought bungalow was situated, and asked whether plans were advanced as he needed medication, pads, a hoist, chair, etc. etc. I was told to get in touch again a couple of days before he was due to leave the assessment centre. This perplexed me so I asked the manageress whether she believed they could sort everything in a couple of days and she was aghast. I then discovered, for the first time, there was a social worker at the assessment centre and they were brought into the discussions. A meeting was arranged with Social Services and it was soon clear that they had seriously underestimated the scale of what was required. Indeed, they wondered why they were being involved at all. Later, there was still no movement so we had a second meeting with Social Services. It turned out that management did not believe they should be involved, were ignoring the situation, and Richard was being left high and dry. At this point Marion and I were completely confused and did not know where to turn to get it resolved, one way or the other. The situation appeared to be drifting and it was left to us to phone around to make something happen. But what?

Serendipitously we watched a television programme that night devoted to the responsibilities of the Health Service for seriously disabled persons and it became apparent that Richard had a very strong case for continuing support from the PCT. We contested the previous decision but it was ruled that the appeal time was over and that this would have to be a new application to the authority responsible for where Richard's new bungalow was situated. Each PCT involved tried to defer responsibility to another and unofficially we were told: "they are all running for the hills because of the cost implications". After round after round of futile telephoning: "she isn't in"; "we'll get back to you", I was advised to ask for the head of department. Amazingly this usually had the desired effect and I was immediately talking to the person who, two seconds earlier, had been "out of the office". After involving the local Member of Parliament and the Chief Executive of the local Health Authority a panel was arranged and Richard appeared before them. The almost unanimous decision was that Richard should never have been referred to Social Services. We have never to this day found out which PCT is responsible for funding his care.

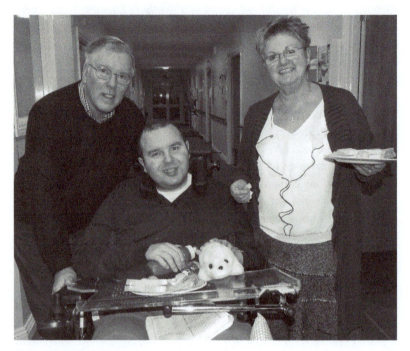

Figure 6.4 David, Richard and Marion.

Watching Richard survive from day-to-day is gruelling. Travelling is exhausting. But dealing with the authorities and often doing their work for them has been an uphill battle all the way. Many seem to believe their job is to withhold vital information, be economical with the truth and save as much money as possible. For instance, Richard was able to drive a powered wheelchair which would have greatly increased mobility. The local Wheelchair Services' policy was a push-chair for three years before eligibility for a powered one. Most people had either recovered or died before then! A further example: Richard had moved into a bungalow and married Karen. We requested a grant towards ramps and other adaptations. The procedure would take at least a year and include a detailed plan to be approved before and after by officials; we would be liable for most of the cost, and it would only be done to their specifications and time. So Richard's uncle and I built the lot, including a hard-core standing for two cars!

After five years Richard's condition plateaued and Karen could no longer cope with the situation so they were divorced. We were advised we could not care for Richard so he returned to the previous assessment and rehabilitation centre. Recently we applied for Mobility allowance because we found out that Richard would be suitable under present rules, even though he was in a residential home. He would benefit tremendously from being able to get out and about easily to restaurants, shopping, etc. etc. However, this was turned down because the home has nursing staff that give Richard his medication. Apparently it is not therefore rated as a home – it is now categorised as a hospital! As a hospital patient Richard would not need transport. As an otherwise healthy person in a home it would be invaluable.

To conclude, Richard has always been well looked after physically. But as well as keeping Richard's and our spirits up, we feel we have had to fight hard for even basic rights against the fiscal policies, and shady, unhelpful operations of the various statutory departments. We haven't described the many forms we have had to fill in requesting how many stairs Richard can climb and how far he can walk. Why are we dealing with various agencies including a private firm, all asking the same kind of questions in the same kind of lengthy form? Can't they draw a line under this after one form has been tearfully completed that Richard can do virtually nothing for himself? And why is the implication in the initial letter that we are trying to defraud the state when Richard would love to still be hard at work.

We used to be happy optimists but the future looks bleak for Richard. We are in our 70s and physically and mentally exhausted. We can do less for him each month. Who will champion him when we are gone? We are happy that he will be physically safe but his hand is clawing and his behaviour is deteriorating; and resources in the care home seem to be shrinking quickly as new management eye the profit margins ever more keenly and/or the state cuts its payments. The social worker has gone, the activity organiser has gone, physiotherapy appears to have been drastically cut and we have not seen an occupational therapist for years – although we are assured they are still on site. On the other hand we live in a country that looks after its disabled better than most in the world and we realise the country has to "cut its coat according to its cloth".

Thomas's story

Thomas is 13 and lives in an old house in Shropshire with his mum who had encephalitis, and his two dogs Lionel and Luca who he loves dearly. They are wire-haired dachshunds otherwise known as 'sausage' dogs; Lionel is 12 now so is a very old man and loves to sleep and somehow manages to snore when awake; Luca is two and is extremely lively and can often be completely crazy. Thomas loves football and pretty much

Figure 6.5 Thomas Tarlton.

everything to do with sport. He plays for his local football club; supports West Ham and enjoys school life. Thomas wasn't quite two when his mum had encephalitis so he doesn't remember much about her illness, but he does know a bit about how to cope if someone you know has had the disease, or if you just want to know how it feels to have someone close to you suffering.

I was 20 months old when Mum got encephalitis. One of the only things that I can really recollect was jumping onto my bed to get Minty and Polo, my two polar bear toys, so that I could take them for Mum. The first time I actually remember thinking of encephalitis properly was at The Encephalitis Society Family Weekend when I was five or six years old. Before then I suppose that I just thought that it was normal because that was the way I had been brought up. I guess it just seemed Mum had a really bad cold and needed to see the doctor. My mum's friends like Wanda made me feel so comfortable when she was ill that it just seemed natural to me.

As I have got older, I think that I have realised just how possible it was for Mum to have died. Also, I now understand how many different ways people can be affected by the illness and that some can be affected so much more than others. I can see that there is no certain trigger for encephalitis and that everybody's experience of this disease is so various that, to be honest, no-one can ever truly predict how fast someone will recover or how quickly they will be able to return home. People can be affected mentally, physically or emotionally, and all these have completely different impacts on those surrounding them.

Of all the words that I could use to describe my mum's illness, I have to say that difficult would be one word that I wouldn't use. However, I do feel that it can be annoying at times. I think that it has made her more protective of me and at times, I think overly so. Often, if I am going into town with some friends, she will want me to be back at the latest by 16.30. I wonder whether if she hadn't had encephalitis this would be any different? These are only trivial things, but they are things that annoy me most. Also, her memory sometimes annoys me as well. She has a good long-term memory, but her short-term is dreadful. On the other hand, it has made her more supportive of me and has really given her a goal to stay focused. I am so pleased that she has done this.

Of course I'm still aware of the effect and damage that encephalitis had on Mum and I know that it is important not to let her get too stressed or tired. Mum gets overwhelmed easily, rarely knows when to stop, and still thinks she can do all the things she could do before her illness. This is something I have to stop her from doing. I realise that she needs to have the freedom, but also the guidance to make the correct decisions. Nonetheless, it has made me more independent and mature. It frustrates me when she can't solve what I think is a simple puzzle such as a word search and can be very irritating when she can't remember events in the short term. In addition, I think her illness meant that I had to mix with much older adults, so now I feel more comfortable in their company. This is something that Mum having encephalitis has given me.

Being part of The Encephalitis Society (www.encephalitis.info) has really helped me to understand how differently people are affected. It has given me the knowledge that actually there are lots of people who do pull through the trauma other than the small few that I have met. Before, I thought that only a minority survive encephalitis; however, I now know that far more people survive than die from the illness. I have met so many people through The Society and heard so many people's stories. Their family weekends and other meetings have helped me to make friends, realise new things, and understand the effects and impacts of the disease better. Also, I feel as though I have a responsibility to make others aware of encephalitis.

I think that I have a much better relationship with my mum because I know that she needs to be cared for. I also have a much better relationship with my grandma because she looked after me for the time that Mum was in hospital and was recovering. She did this almost single-handedly and therefore I have a greater respect for her as well. I've spent more time with Mum because she doesn't have to work so we have had lots of time to develop our relationship and become better friends than anything else. I now value health and especially mental health more because people only see what is on the outside which is generally completely different to the inside and this is what counts the most.

The main piece of advice that I would give to someone else in my situation is that it may seem dreadful at first, but it is vital to stay positive; once you dig yourself into a ditch, there is practically no escape. There is a higher chance that your parent will pull through and, like I said before, you will have a much better relationship with your mum or whoever it is. It will make you much more sensitive, independent and understanding of those around you. It is important to always keep in contact with The Encephalitis Society because I felt they helped me so much more and really gave me something to enjoy. Also, someone younger than me would perhaps find it useful to read books like Gilly the Giraffe (www.encephalitis.info), My Best Friend Buddy (www.childbraininjurytrust.org.uk) and Tim Tron (www.thechildrenstrust.org.uk). They helped me to comprehend encephalitis better and made me realise actually what was going on: I could put it into perspective.

If I was to give health professionals any advice I think one of the main things I would tell them is not to be patronising. Although you are told to be caring and loving as it is part of your job, it is important to remember that sometimes, children just want to be left alone rather than constantly being asked if they want a drink or something to eat. It may seem that you're being helpful, but children often just want to have a good think or be on their own to

Figure 6.6 Thomas and his mum, Rachel.

visit their parent or whatever they want to do. However, it is still very necessary to be welcoming, but most of all, make them feel quite normal; they might not want all the fuss. Otherwise, some children do not like to be thought of as different, they just want to feel like everyone else, normal.

For me encephalitis is a thing of the past and it will most likely not affect me or my family's present and future, again. On the other hand, it is important to make sure that I don't lose sight of what Mum having encephalitis did for me and to always understand what those affected by it feel like. I know that the repercussions will never disappear entirely, and I'm not going to try and make them. I also know that Mum can pretty much only get better from now on so I don't think of it as something that really worries me. It is important for me to keep looking after her and keep looking ahead to the future, where the hopes and dreams lie.

Dr Audrey Daisley

Dr Audrey Daisley is a consultant clinical neuropsychologist specialising in working with families affected by neurological illness and injury. She is passionate about improving outcomes for families and helping the professionals and teams around them 'think family' and take a more relational approach to the services they provide.

Audrey trained at the University of Newcastle, qualifying in 1992 and took up her first post in a

Figure 6.7 Dr Audrey Daisley.

Paediatric Clinical Psychology Service at South Manchester University Hospitals NHS Trust. There she worked with children and families affected by a wide range of health conditions (such as neurological disorders, acquired brain injury and diabetes) and it was from this work that her interest in how families manage the impact of illness and injury developed.

In 1995 she took up the post of clinical neuropsychologist at an NHS neurorehabilitation service in Oxford (known then as Rivermead Rehabilitation Centre and now renamed the Oxford Centre for Enablement). She remains part-time in this role as a consultant clinical neuropsychologist (in addition to working in private practice) and is both the consultant lead clinical psychologist for the Neurorehabilitation Service and for the unit's Family Support Service; she has led the development of innovative and individualised family-focused support services in this context and has a particular interest and expertise in working with children affected by brain injury or neurological illness in a parent. She is committed to offering strength-based, resiliency-focused interventions that build on the existing skills that families bring to difficult situations. She is also interested in Emotionally Focused Family Therapy and Narrative Therapy approaches.

Audrey has shared her work extensively with colleagues through teaching, training, workshops for families and staff groups, conference presentations and research. She also has experience in acting in a consultancy role in relation to family focused service developments and in providing advice regarding family adjustment issues to a wide range of health and social care professionals. She was a founding member of, and remains actively involved with, the Oxford branch of the United Kingdom Acquired Brain Injury Forum (www.ukabif.org.uk).

A clinical neuropsychologist's perspective of Kay, David and Thomas's stories

The onset of serious illness in a child, or other family member, is typically a life changing experience for all involved. The effects of acquired brain injury (ABI) on the survivor and their family have been extensively studied and, in short, we know that for many the experience can be a devastating one. In this chapter three relatives of people with encephalitis describe, in their own words, how their lives have been deeply affected by the illness experience. The first two accounts are by parents whose children were affected by encephalitis; one child already an adult, the other a teenager just entering adulthood. The third account is by a child whose parent (his mother) had encephalitis; the experiences of children who have brain injured parents is rarely given voice (Daisley and Webster, 2008) and the inclusion of his story here provides an important and unique contribution to the encephalitis literature.

All three accounts provide honest and poignant reflections on what happened to their relative and we hear about their life before encephalitis and afterwards and how the experience of the illness both disrupted and shaped who they are today. Their narratives remind us of the highly individual and personal response of each family to the seemingly same situation and bear witness to the struggles families face and the strengths they bring. They highlight the unique and complex adjustment challenges that encephalitis presents and how, in particular, in this context, stories of despair and grief can stand alongside those of hope and resilience.

Consistent with the wider ABI family literature (Buteri-Prinzi et al., 2014) themes of loss permeate the parent stories of encephalitis. These are complex losses that vary and change with time as new understandings about their children's situation emerge and as the parents themselves journey through their own adjustment. We hear about the abrupt, acute, painful and immediate losses that the onset of encephalitis brings about. Both parents allude to having been propelled into a crisis without knowledge or time to prepare. They describe having to manage the sudden loss of roles, routines, expectations as well as their own complex range of emotions. However, as the parent/protector the priority must be the child and they are driven by the strong need to 'do something' (and for many parents this is akin to going into 'battle'). Meanwhile, others in the family (e.g. siblings, spouses or the children of the ill person) typically look to them for support and parents can quickly become overwhelmed by the sudden demands on them. For those with adult children this can be a complex undertaking; the direct parenting demands have typically lessened and different ways of relating to their children (who may have partners and children themselves) will likely have developed; parents may now be pursuing their own life-long plans for retirement and the onset of encephalitis requires the suspension (and possible eventual loss) of these goals (Minnes et al. 2010). The parent may need to step back into previously held roles of care taker, protector and advocate for their child without choice, preparation and knowledge of what is being faced. This can be accompanied by a myriad of complex and often conflicting emotions such as anger, sadness, fear, resentment and guilt. For those with younger children, 'normal life' as well as future hopes, plans and dreams are all suspended while the focus moves to the immediate crisis (Wade et al. 1998). In essence, when brain injury enters their lives, families lose their normalcy along with their sense of who they are; the telling of the story of their lives before (and the 'before' is often emphasised) and after encephalitis serves to urge the listener to listen to, hear, appreciate and feel their loss and to know 'this is not who we are, this is not our lives!' And so, when seemingly unheard or misunderstood, parents will continue to tell their before and after story (in the hope that we will 'get it') and can become stuck managing this distressing discontinuity if we do not indicate that we understand.

Clinical experience and the stories provided here suggest that sadly some brain injury professionals may not always fully appreciate the challenges facing parents. Staff expectations of parents can be high, but the parameters for their involvement are not always made explicit nor the 'rules of engagement' with the teams (and indeed their own child) made clear. Parents may feel they are seen as 'over-involved', 'taking over' and even as 'inappropriate' (e.g. if they wish to carry out personal care for their adult child) by the teams caring for their relative. Or they may be seen as 'disengaged' (when they stand back in fear or uncertainty) or in 'denial' when they challenge difficult issues such as prognosis or the amount of therapy their child is receiving. Parents describe feeling as if they are 'in the way', 'a nuisance' because they ask frequent questions or as 'struggling' to feel heard and understood. There is typically little guidance provided to families on the roles they should assume and how they 'should be' when working alongside health professionals and given that they are in the midst of crisis it is unsurprising that their confusion and distress might manifest as behaviours and emotions that some staff can find challenging. Morris (2004: p. 15) reflects on this issue when considering the content of many rehabilitation programmes; he notes that it can be a challenge for some brain injury professionals to "speak to the identity dilemmas" (facing patients and their families) and instead opt to focus directly on the manifestations of these deeper issues by offering interventions such as anger management, stress reduction. Whilst helpful for some families they do not address the issues at the core of the crisis. However, many brain injury services do take and work from a more relational perspective and can work alongside families in meaningful ways that embody partnership, collaboration and shared understandings.

For some families, however, there can remain a strong sense that they must 'fight' – fight back at the medical profession, health and social care services and those who make decisions about the future care of their children. This theme is strongly captured in David's account of his experience of the wider formal networks around his son. He alludes to feelings of anger, bewilderment and mistrust in the system and a strong fear about who will 'fight' for his son when he is no longer able to. Struggling against the system is a common theme among families of people with brain injury (Chamberlain, 2006) and in the post-Francis NHS (Francis, 2013) we must endeavour to support more brain injury teams to continue building their capacity to offer compassionate care that fits with families' lived experience of encephalitis.

Returning to the theme of loss and how this can vary with time for families, stories of loss in the early stages of recovery typically co-exist alongside hope, or restitution, narratives (Frank, 1997) – parents have acknowledged that their child is seriously unwell but remain firm (or at least hopeful) in the belief that recovery will occur and they and the family will be restored to what they once were. However, as a child's recovery slows and the permanence of the situation starts to become a possibility, parents (and other family members) are faced with new adjustment challenges. The loss that parents experience as recovery slows is complex and difficult for them to comprehend – their child is changed by the effects of the encephalitis – this may be physically, cognitively, emotionally and behaviourally; the 'old' child seems lost – yet they remain; the loss is incomplete and unclear. Parents are tasked with having to hold competing viewpoints of their child and their situation – "she is here physically, but her 'old' self is gone". Boss (2000) termed this type of loss as 'ambiguous' – the person with the brain injury is both absent and present at the same time; for parents this possibility is highly distressing, confusing and difficult to comprehend. Boss (2000) notes that without meaning families struggle to know how to cope; previously useful strategies may no longer be helpful and the effect is that they can become immobilised, stuck and exhausted. Coping and adjustment processes are blocked and they can experience an increase in emotional distress and in particular, hopelessness. Boss (2000) talks about the importance of helping families explore and find new meanings in the situation, to work on reconstructing their identity, to manage the contradictions in their story (e.g. I am both thankful he is alive and yet burdened by the guilt of his life as it now is), accept uncertainty and to re-evaluate relationships. In doing so families may be supported to move from this ambiguous position to a point where they may rediscover hope in different ways than previously. However, this is specialist intervention and many brain injury services are not equipped to provide this type of psychological care to all families.

It is not all bleak though! For many families strength and resilience are also present in their injury stories but these themes are typically more difficult to elicit (or be offered) in some, more problem-focused cultures. Walsh (2006) refers to resilience as not simply "bouncing back" from a crisis but rather "bouncing forward", strengthened and more resourced than previously as a result of having faced the injury challenges. The development of resilience- and strength-based interventions with families following acquired brain injury in both adults (Godwin et al., 2014) and children and adolescents (Gan et al., 2010) are becoming integral parts of many rehabilitation programmes in the USA and Canada and more and more UK teams are working from relational and family-focused frameworks. Patient organisations also support families in seeking the kinds of help they need and have given a voice to the diverse experiences of those affected by encephalitis and brain injury.

Such themes of hope, resilience and optimism prevail in the final narrative by Thomas, aged 11 years, whose mother had encephalitis when he was a baby. His voice in this book is unique as the needs and experiences of children affected by parental brain injury are typically unnoticed and as such they have been regarded the forgotten victims of brain injury (Daisley and Webster, 2008). A small, but growing, research and clinical literature suggests that in the context of parental brain injury children are faced by similar challenges to those of their adult counterparts; they too must manage the initial shock of the parent's illness, understand and cope with the changes they see in the parent and in their own lives as a result, consider what this means for them since parents typically provide important role models for children and then manage the wide range of emotions that arise in response to these challenges. This is typically undertaken by children in a private and unsupported way as the services that care for their adults rarely have the skills to address children's issues (Webster and Daisley, 2007). Children in this context may be vulnerable to emotional distress, can develop thoughts of self-blame for what has happened to the parent, and hold many misconceptions and misunderstandings about the parent's ability to recover and resume roles (Daisley et al., 2009). Few opportunities are provided for them to tell their story, for them to talk about the discontinuity they are experiencing as they try to relate to the 'new' versus the 'old' parent. Narrative-informed therapeutic approaches can be helpful in aiding children to explore and cope with these changes (Daisley et al., 2014).

Thomas's mother developed encephalitis when he was a baby and her living with encephalitis is primarily what he knows as 'normal'. In his account we do not experience him facing the discontinuity in parenting forced on other children whose parents sustain illness when their children are older. However, he does bear witness to some of the post-illness issues that challenge children in these situations – the irritation (and sometimes embarrassment) at the parent's reduced cognitive abilities, the over-protection that injured parents can show so that no further harm will befall their children and the acknowledgement that as a family there is now a need to do things differently due to the encephalitis. He also raises the issue of altered and reversed family roles that can follow encephalitis; he relates that he must at times be his mother's carer and talks of the importance he places on this role. He has re-defined the complex issue of young people as carers in a way that is meaningful and enriching to him. Despite these challenges Thomas has been able to take his experience of his mother's encephalitis, assign positive meanings to aspects of it that might otherwise have had the potential to distress (i.e. the reframing of her not being employed as an ongoing opportunity for them to have increased time together to develop their relationship) and create a rich and positive account of their life together. This is a hopeful message for parents with brain injury who worry enormously about the impact of their situation on their children (Edwards et al., 2014) and to other children facing such challenges.

There is learning here for support services to first attend to the stories that children who have parents with encephalitis need to be able to tell; like adults they benefit from having their fears, worries and concerns witnessed and then for them to be supported to consider this situation as a possible opportunity for new learning, positive growth and the development of resilience (Butera-Prinzi and Perlesz, 2004). However, this can be a challenging undertaking for services who typically take a problem-focused viewpoint and who regard brain injury as a set of problems to be fixed rather than as a springboard for growth.

Thomas told me that this was the first time he had ever "properly" told or reflected on his own encephalitis story – and that he had enjoyed and benefitted from the process. He told me he "might write some more in the future" as he would like to go on telling other children that encephalitis does not need to be "awful" and that he wishes to help. Andrew Solomon, US writer on politics, culture and psychology, in a presentation on 'how the worst of times makes us who we are' (TED

Talks, May 2014) urges those with a story of hardship to tell "to forge meaning, create identity and then invite the world to share your joy" This has surely been achieved by Thomas.

The three stories presented here bear witness to how parents and children can both struggle and thrive after encephalitis. In their own words they have shared their experiences of the personal and relational impact of their relative's illness and how they have negotiated their journey from diagnosis through to the present day – through sharing their direct experiences they have conveyed to us a very individual sense of what it is like to be them. The enormity of the changes they have experienced in key aspects of lives (in particular their roles, relationships and identities) were shared alongside stories of recovery, gain and resilience illustrating the complex adjustment challenge that encephalitis presents.

There is much learning in these types of accounts for the authors of these stories and for those who read them. Similarly, affected parents and children may derive comfort, knowledge and hope from these experiences whilst at the same time bearing witness to the struggles of others (Butera-Prinzi et al., 2014). Crucially, health professionals may gain a richer understanding of the lived experience of those living with encephalitis and use this knowledge to further develop support services for families that address the issues that are central to their concerns. If families can feel that we, as health professionals 'get it' (and many do!) – that we appreciate and honour the losses they have experienced through supporting the telling and re-telling of their stories we may be able to create a space for them to move forward feeling more understood, more resourced and more hopeful. As Kilty (2000) notes, "as more stories are told each individual becomes empowered and the community of story tellers becomes enriched by the diversity of the human capacity to adapt and develop".

Conclusion

Kay, David and Thomas have all shared their narratives in heartfelt ways. Their three experiences of the same condition are all vastly different, with Laura making a relatively good outcome, Richard much less so, and Thomas providing us with the unique experience of a child who has a parent affected. Kay touches upon the guilt parents can sometimes feel when one child is seriously ill and siblings might need to shoulder responsibilities they otherwise would not have been expected to. David also reminds us of the fears about the future experienced by ageing parents whose children have profound needs. Thomas provides us with some interesting guidance for professionals working with children who have a relative affected by acquired brain injury. Dr Daisley provides a good deal of theoretical evidence which frames their experiences and provides us with insight into the implications of their experiences in a more broad way. Dr Daisley reminds us of the importance of including the narratives and experiences of children, be they of parents affected or those of brothers and sisters. In the next chapter we hear from Tiggy about the loss of her son Johnny and the impact that had on her, and her family.

Key messages
- Outcomes in encephalitis can vary enormously from good recovery to profound disability.
- Brain injury in the family is a life-changing experience.
- Offspring and siblings can be unintentionally overlooked in the trauma of acute illness.
- Parents have fears about the future, particularly as they get older, and their adult child has moderate to severe disabilities.
- People can find the health and social care systems difficult to navigate and frustrating to deal with at times.
- Health professionals can gain a richer understanding of people's lived experience by listening to their narratives.
- Providing opportunities for children to share their experiences and to hear their narratives is important.
- Sometimes children, like adults, just need space, or to feel 'normal'.

References

Boss, P. 2000. *Ambiguous Loss*, Cambridge, MA, Harvard University Press.
Butera-Prinzi, F. and Perlesz, A. 2004. Through the eyes of a child: children's experiences of living with a parent with an acquired brain injury. *Brain Injury*, 18 (1), 83–101.

Butera-Prinzi, F., Charles, N. and Story, K. 2014. Narrative family therapy and group work for families living with acquired brain injury. *Australian and New Zealand Journal of Family Therapy*, 35 (1), 81–99.

Chamberlain, D. 2006. The experience of surviving traumatic brain injury. *Journal of Advanced Nursing*, 54 (4), 407–417.

Daisley, A. and Webster, G. 2008. Familial brain injury: impact on and interventions with children. *In:* Tyerman, A. and King, N. (eds) *Psychological Approaches to Rehabilitation After Traumatic Brain Injury*, Oxford, BPS Blackwell.

Daisley, A., Prangnell, S. and Seed, R. 2014. Helping children create positive stories about a parent's brain injury. *In:* Weatherhead, S. and Todd, D. (eds) *Narrative Approaches to Brain Injury* (pp. 143–164), London, Karnac Brain Injury Series.

Daisley, A., Tams, R. and Kischka, U. 2009. *Head Injury: The Facts*, Oxford, Oxford University Press.

Edwards, A. R., Daisley, A. and Newby, G. 2014. The experience of being a parent with an acquired brain injury at a neurorehabilitation centre 0–2 years post-injury. *Brain Injury*, 28 (13–14), 1700–1710.

Francis, R. 2013. *Report of the Mid-Staffordshire NHS Foundation Trust Public Inquiry*, London, The Stationery Office.

Frank, A. W. 1997. *The Wounded Storyteller: Body, Illness and Ethics*, Chicago, University of Chicago Press.

Gan, C., Gargaro, J., Kreutzer, J., Boschen, K. and Wright, V. 2010. Development and preliminary evaluation of a structured family system intervention for adolescents with brain injury and their families. *Brain Injury*, 24, 651–663.

Godwin, E., Chappell, B. and Kreutzer, J. S. 2014. Relationships after TBI: a grounded research study. *Brain Injury*, 28 (4), 398–314.

Kilty, S. 2000. Telling the illness story. *Patient's Network Magazine* (International Alliance of Patient Organisations), 15 (3). www.aissg.org/articles/TELLING.HTM (accessed 7 January 2016).

Minnes, P., Woodford, L., Carlson, P., Johnston, J. and McColl, M. A. 2010. The needs of aging parents caring for an adult with an acquired brain injury. *Canadian Journal of Aging*, 29 (2), 185–192.

Morris, S. D. 2004. Rebuilding identity through narrative following traumatic brain injury. *Journal of Cognitive Rehabilitation*, 22, 15–21.

Solomon, A. March 2014. How the worst moment in our lives make us who we are. Ted Talk extracted from www.ted.com/talks/andrew_solomon_how_the_worst_moments_in_our_lives_make_us_who_we_are?language=en (accessed 30 October 2015).

Wade, S. L., Taylor, H. G., Drotar, D., Stancin, T. and Yeates, K. O. 1998.

Family burden and adaptation following traumatic brain (TBI) in children. *Paediatrics*, 102, 110–116.

Walsh, F. 2006. *Strengthening Family Resilience* (2nd edn), New York, The Guilford Press.

Webster, G. and Daisley, A. 2007. Including children in family focused acquired brain injury rehabilitation: a national survey of practice. *Clinical Rehabilitation*, 21 (12), 1097–1109.

Chapter 7

The one who didn't make it

Tiggy Sutton, Michelle Hayes, Ava Easton

How do you do justice to your son's life, or describe his dying?
How do you show how you felt? How can you hope to comfort
parents who suffer the same loss? All in a few thousand words...

Tiggy, Johnny's mother

Introduction

In the three chapters that have preceded this one we have heard a range
of accounts from survivors, and family members. This chapter is different in many ways. We hear from Tiggy whose family lost their son
and brother Johnny to encephalitis. This is a powerful narrative and
one without which this book would not be complete. We also hear from
the intensive care consultant who was in charge of Johnny's care as he
became increasingly unwell and oversaw his departure from this world,
and the family's grief. Death is the very sad and unfortunate reality of
encephalitis for some families and this chapter helps us understand that
pain, loss and how families make sense of, and find ways to cope with,
what has happened to them.

Tiggy's story

Tiggy was born and brought up in Dorset. She worked in the arts before starting her own antique dealing business in 1982. She married in 1981 and had three children before moving to live in Hampshire. She was a full-time mother and spent 20 years fund-raising for the Youth Clubs of Hampshire. An idyllic country life full of children, dogs, cats, ponies and chickens, divided between

Figure 7.1 Tiggy Sutton.

schools, sports fields, holidays and family, was changed forever in 2008 when Johnny, her youngest son, fell ill and four days later died of encephalitis. She keeps herself busy now by walking her dogs, playing golf and tennis and travelling with her recently retired husband, and Johnny's father, Robert. She is a keen gardener and bridge player and is now regularly involved with The Encephalitis Society. Tiggy says she is bad at writing but hopes her contribution will help others.

This is Johnny's story, written in his honour – our tribute to him – a son loved, a life lived, a life lost. It is a story of love, remembrance and the survival of his family by filling the chasm with positive action, and channelling grief into something other than a black hole.

Johnny made an impact on people in his short life, and in his death he has also made a difference.

Johnny was our third, and youngest child, born in south London in 1990, a strapping nine pounder. He was a happy baby, and being the youngest, he was soon laughing with his family. He pushed himself to keep up with his siblings, Patrick and Joanna, and this continued throughout his short life. From walking at one, to leaving school and dying at 17, he made the most of life and embraced whatever came his way, always with a smile on his face.

Johnny's first four years were spent between London and Dorset, where he would happily roll around in the sand and sea, crabbing and building sand castles, with his family and cousins: an idyllic childhood. When he was four, we moved to Hampshire. He worked hard at school, played hard at sport and loved parties, but mostly enjoyed being at home with his family. Johnny was popular with his peers, both boys and girls, and with people of all ages. He was kind and thoughtful, gregarious and sensitive. He had a ready smile and was happy in his own skin. His position in our family meant he had by turns been teased, made to run errands, been spoiled and been the object of his siblings' jealousy, but he was ever the diplomat and kept the peace; he learned tolerance and gained wisdom beyond his years. He loved to play family games, whether it was tennis, cricket, rounders on the beach, or 40/40 in the garden. He also loved backgammon, Cluedo and especially Monopoly; there would be much shouting and sometimes sulking. Although energetic, he was often tired, and would stretch out on the sofa and watch television: South Park and The Simpsons appealed to his sense of humour; he recorded all the James Bond films which he watched many times over. He loved food not only to keep his fast-growing frame fuelled, but also for the pure pleasure of eating. However, he was a poor sleeper; it was as if he had difficulty turning his brain off, not helped by a vivid imagination and being scared of the dark.

Despite the fact that he was fit and full of energy, Johnny's immune system was not strong and he would often get ill for a couple of days with a temperature. He was stoic about this; it was just part of his growing up and at the time I didn't worry, but in retrospect, I am far more aware of his weak immune system. I now know that the immune system repairs itself with sleep.

Johnny developed glandular fever at 12, but this was short lived and he was soon back on the sports field playing college football. In his last year at school, he trained hard to be picked for the team. He ran, weightlifted and swam, and turned from a gangly 6' to 6'2" with a broad set of shoulders and a well-honed six-pack! His team won and he was declared man of the match. After he died his team mates created the 'Johnny Sutton Cup' for 'Man of the Match', which is still awarded each year.

In his last summer holidays before his A-level year, Johnny climbed Mount Kilimanjaro with his great friend Edmund. He did minimal training for the expedition and his only worry was about the altitude. Sure enough, both Johnny and Ed were sick halfway up the mountain. Even so, they made the summit, much to their relief, through sheer grit and determination. He raised £3,000 for local youth clubs.

When he left school in 2008, there followed a flurry of friends, beaches, parties and celebrations after the hard slog of A-levels. Going to bed in the small hours in Cornwall, Portugal and Corfu, Johnny was up again after a few hours' sleep, in order not to miss out on the sun,

Figure 7.2 Robert, Johnny, Tiggy, Patrick and Joanna.

*the sea and the fun with his friends and family. We had what turned out
to be our last family holiday in Corfu. His hands were a bit shaky and
he did complain of headaches, but I didn't worry unduly and put it
down to too little sleep and too many parties.*

*The rest of Johnny's life was beckoning: he had applied to Trinity
College Dublin to read Geography and Philosophy. After a stalking
trip to Scotland, he had a temperature on A-level results day. He had
achieved three A grades, and Trinity confirmed he had gained a place
for the following September 2009. His temperature was down in the
evening, so he went into town to celebrate with his friends, returning
early, having had nothing to drink as he was driving. They were a
close-knit gang, many of them having been through two schools for ten
years. There was always fun, joshing and laughter, especially when
Johnny was around.*

*The following day Johnny and his friend Charlie went to London to
plan their gap year together in South America. He was going to learn
Spanish for a month and had work organised for the autumn to earn
money; his gap year was taking shape, he was a happy boy.*

*He was obviously not feeling 100 per cent that Friday evening; the
boys were back early in our house in London, after a quiet supper,
alcohol-free. However, Johnny had difficulty sleeping that night, and
Charlie found him on the sofa on Saturday morning, taking 20 minutes to
rouse him. Charlie's father rang and spoke to my husband, Rob, to tell
us. I did speak to Johnny, but got no sense out of him. We told Charlie to
take him straight to Accident and Emergency in a taxi. He was sick, very
disorientated and confused. Charlie was terrified and knew something
was badly wrong. Rob rushed up to the hospital. Johnny was being examined; he had bitten his tongue and had clearly had a fit. By the time I got
there he was in the Acute Medical Ward. He had his eyes closed and was
moving his head from side to side a lot, and when I asked how he felt, he
mumbled "I am bored". The doctors had tested for drink and drugs, in
spite of Charlie insisting they had had nothing to drink the night before.
But two young boys arriving at the hospital on a Saturday morning
looked otherwise. The drink and drugs tests were negative. A newly
qualified young doctor came in to do his vital responses, which she said
were alright, but Johnny was far from responsive, mumbling incoher-
ently. I never heard him speak again.*

Suddenly Johnny sat up staring at the corner of the room with veins bulging in his neck and had a fit that lasted for a long five minutes. Doctors rushed in; we had to leave the room; it was too distressing to witness and hear. They stabilised him and eventually a lumbar puncture was performed, with me holding him steady. The doctor rang much later to say it was clear, no sign of meningitis and he still thought it must be drink or drugs. I felt quite sick, but it was going to be alright: he was in hospital. I hadn't heard of encephalitis, and there was no mention of it, although it turned out it had been put down as a question mark when he was in the accident and emergency department.

At 05.00 on Sunday morning, we received a phone call to say that Johnny had had another fit and was being moved to the Intensive Care Unit. We rushed there to find him wired up to every possible machine, in an induced coma and on full life support. It was heart-stopping; our beautiful boy lying there covered in tubes and wires. This was something you saw on television; this couldn't be happening to us. A registrar told us there had been an error in administering the drugs and the anti-epileptic drug had only been given for 24 minutes not 24 hours, but this wouldn't have made any difference, he said. We were in a surreal fog, we didn't know what questions to ask, but just went into a trance, sitting beside him, mesmerised by the machines. The nurses were working on him continuously, taking blood for analysis, keeping his stomach working, pumping green liquid in and sucking it out. Encephalitis was beginning to be mentioned but we still didn't understand what that was or the possible implications. In retrospect, ignorance was bliss at that point. It was my birthday; somehow we left his side and got some lunch, and I even shopped for an hour with my daughter. Johnny did not know or would not mind; he was asleep and he was going to be alright.

Monday morning brought no change except his kidneys were not functioning properly. A new consultant came on duty, and told us she was going to reduce the anaesthetic to see how he was out of a coma, but his body was in a continual fit and tremor. Rob asked her if "Johnny's life was in danger?" I was cross with him for asking such a silly question, and was shocked when she replied that she "couldn't give an answer to that question". We stayed by his bed, holding his hand and watching his every assisted breath, always with a tremor in his body.

He had a brain scan that afternoon, which showed no tumour, no swelling, nothing out of the ordinary.

On Tuesday his blood levels showed far too much potassium and then far too little. I learnt the levels have to be just right to trigger the heart muscle. As we were taking a break and texting family and friends with updates, Johnny's heart stopped and the consultant and nurses rushed to him. We ran the ten yards, my legs buckling as the crash team arrived and massaged his heart into pulsing again. We were shaking and without spelling it out to each other, Rob and I began to acknowledge how dire things were for him.

Later that night, Joanna came to see her brother and was as upset as we had been by the sight of him wired up to life support. She was brave, though, and Rob took her home, whilst I spent the night in a side ward. Patrick, our eldest son, was coming back from a holiday in America that night. At about 03.00 I was called to Johnny's side. His heart was beating irregularly again and the consultant came in and a surgeon gave him a pacemaker. I called Rob and instinctively rang my sister and her husband, who immediately set off to us, arriving at 06.00. By now I was on automatic pilot, acting normally, even smiling and asking the consultant if she had gone back to sleep. Rob picked up Patrick from Heathrow and brought him straight to see Johnny. He was distressed at the sight of his beloved younger brother lying inert, bare-chested, covered in wires, especially as we hadn't told him how serious it was until his return from America. To be fair we hadn't known ourselves.

My brother-in-law, Nick, a vet, was asking all sorts of technical questions about the drugs they were using, and he could see they were trying everything, including by this time, steroids. A priest came by, but I told him we didn't need him. Did I say "yet"? I can't remember. We had been to the hospital chapel that morning, praying like we had never prayed before. We were still in this vacuum of a twilight world, just existing and not thinking backwards or forwards. There was talk of a neurologist coming from another hospital to see Johnny and give an opinion. Not that it would, or could, change anything, but someone else to ask why, what is happening? We were told his car was stuck in a car park; how could such a mundane occurrence take place, when we so desperately needed something ... anything ... to cling on to. In a trance we went to a café opposite the hospital, not that we had an appetite, and were there when the call came. Come back.

We raced back, willing the slow lift to speed up. By the time we reached Johnny, the consultant and nurses were surrounding him and shaking their heads. My legs gave way again and I wailed, Johnny had taken his last aided breath. The nurses were crying, they had tried so hard to save him. Our boy ... how could this have happened? This was a nightmare and we were going to wake up from it. Shock came down and silenced us and we moved in slow motion like robots. He died at 14.10 on 20th August 2008. The priest came, we gathered round Johnny and knelt and prayed.

We drove home to break the news to Patrick and Joanna; Patrick demanding to know how, and why so quickly, Nick gently trying to explain in laymen's terms. They wanted to see their brother and we returned to the hospital to say goodbye to Johnny in the Chapel of Rest. The consultant spoke to Patrick and Joanna and told us that his organs had stopped functioning, but my impression was that they were as baffled by the whole traumatic four days as we were.

We had all turned our phones off in the last few hours, but now that Johnny's death was for real, we had to break the news quickly before the 'wonders' of social media took over. The outpouring of love we received was immense; friends simply turned up at our house. There wasn't much talking, just crying, hugging and a mutual feeling of dis-belief and shock.

Charlie had gathered many friends together locally and they all spent the night huddled together. Next morning the College Chaplain who had known Johnny well, held a simple service in the medieval chapel. Johnny's friends lit candles and hung little messages on a tree and began to write on Johnny's Facebook page. It was their forum for expressing their grief; for the next couple of years, mostly on Johnny's birthday and anniversary, messages continued to be sent. It is a comfort to know that he will always be remembered.

We got ourselves back home and began the process of living minute by minute, hour by hour, day by day, without our treasured Johnny. Our close family and friends and many of Johnny's friends came to visit in a constant flow. Emily and Vic, daughters of close friends, came to stay, to open the door, make cups of tea, cook meals and answer the phone. A week went by in a blur of flowers, letters and people, but mostly grief and love. The letters made us realise even more who we had lost. We discovered much about our son that we didn't know, and the comments made us both smile and weep. Edward brought round a photo collage with Johnny beaming out of each one, taken just three weeks before in Portugal. In hindsight, I regret we didn't give more time during those first few days to just Patrick and Joanna. They had to share us with the stream of visitors, but we didn't want to say no and batten down the hatches. There are no rules for this situation; you just muddle through, and for me consoling Johnny's friends helped me to stop thinking about myself. This must be the definition of 'heartbroken', it felt like carrying round a lead weight in my chest. I had little time alone except having a bath to soak away the tears and ease the pain.

Rob spent time in his study on the phone to the hospital and coroner about Johnny's post mortem. What exactly had killed him? Samples of his brain were sent away for analysis; they tested for Lyme's Disease, herpes, measles and all the known viruses that can cause encephalitis. They never found a definite answer.

We began to plan his funeral. The service took place in the little parish church next to our house. We chose hymns he knew; my brave children read lessons and we, his family, his many aunts and uncles, grandparents, cousins, godparents and very close friends all managed to sing and bid him farewell. The sun was shining as we buried him and we all threw flowers picked from the fading summer garden on top of his coffin, including a letter to him from the daughter of some family friends. It is a comfort to have him so close to us, and I visit him often, keeping the flowers fresh by the white headstone. I attend the church regularly and recite the Creed, but wish I did believe in eternal life.

It was at this stage we contacted The Encephalitis Society. We met Ava Easton in Winchester that autumn; they reached out to us and it was the start of our close relationship with them, which still continues. They knew what we were going through and they understood our trauma, lack of knowledge and bewilderment. Sadly they had seen it all before. Very kindly, they went through the post mortem to see if they could shed any light on what had triggered Johnny's death and tried to answer some of our questions. Much of it was too technical for us to follow but we slowly began to understand the truth about encephalitis and its vagaries.

We wanted to hold a memorial service for Johnny quickly, before everyone dispersed to university, school and jobs. The College Chaplain conducted the most extraordinary service in Winchester Cathedral. Joanna lit a huge candle and Patrick read a lesson. The Chaplain's address was full of hope for Johnny and us, it was about love. Three tributes gave a varied view of Johnny's short life, and brought tears but also smiles to the entire congregation. His form master described Johnny as 'hilarious'; Charlie, his friend, said 'Johnny was the guy everyone secretly wanted to be' and his uncle Nick told the mostly young congregation 'to lead their lives to the full and a bit more, in part for Johnny'. A thousand people left the Cathedral to Coldplay's 'Viva la Viva', Johnny's favourite tune of the summer, and for everyone there, Johnny's song.

Now for the rest of our lives without Johnny.

Joanna went back to university for her last year; Patrick started his first job and Rob went back to work in London. Since Johnny was born I had been a full-time mother; now one of my limbs had been chopped off. My family and close friends nurtured me with love and kindness. I found I had to keep incredibly busy, mostly being with people. I have never been a solitary person at the best of times, and being alone with my thoughts left me in a panic. Driving alone was quite dangerous, with tears streaming down my face and beating my hands on the steering wheel with pain and grief.

At first Johnny was at the forefront of my mind, constantly thinking about him and visualising him. When I closed my eyes the hospital scenes flashed up; when I woke or went to sleep, there he would be. Gradually, however, over the weeks, months and now seven years later, some, but not all, of the images have faded. The thoughts come less often, with a song or a place triggering an image or a memory, catching me by surprise, and making me start with disbelief that he is no more.

I wanted so much to keep Johnny alive and include him in conversations, even though there was nothing new to say about him. I always dreaded the question, "how many children do you have?". To tell the truth was painful for us both; to glance over it was to deny Johnny. I vary the answer depending on how strong I feel.

Our grief has eased, but it has never disappeared. The shock of Johnny's death helped to numb us for the first six months or so, but then the hard grind of living with our loss began.

We had already decided to take a holiday – a far-away escape. One girlfriend said "hold Johnny in your heart and take him with you wherever you go". Good advice.

Off we went to Buenos Aires. The Plaza de Mayor had special resonance: the mothers of the 'lost sons' who disappeared during their civil war hold a moving vigil, every Thursday. In the huge cathedral we lit a candle to Johnny, something we still do in any church we go into wherever we are in the world. We felt the pain of families in the famous Recoleta cemetery. We were on a journey both physically and mentally. The enormity of the Andean landscape, the majesty of the Iguazu Falls, the blue of the glaciers in Patagonia, the flight up the length of the Andes, all helped to lift our spirits. Most memorable of all was the immense sculpture of an albatross standing 40 feet high on Cape Horn; it is a memorial to mariners who believed that the albatross took the spirits of drowned sailors up to heaven. Two days later it would have been Johnny's 18th birthday, on 10th November 2008; surrounded by sea and hills, on that unbearable day, I began to plan a memorial garden at home.

The trip had been an escape and a distraction. The open spaces and physical exercise were soothing; we walked and rode, kayaked and drove through hills, gorges, rivers, glaciers and deserts, but it was time to return.

We missed Patrick and Joanna and worried that we were being selfish, not being there for them at this time. We communicated often by phone or email, each of us putting on a cheerful voice or brave face. This has been the pattern with us; we would grieve quietly in our four corners and come together to buoy each other up. If I become too emotional or build Johnny up as a 'wonder boy', I am reminded that he wasn't so clever, so talented and marvellous, just Johnny ... his unassuming self. They loved their brother as much as we did, but I don't think we really let them realise enough that we knew that it was as hard for them as for us. Rob lost his older brother William at 21, and so as a sibling he had been through this before. We have never thought of it as 'our' grief, we have shared it liberally around, and we continue to be impressed and proud of the way Patrick and Joanna have handled the loss of their brother so bravely and stoically.

We returned from our travels and faced our first Christmas without Johnny. Kind friends, whose family had grown up with ours, had invited us to their ski chalet. I could hardly speak on Christmas Day; but again physical exercise was a lifeline. Johnny loved skiing and there were many places on the slopes that reminded me of a certain jump or crash or bomb that he had done in previous years. We let off floating lanterns that night, all of us remembering and saying prayers to him. We were surrounded by love.

In March 2009 the inquest was held. We had an appointment with the consultant at the hospital beforehand, to go through the post mortem. Samples of Johnny's brain had proved inconclusive as to what had caused the encephalitis, so we were not expecting any great revelation, but they gently and in laymen's terms explained that his organs had all failed and the cells had died. The post mortem had revealed that the stem of his brain was inflamed with encephalitis. The inquest was a surreal, out of body experience, looking down on the coroner talking about Johnny, and the experts giving evidence. It was confirmed that his glandular fever, five years earlier, was not the cause of the encephalitis. I asked why he was only given steroids on his last day, and maybe I should have asked about the 24 minutes rather than 24 hours of anti-convulsant drug, but by this time I knew that nothing would have made any difference to the outcome. After about half an hour, it was recorded that Johnny had died of 'non-specific sclerosing encephalitis'.

We were back in touch with The Encephalitis Society again after the inquest. I had read every newsletter and every story of those who had died or were affected by it, trying to understand this illness that had so quickly robbed us of our boy. I needed to do something for Johnny, to keep his name alive, his memory vivid.

His garden has evolved over six years into a magical area: an informal circular space surrounding a bronze sculpture of a merlin in full flight. It's a natural oasis, a place to sit and reflect, the birds always singing in the now mature shrubs and trees, all given in Johnny's memory, and a happier place to be with family and friends than standing tearfully around Johnny's grave.

The College allowed us to erect a commemorative plaque to Johnny in a medieval cloister. My younger sister had found just the right words on my grandfather's headstone:

"To live in the hearts of those you leave behind, is not to die"

We held a service around the plaque; the family, cousins and a crowd of his friends came back for a gathering in our garden. It was a year to the day after the memorial service; they brought with them stones, pebbles, shells and even earth that they had carefully chosen with love and remembrance from around their travels, to put in the trough in Johnny's memorial garden. Rob and I still bring bits and pieces back from wherever we are in the world.

That year we set up a travel award in Johnny's name. The college boys selected would raise awareness and money for The Encephalitis Society during the year and in exchange would be helped with funds for a project in their penultimate summer holidays. In the first year, Ollie raised £12,000 and climbed nearly to the summit of Stok Kangri in Ladakh. The following year, three boys bicycled down through Italy, raising £10,000. Everyone benefitted from this: the boys, The Encephalitis Society and us, feeling we were doing something positive in Johnny's memory. The award ran for five years, meaning that a generation of his peers who knew of Johnny, were also made aware of something called encephalitis. Now the fund supports boys doing charity work in Ladakh.

Johnny's friends have also individually raised money for The Encephalitis Society by running marathons; two of Joanna's friends ran a half-marathon; Ed took up the Tough Mudder challenge; Nick is going to do the marathon this year; and Ed is going to organise a football match. They carry out these challenges for Johnny and it helps them too.

Patrick, Joanna and two of their friends decided to put on a charity party in London in memory of Johnny in aid of The Encephalitis Society. The 'Red and Blue Ball' took shape, the colour coordinating with the red and blue jigsaw logo of The Encephalitis Society. They cajoled friends and contacts to come up with a dozen great auction prizes, and Rob helped produce a glossy brochure, with advertisements paid for by city firms. A total of 220 friends arrived in red and blue party clothes. Patrick bravely made a speech and we all drank a toast to Johnny. The evening raised an astonishing £32,000, an amount beyond their wildest dreams.

The pinnacle of our fund-raising came with The October Club Dinner in 2013. Thanks to Ava, The Encephalitis Society won the pitch to be the Club's chosen charity that year, by showing how a significant sum of money could make a real difference to it. More tears of joy from the three of us! The Club also fixed a Race Day at Ascot in July. There wasn't much explanation about encephalitis at the lunch and afterwards, at the paddock, I overheard a group saying "what is encephalitis, is it a tumour or water on the brain?". I sidled along the rails and told them my story. One of them pledged to make up the difference between the amount raised and £500,000.

Four hundred city bankers and stockbrokers filled The Savoy, a glamorous affair, but rather nerve wracking for us. After the dinner a short film was shown introducing The Encephalitis Society and its work. It showed three smiling girls chatting at an Encephalitis Society weekend about how their lives had changed after contracting the illness. Tim Bond talked about his experience post-encephalitis, and, filmed in his memorial garden, I talked about Johnny.

Professor Tom Solomon gave a brilliant talk, and many of The Society's Ambassadors (all of whose lives have been touched by encephalitis in one way or another) contributed in some way: Simon Hattenstone lent his support by providing an auction prize; Aliki Chrysochou sang beautifully; Mathew Bose and Rebecca Adlington chose raffle winners and gave out awards. Then it was time for Rob to speak. Although he is an experienced public speaker, this was as hard as it gets, talking about his beloved son; you could have heard a pin drop as his gravelly voice wavered. The ensuing auction was a huge success and by the end of the night we had raised £400,000, plus another £100,000 from my Ascot friend, and we knew this was going to help transform The Encephalitis Society. We felt proud to have helped even though it was hard for us to speak publicly. Johnny's death has made a huge difference to The Society which has created an annual bursary in his name.

'Life goes on' and it does. We support one another and are supported by friends and family. Wilfie, a black cocker spaniel puppy arrived and breathed a new energy into our house, giving a reason to get out of bed and puts a smile on our face.

A huge blow came with the news that a good friend of Johnny's had died suddenly in a tragic accident on his gap year in India. Adam's mother and I console each other and as with a couple of other mothers who have lost children, we can bare our grief to each other in a way that only we can understand. It is a grim club of which to be a member, but we are a comfort and support to each other. These friendships are precious, and it is not all gloom. We have a cry, a laugh and a drink or two and we keep smiling for all our sakes, the dead and the living.

2014 has been a particularly poignant year, the 100th anniversary of the First World War. We went one cloudless morning to see the poppy installation at the Tower of London, and were captivated and moved by the sea of red: one poppy for one life. We empathised with those young soldiers' parents, their sons so far away and no body to bury. We are luckier than them and many bereaved. Johnny knew no pain, he knew no fear, he was not in some foreign country, he was at home, he was happy and we were with him when he died and he knew nothing about it. We did not have to say long heartfelt impossible goodbyes, or watch him die a slow, painful and frightening death. Shocking, yes, but no wounded disfigured body, and his handsome face without a mark or line.

"He shall not grow old, nor shall age weary him. We will remember him."

The clichés "time is a healer" and "it never gets better, you get better at it" hold true for us. Life will never be the same, but we continue to learn how to cope with our loss, though it is the hardest of tasks to endure. We all miss him beyond words, but we have survived; the human spirit is a powerful and remarkable thing. We do enjoy life as best we can, living it to the full, as he did, and in part for him – he would hate us to be unhappy. We have tried to be kinder and more thoughtful, and by helping others, we endeavour to heal ourselves. We have been loved by all around us. If there is a God, it is love.

Dr Michelle Hayes

Dr Michelle Hayes is the consultant in Anaesthesia and Intensive Care Medicine at Chelsea and Westminster Hospital, London. Dr Hayes was the consultant in charge of Johnny's care in the final two days, hours and minutes running up to Johnny's death. It was also her responsibility to communicate with the family and help them understand why their son had died.

Figure 7.3 Dr Michelle Hayes.

An Intensive Care perspective of Johnny's illness, death and the family's experience

Looking back I remember so clearly the time that Johnny was in the Intensive Care Unit. When I mention his name to other staff, they also remember him, as his death had such a huge impact on all of us. He was so young, barely a man and we were all devastated when he died.

I took over Johnny's care as the consultant in charge of the Intensive Care unit on a Monday morning after his admission with confusion and fitting the previous weekend. Unfortunately, there were already some signs that the course of his critical illness would not be straightforward. He was continuing to suffer from fits despite many different anticonvulsant medications and as time went on he was developing signs of multi-organ failure. The provisional diagnosis was encephalitis and the key things to be performed on that first Monday were both supportive and specific to the encephalitis. We agreed that continued treatment of the encephalitis, control of convulsions and further diagnostic tests were a priority along with communication with his parents.

One of the most difficult parts of my job is to impart bad news as sensitively as possible. It's not easy to tell a devoted caring family at first meeting that their beloved son may not survive. It's crucial that you can separate your professional responsibility from your emotions.

As the clinician in charge you must be able to push forward with care whilst offering support to a family in turmoil.

The journey from that Monday morning until Johnny's death on Wednesday afternoon was a roller coaster for everyone. It's unbelievable to realise that my involvement in his care only lasted 48 hours or so – looking back it seems so much longer.

Encephalitis is most commonly due to a viral infection in which the virus crosses the blood brain barrier and replicates within the neuronal tissues. In Johnny's case encephalitis was wreaking havoc in his brain and despite all measures his condition was deteriorating. In fact by Tuesday, Johnny was receiving artificial support for his lungs, heart and kidneys. As is sometimes the case, the diagnostic tests weren't particularly helpful. We called in experts from all specialty areas within the hospital to offer advice and we particularly involved experts from other specialist centres in the hope of finding some means of stabilising his condition. Sadly his deterioration was relentless with too little time for Johnny's family to be in any way prepared for his eventual cardiac arrest and demise. The end came all too soon – it was truly painful to witness the family's distress and we all felt devastated that we hadn't been able to save him. Many of the staff were unable to hold back their tears and cried for the family and their huge loss.

After Johnny's death we discussed his case at our internal meetings and continued to pursue the cause for his encephalitis but the underlying trigger for his illness eluded us. We see many cases where encephalitis is part of the differential diagnosis but it is extremely rare to see a case such as Johnny's. The inquest described the resultant destructive process as a result of 'non-specific sclerosing encephalitis' and it was clear from this that there was little that could have been done to arrest the process and save him.

It has been both painful and, at times, uplifting to read Tiggy's narrative. The account of Johnny's time in hospital and the family's subsequent loss reminds me of our own limitations. We know that providing intensive care will not save everyone but it was particularly hard to witness the death of such a young man. It has, however, been heart-warming to see how the support of friends, family and The Encephalitis Society has helped all of those who knew and loved Johnny move forward.

Conclusion

This is a tragic story as encephalitis stories can sometimes be. Despite everyone's best efforts Johnny died and his family and friends live with the consequences every day. We thank Tiggy for having the tenacity to share her heartfelt and brutal, yet inspiring, story so very openly, in the hopes it might give just one other family some comfort, or at the very least to know they are not alone. We also thank Dr Hayes for similarly reminding us how these tragic deaths can also impact upon those providing care and treatment in our health services. It seems perhaps trite to write more concluding remarks. Tiggy's story and Michelle's sincere supporting narrative really don't warrant anything further to be said.

Key messages

- Encephalitis can result in death and in many cases the cause remains unknown.
- After a death from encephalitis family members have many questions, and need to be supported to help find answers, where they exist.
- The human condition is fragile and yet, at the same time, resilient.
- Bereavement is experienced by people differently and individuals will find diverse ways of coping.
- Doctors and nurses also feel the loss of their patients, and can often be frustrated that our knowledge doesn't yet extend to being able to save everyone.

Chapter 8

Neuro-narratives

Authors and readers

It's almost like you're a life member of a club that you had, that you didn't actually choose to join, but you are and because of that you will never leave it because you can't...

Pauline, wife of a survivor

Introduction

So far Chapters 1, 2 and 3 have created the foundations for understanding encephalitis, its consequences and the role of narratives in medicine throughout history. Chapters 4–7 shared honest, searing and at times brutal accounts of survivors and family members which, at the same time, provided some comfort, inspiration and hope. These central chapters also contained analytical commentaries by experts in the field who clarified aspects of encephalitis in action and its consequences for survivors and their families. Chapter 8 looks in more detail at the use of narratives, and their effect upon authors and readers.

A person's sense of self and identity are concepts that usually endure through time (albeit with varying degrees of success as we progress through life's ups and downs); however, there are certain conditions under which they may be disrupted, such as neurological illness and injury to the brain (Biderman *et al.*, 2006; Chamberlain, 2006; Charmaz, 1994; Fraas and Calvert, 2009; Hyden, 1997; Lawton, 2003; Muenchberger *et al.*, 2008; Nochi, 1997, 1998, 2000; Ownsworth, 2014; Polkinghorne, 1991; Segal, 2010; Whitehead, 2006), and of which Chapters 4, 5 and 6 in particular provide empirical evidence.

The use of narratives as a primary resource for creating meaning and purpose, along with their capacity to bring structure to complex and unexpected events is discussed at length in the literature (Alheit, 2005; Atkin *et al.* 2010; Bell, 2000; Bruner, 1994; Jones and Turkstra, 2011; Hyden, 1997; McAdams, 2001; Phillips, 2003; Polkinghorne, 1991; Riessman, 2004; Skultans, 2000; Teske, 2006; Williams, 1997; Woody, 2003). Their role in framing "the exceptional and the unusual into a comprehensible form" is also reinforced by Bruner (1990: p. 47) when he says that our motivation to write stories comes from a desire to understand the world around us, particularly when that world takes an unpleasant or unexpected turn (Aronson, 2000; Bruner, 1994, 2002; Carey, 2014; Pennebaker and Seagal, 1999; Riessman, 1990; Teske, 2006; Williams, 1997). Therefore it is easy to appreciate that people's stories have an important role to play when people are affected by illness. The importance of telling one's story and being listened to enables a person to gain some distance from and perspective of their experience.

Narratives following illness allow the authors to decide for themselves what is important and which words they will use to describe their experiences, enabling not only structure and meaning to be created. In being heard people also gain a sense of validation. Stories of illness allow people, as we have seen in detail in Chapters 4–7, to document how their illness has impacted upon their lives and often the lives of those closest to them, facilitating opportunities to reconcile and come to terms with what they have experienced (Harrington, 2005; O'Brien and Clark, 2006). Narratives not only enable us to better understand individual illness experiences but also how they are rooted among people's relationships with others, their social networks and society at large (Skultans, 1998). By organising our narratives we not only better understand our present, we control and manage our experiences, and can plan for the future (Nochi, 1997) by reflecting on what has worked well, less well and what we might do differently in similar circumstances. In the same way that acceptance and adjustment following neuro-disability is constantly changing, so too then do people's stories (Segal, 2010).

Thus we can say with some degree of certainty that writing one's story or perhaps reading those written by, or about people, following encephalitis or other neurological illness or injury contributes to people making sense of their experiences and their ongoing recovery journey.

This chapter considers some of the theoretical and empirical evidence as to why people use narratives following trauma and ill-health (in particular those in response to encephalitis and its subsequent brain injury); the impact upon both readers and writers; identifies some factors that complicate our understanding; and concludes by highlighting the need to approach narrative use with caution in some cases.

Narratives and authors

In this section we look at authors and their narratives. The theoretical evidence is inter-woven with empirical evidence from the qualitative element of a study that considered in detail the role of narratives in the recovery of people following encephalitis (Easton, 2012).

People who write their stories do so in two broad domains generally: writing for personal and private reasons, and writing to effect some external or collective change. We consider the first of these.

Writing stories for personal reasons

Dealing with, or making sense of one's experience, is a substantial finding in the literature with many authors identifying this as having a significant role in why people write their narratives (Aronson, 2000; Baikie and Wilhelm, 2005; Bruner, 1994, 2002; Charmaz, 1994; Charon, 2001; Chesson et al., 1999; Hyden, 1997; Jones and Turkstra, 2011; Lillrank, 2003; Luria, 1987; Medved, 2007; O'Brien and Clark, 2006; Phillips, 2003; Pinhasi-Vittorio, 2008).

> ... if somebody asks me about it [prosopagnosia], you know, I can maybe explain it better ... because I've come to understand it better.
>
> (Claire, person affected, age 34[1])

This suggests that people's stories are perhaps less about solving their problems or finding solutions but more about their process: the journey as opposed to the destination (Bruner, 2002). The process of telling one's story can be a cathartic experience (Aronson, 2000; Robinson, 2000) and a way to deal with and extinguish fear (Kemp, 2000). In some cases writing one's story can be an attempt to reconcile feelings of alienation and estrangement which exist when people compare themselves to the way they were before their brain injury (Frank, 1997b).

> Writing it down made it real and I could say 'actually, you know, this is what happened' … this is what happened to me, this is how I felt…
>
> (Rachel, person affected, age 26)

This concept of 'reconstruction' is not unusual in the literature. Following a sports-related horse-riding incident which led to her own brain injury, one author who considered the impact of narratives and other creative interventions in detail, describes her doctoral thesis as the final chapter in a journey started in order to 'resume authorship' and 'commence construction' of her own altered life-story (Smith, 2007). Illustrating her paper are case studies of fellow brain injury survivors, one of whom, Diana, describes her old self having died and been replaced by a 'new self'. Smith argues that this loss of sense of self and accompanying loss of one's self-esteem are not only *consequences of* brain injury but *contributors to* the changed psychosocial circumstances in which people find themselves following brain injury. The narratives of Roy, Sophie and Ross, along with Jean's story in Chapters 4 and 5 repeatedly raise the issue of a different sense of self.

Some authors suggest that it is loss which people affected by brain injury/illness attempt to reconcile through writing (Durham, 2005; Morris *et al.*, 2005). It is possible that people's stories may act as a eulogy to their former self, a way of saying goodbye and accepting their altered/new sense of self, in order to make sense of their experiences. Poetry enabled Ned to find a new way to express himself, and he says that writing his poetry allowed him to organise his thoughts and reflect on them, and that through this process a 'new' Ned began to emerge (Pinhasi-Vittorio, 2008).

The process of writing and the structure that is required, even at a most basic level, may provide orderliness to people's accounts. Most people are aware of the conventions of a beginning, a middle and an end, and if the experience of those stories received by The Encephalitis Society are any indication then it is notable how many of the stories received follow a convention of 'this is who I was before', 'this is what happened to me' and 'this is who I am now'. Roy, Sophie, Jean, David and Tiggy's stories in Chapters 4, 5, 6 and 7 very much follow this convention. It is perhaps therefore the process of structuring a narrative into some kind of sequential monologue that provides those writing them with a sense of order from which understanding and acceptance can begin.

The Man with a Shattered World (Luria, 1987) is one of the most famous neuro-narratives (neuro-narratives are discussed in more detail in Chapter 3) of the twentieth century, documenting over the course of 26 years the struggle of Zasetsky, a Russian soldier who sustained a brain injury in the Second World War. Zasetsky is intensely occupied in documenting his experiences in his journals and notebooks (there is some similarity here to Clive Wearing's intense desire to document his 'awakening' following encephalitis: see later in this chapter) despite the creation of each word, the construction of each sentence, paragraph or conclusion being a battle. He himself struggled to understand why this compulsion to document was so important and concluded it was because it not only allowed him to assemble his past, but also to compare, arrange and consider his present experiences and desires. His documenting of lost memories was his only way of thinking and he hoped it would develop further his ability to think, and that he might once again be able to contemplate a future. Zasetsky is one example of narrative being used to create structure and coherence for experiences which are outside the control of the individual. Whether spontaneous narrative creation is useful for, or even used by, the majority of memory-impaired people, remains unknown; however, both Zasetsky and Wearing (as we see later in this chapter) demonstrate that narrative may be a tool to which some memory-impaired people turn.

Documenting a story may also result in externalising feelings: to make concrete something outside of one's own mind/self.

Um, I think initially it was sort of really hard because it would bring back so many memories, um, and make it real again and all that kind of stuff. Um, but then after that initial 'oooh', um, I dunno, I think it was just a really good way for me to get it out of my head.

(Rachel, person affected, age 26)

If you can externalise and potentially distance yourself from something then perhaps it means you can, however temporarily, stop living it. As a critically ill person you often have no desire or ability to coordinate a fact-finding mission that will enable you to make sense of, or participate in, what is happening (Rier, 2000). You are simply too ill. Therefore people's subsequent desire to explore and record the 'story' of what happened is quite possibly one attempt at making sense of that which they were too ill to do at the time, and for which they have very little clear memory.

The process of writing and publication provides validation and in some instances is a request for understanding and support from others (Frank, 1997b, 2000; Hyden, 1997; Lawton, 2003; Murray, 2000; Skultans, 2000). "Witnessing and receiving testimony are not solitary acts but depend on relationships to activate and sustain them" (Sparkes and Smith, 2002: p. 279). We are by nature collective beings and the groups we belong to shape our identity, yet isolation following brain injury is a well-documented outcome (McLean et al., 2012). Knowing there are others who have experienced similar situations is important in helping people make sense of their experiences and also as a source of hope and inspiration (Smith and Sparkes, 2006; Whitehead, 2006). Groups can also provide us with stability, meaning and direction (Haslam et al., 2009; Jones and Turkstra, 2011) and this may form part of people's decisions to join patient support groups or internet message boards, for example. Some authors suggest that narratives are a 'social glue' that brings people together in a 'common identity' through the process of sharing their narratives (Marshall, 2011). Both readers and authors report that narratives make them feel less isolated and in particular that reading other people's stories provided a sense of collective belonging (Easton, 2012).

In making sense of one's experience there also comes the opportunity to turn the 'negative' into a 'positive' (Fraas and Calvert, 2009; Glover, 2000; Kemp, 2000; Noble, 2005; Price-Lackey and Cashman,

1996). This is what Frank (1997b) calls a restitution narrative and which is similar in some respects to Nochi's *grown self* model (Nochi, 2000). The desire to positively reframe is evident in the online diary of Ivan Noble which reached international prominence on the BBC News website (http://news.bbc.co.uk/2/hi/health/4211475.stm, accessed 31 May 2015). Ivan, suffering from a malignant brain tumour, admits that, like so many, when he began writing he had no idea why he wanted to document his experiences. The closest Noble gets to providing a reason is "an urge to keep going and to try to make something good come out of something bad" (Noble, 2005: p. 81). Similarly, following his operation to remove a brain tumour, Martin Kemp (2000) described writing his book as a way of remembering and replacing the bad with the good times again. Jenny, who sustained a brain injury, kept a diary "to process thoughts and feelings that could not be openly expressed" (Price-Lackey and Cashman, 1996: p. 308). The authors went on to suggest that Jenny's narratives were not simply a documentation of her experiences but they were also useful in her interpretations of her experiences: creating positives from negative circumstances, aiding her recovery and enabling her to reconstruct her identity.

Narratives exist following neurological disease and brain injury, and they help frame, and reframe complex and traumatic events so people can better understand and make sense of them. Writing one's story and the process of being heard provides structure and meaning to one's experiences as well as validation and perspective. People's narratives also play a part in reducing their sense of isolation and creating opportunities for them to engage with others who understand. As a result the desire to write and share one's story can be important in people's recovery. In this next section we look in more detail at when people author stories for reasons outside their own personal development: writing stories for others to read.

Writing stories for others

In contrast to writing stories for personal reasons, some authors write for more collective or public outcomes, and they are often written with a specific audience in mind. They appear to be often preconceived, and with a clear desire to achieve certain outcomes by putting pen to paper.

Some authors identify communication as being an important outcome from writing their stories. Communication skills can be impaired following neurological illness/injury and can pose a major problem when attempting to re-engage with one's family and community (Galski *et al.*, 1998; Hyden, 2008). The ability to communicate effectively with other people is not simply a way of making your feelings known, although this is by no means an insignificant point. Effective communication is also about being listened to and, in particular, being taken seriously by other people.

> ...it was only for two people, people closest to me, my mum and my wife, just so that they understood what I was going through. I don't think I probably ever had a conversation with my mum about, about the time as such, until the story was written and we, er, then we had a good chat about it and boy did we have another good cry about everything that had gone on so it was good on that front so she could understand where, what I was feeling at the time, because at the time I couldn't express my feelings in any way let alone string a sentence together erm so it was good for her to understand.
>
> (Andy, person affected, age 34)

A further example includes a patient reciting a poem during a primary care consultation in order to express her difficulties. This prompted an extraordinary divergence from normal primary care custom when the doctor's practice concerned developed and ran poetry workshops for patients (Opher and Wills, 2004), resulting in improvements in patient-practitioner communication, and reduced levels of patient-reported isolation and loneliness (this is discussed in more detail in Chapter 9). Consequently, for those whose ability to communicate in conventional senses has been impaired, or who struggle to express themselves, it would seem narratives offer an alternative medium.

Power imbalances can exist between patients and practitioners in medical and healthcare environments (Atkin, 2003; Bell, 2000; Bury, 1991; Frank, 1997b; Lillrank, 2003). Narratives in medical settings are further complicated because people do not exist in isolation. Clinicians are part of not only the patient's narrative but also their own. Stories are made as well as told in clinical settings and being temporal in nature they are subject to changes in plot that might never have been imagined: conflict is therefore present and outcomes uncertain (Sorum, 1994). Consequently stories that are part of biomedical time, which is shaped by disease and treatment, as opposed to human time, which is influenced by motive and intention, can result in the main focus becoming pathology rather than the person being at the centre of their story (Bell, 2000; Carbaugh, 2007; Frank, 1997a; Mattingly, 1994). Consequently, health services, as well as those who are responsible for providing them, may be at significant risk of ignoring the patient's own understanding of their illness and disease. This results in the 'patient' attempting to find other ways to guarantee their experiences are heard. Johansen (2002: p. 56) illustrates both these points when documenting the story of her son's brain injury:

> although this medical institution existed for the welfare of its patients, all of whom relied on it for their healing, they were often reduced to objects submissive to the will and convenience of the attending experts. Patients' voices and personal agency were disregarded as largely invisible decision makers manipulated their body parts and organs. The vocabulary and tone of voice with which many staff communicated to patients was frequently condescending or patronizing.

She goes on to describe the chasms between the medical case notes constructed by the doctors which she describes as based firmly in the present, disregarding the past and the "biographical narrative we had lived with our son", therefore "contributions we as parents might have made ... were not sought by the medical professionals, social workers or chaplains" (Johansen, 2002: p. 45). This experience is reflected by members of The Encephalitis Society: "The doctors and nurses didn't understand – they didn't communicate with my family, even before they had confirmed the tests. Only one seemed to understand encephalitis at all – the nurses had no idea" (Hare, 2005: p. 33).

Adams (1995) further illustrates the desire to be seen as a person first and patient second. He was asked by Tom, an in-patient survivor who was hospitalised in 1931 following the pandemic that was encephalitis lethargica (circa 1915–26), to record his experiences. Tom's request was because he wanted their experiences as people acknowledged as opposed to what he described as "patients with a rare and strange pathology" (p. 79). He wanted his experiences of life in a hospital for over 50 years, recorded in their own right rather than as documentation of his disease and its progress. In other words he wanted his experience balanced with what he considered to be an overtly biomedical focus. Oliver Sacks (1991) described similar exchanges with his encephalitis lethargica patients urging him to tell their stories, lest they should never be known.

The paper co-authored by a father and survivor (Egdell *et al.*, 2012) referred to earlier in Chapter 4 by Professor Solomon illustrates a family's frustration at not knowing if their son would survive and, when he did, no-one had prepared them for the changes in his personality and behaviour. A further paper by Crow (2006) documents her brother's brain death, their end of life decision-making, and attempts to de-medicalise a situation that had profound social and emotional, as well as clinical, implications. Recounting her family's experiences of their interactions with the medical professionals involved, they reconstructed medical and often brutal communications into narratives that were more meaningful for them. For example, the news from the doctor that her brother's brain injury was "the worst injury he'd ever seen" (p. 178) was translated by the family as evidence of his tenacity, that he was a fighter, and perhaps more importantly a potential survivor. Crow's narrative describes her anger with the medical profession, both in their treatment of her brother and of their inaccessibility to them as a family. Other papers (Jumisko *et al.*, 2007) urge professionals to pay more attention to the voices of relatives: it is not only important in understanding them, but also in alleviating their suffering (Man, 2002; Ponsford *et al.*, 2003). David's narrative in Chapter 6 is a further eloquent expression of a relative's frustration with healthcare services and the often associated bureaucracy.

These accounts raise a potential gap between the practice of health professionals and physicians and the expectations and experiences of patients and their families. Often recipients of healthcare want their opinions sought and listened to. Where information is provided it is sometimes felt to be insensitive, overtly medical in its use of language, and delivered with little regard to the impact it might have upon the recipients, who, in turn, are struggling to come to terms with the unexpected and unfolding trauma before them. The responses of doctors and other practitioners also impact upon a family's ability to cope with what may be the return of a relative who is very different to the one who became ill. Narratives can be a medium through which people document their experiences in response to what they consider overtly dominant medical communications and which demonstrate their desire to influence and change understanding, behaviour and practice.

Living with hidden disabilities (as outlined in Chapter 2, and as described in more detail in the survivor narratives in Chapter 4) often means not being believed. This can mean struggling to access rehabilitation and treatment, as well as experiencing professionals who may be insensitive and lacking in empathy (Lorenz, 2010). Perhaps for these reasons some authors write with a view to changing professional and public understanding, behaviour and practice (Crow, 2006; Foust, 2008; Glover, 2000; Hill, 1999; Hogan, 1999; Lanza, 2006). In a single brain injury case study, the author thanks the case study for "bearing [*sic*] his soul in the hope that his story would help to further understanding" among health professionals and rehabilitationists (Glover, 2000, p. 476). Foust (2008) documents the gap between the reality of family members' experiences following brain injury, and the superficial analogies used by the doctors which in no way prepared her for the depth and gravity of her experiences.

Desire to make changes in professional understanding, behaviour and practice needs, however, to be a subtle one in order to be published in peer-reviewed journals, by those whose practice and behaviour is challenged and is the desired focus of change (Smith and Squire, 2007). One nurse's experience of her medical and therapeutic treatment following a stroke (Lanza, 2006) included a 13-point 'Lessons Learned For Nurses' – an example of an attempt to improve understanding and practice among colleagues. Clinicians who experience a clinical situation of such magnitude also sometimes write papers to encourage more mindful practices among colleagues (Wilson *et al.*, 2001). This paper describes the author's shock at finding a patient emerging from a vegetative or minimally conscious state with severe physical and communication problems but who was completely cognitively intact. Such was the horror described by this young woman of her experiences with those responsible for her care, the authors felt compelled to write a paper including some of the young woman's own narrative. The authors were explicit in their desire to urge the medical profession to review their practices in the care of such patients. Writing to challenge, review, reflect and effect changes in practice is important.

Patient narratives can also be useful in educating other patients and families about the recovery process (Fraas and Calvert, 2009). There is evidence of authors writing to provide guidance for people directly affected or family members experiencing the trauma associated with neuro-illness/disability (Hogan, 1999; Lillrank, 2003). Markham (2014) explicitly states her book about her husband's brain injury is written in the hopes of bringing "comfort and help to people that have suffered or lived with brain injury" (p. 5). Pape (2005) describes the author's recovery having sustained life-threatening head injuries following a motorcycle accident. His primary intention in writing the book was to give direction to others, because "Carol [his wife] often said she would have benefited from reading a book like this whilst I was so ill in hospital, to give her an idea of what to expect, if and when I recovered" (p. ii). Many other texts exist for similar reasons (see Durham, 2005; Hammond, 2007; McCann, 2006). Understandably, traumatic experiences can foster a desire to provide direction and guidance for others and it may be one of the few positive things people believe they can do when they feel their lives have lost control.

We have considered the motivations and intentions with which people write: for personal and public reasons, and to influence or support others. In the section that follows we take the unusual step of looking at the impact of narratives not upon those who write them, but upon those who read them.

Narratives and readers

Little research has looked at the impact of reading stories written by, or about, people affected by neurological illness and injury. What follows is a brief look at findings from a study (Easton, 2012) that considered this subject among a post-encephalitic population.

Most people's experiences of encephalitis narratives are positive, with a minority for whom they are negative (more of this later in this chapter) and a small number whose feelings fluctuated (Easton, 2012).

Similarly to authors, readers tend to turn to stories for both personal and more public or collective reasons. What follows is a consideration of each in turn.

Reading stories for personal reasons

Improvements in understanding and making sense of their own, or that of a family member's experiences following encephalitis, was a common expression:

> ... I'd never ever heard of it before ... I was on a school trip in Stratford and then the next minute I was in hospital for five months. For me it was such a big, life-changing thing but I did want to read, when I could, I wanted to read them just to try and make sense of it all, and try and understand what was going on and that I wasn't some weird person and it was the only one that'd ever happened.
>
> (Rachel, person affected, age 26)

Whilst those directly affected by encephalitis use stories to help them understand what is happening to them, family members use them to understand the affected person and how they are feeling:

> He has, he's very, very limited communication ... so I'm actively trying to find ways, you know, maybe to understand J more and to be able to move deeper into his world, if you know what I mean, so that I can bring him into ours.
>
> (Susan, parent, age 40)

And to check they are doing all they can for them:

> I just wanted to understand how other people feel when they've got this problem. I think you fill up with what you can take in on encephalitis and then you understand it on your level then I wanted to know about epilepsy, you know am I doing everything I can?
>
> (Ginny, parent, age 47)

Some family members use reading stories to communicate and to accept and cope with challenging behaviours, reminding themselves and other family members that the person affected cannot help the way they are. They are in effect using the stories to embrace and legitimise behaviour as a result of the injury to the brain which in other circumstances might be considered unacceptable:

> If there is anything I read and think "oh wow this is just like T or this is just more to do with his behavioural issues" ... I'll say "you need to read this" to my husband or even to his brothers or read it out and say "look this is why T acts as he does, we need to be a bit more understanding because of this, that, and the other".
>
> (Brenda, parent, age 46)

Some people used stories to better understand the experience of their relative affected by encephalitis, and in turn have been able to initiate discussion with them about issues, in some cases prompting the person affected to disclose or discuss things that might otherwise have remained hidden:

> They, they helped me to understand them and in turn it's helped me to help G because there would have been things he wouldn't have told me that he was experiencing but other people have and then I've been able to go to G...
>
> (Pauline, wife, age 49)

Reading other people's stories to improve understanding and make sense of their experience, to assist in communication, and as a tool to better cope with the difficulties presented by brain injury, were clearly important to people. In addition people also read stories for more public or collective reasons (i.e. looking outside of themselves, comparing their experiences and the importance of being part of a group), and we consider this now in more detail.

Reading stories for collective reasons

In particular readers describe using stories to compare their own experiences with those of others:

I think there's always hopes and intentions when you're reading, erm, certainly a story, and I'm, I just can't really explain myself with this, I know certainly I often read and you're often looking to find a mirror image of what you've been through, somebody else who's been through exactly the same and I don't know why that is, you just hope to find somebody...

(Susan, parent, age 40)

Some people, usually family members, use the experiences of others to make very specific comparisons, for example looking out for new symptoms, comparing their treatment with that of others:

Well in the back of your mind, you're only really looking out for yourself and um, and you want to look at, read other people's stories about their level of problems and their level of recovery and you're trying to compare it with your own and really you're just trying to get something for yourself out of it. It's quite a selfish thing really."

(Vince, parent, age 45)

Readers report a range of positive effects and impacts from using stories to compare their experiences, with some people experiencing a sense of feeling validation:

...it does, it sort of, you're not making memories up but you sort of say 'yes, that did happen'. It is that, that, diary thing you know, it definitely is like erm, finding that you're just not the only one it's happened to, obviously. I knew that before but it's the proof isn't it? I would say it does make it more real. Yeah. Cos it's so long ago you sort of, what you think you can remember mightn't really be real, just what you've heard. So, yeah, I think it does validate it.

(Martin, brother, age 47)

And also in response to feelings around not being believed:

Probably because it felt like you'd found keys that were opening doors, erm, for awareness, confirmation, erm, to validate and I just needed others to know what I was reading, what G was reading, and I think it's because it stems from not being believed. So that's what we were actually using it for, erm, and helping them to come to terms that you know, you're not on your own either going through this. Other, others have experienced it very similar but again it's quite a recurring thought that all the time it was validating, proving, we are telling the truth!

(Pauline, wife, age 49)

People also use stories to gain perspective:

I think it sustains you more than anything. I think it gives you just a bit of perspective on what has gone on in your own and keep you, keeps you fixed, so you know, you know what you've got to go through, you know what you're going through.

(Charles, husband, age 67)

Like Sophie in Chapter 4, many survivors and family members describe a lack of understanding or respect for their post-encephalitis difficulties. For many reading other people's stories reduced their sense of isolation and made them feel part of something: a collective, a group:

...it's brought me into a fold. I know that somebody else is out there suffering the same as me, even if it, nobody else knows it, but I know it. I know there is somebody else out there the same as me...

(Harold, person affected, age 74)

In some cases that sense of being part of something is subject to conflicting feelings:

Because we're still tied together. We're still what … what happened to G and myself, dealing with what's happened to G still links me with other individuals who've gone through the same. It's almost like you're a life member of a club that you had, that you didn't actually choose to join, but you are and because of that you will never leave it because you can't, you can't take away what's happened so it's, it's like a forced membership really, erm, so you would never turn your back on individuals who are going now through the same process...

(Pauline, wife, age 49)

Many readers of encephalitis narratives describe feeling uplifted, encouraged, inspired, motivated and hopeful having read stories authored by those who had the same or similar experiences as themselves:

I think other people with encephalitis is a great source to you because no matter what type of encephalitis or how you feel about it or what you do yourself, whether you are upbeat or down or whatever, if you read about somebody else there's always something in that story you pick out that can make you think "oh, they did that, maybe I could do that, maybe that's a good way to cope".

(Belinda, person affected, age 53)

Clearly stories, for many readers, provide understanding and help them make sense of their experience, in addition to providing a sense of belonging and reduced feelings of isolation, encouraging people not to give up: others had come out the other side. Similarly the survivor narratives in earlier chapters are in many ways sources of comfort, hope and inspiration. The importance of this in a condition, like so many other neurological conditions, which up until this point had no personal or collective meaning, should perhaps not be underestimated. To suddenly encounter others speaking the same language, describing experiences similar to their own and to which they could relate must be both powerful and empowering, and was a primary reason for ensuring survivor and family member stories formed a significant element of this book.

This chapter has demonstrated the use and usefulness of narratives for both readers and authors. It would however be remiss not to consider in more detail areas of knowledge that require further development, and issues that complicate the use of narratives.

Missing voices and factors that complicate narratives

There seem to be a number of patient voices missing from the literature and the research more generally that considers narratives and patients with neurological conditions and brain injuries. This section covers some of these issues, in particular working with people who have memory problems; working with people who have more than mild cognitive injury, and communication problems; where capacity and consent may be an issue; the bias presented by some research; and finally when we should consider caution in narrative use.

Memory

Like Frank (1997a), some other authors suggest that the making of memories is assisted by the telling of stories (Green *et al.*, 2002); that the process of creating stories enables a memory blueprint to be made without the need to remember the story verbatim. However, others state that people who do sustain memory problems following acquired brain injury have problems in "maintaining a coherent and continuous narrative" (Segal, 2010: p. 300), and that loss of memories can not only be devastating when attempting to recall one's narrative history but also in creating a current and future narrative (Yeates *et al.*, 2008). The implication is that to be without memories and thus stories is "like being without a self", and that "to be without one's stories is to be without knowledge of one's life" (Young and Saver, 2001: p. 74).

Memory impairment in adults affected by encephalitis spans between 45 per cent and 61 per cent depending upon the aspect of memory affected (Dowell *et al.*, 2001). This may go some way towards explaining a desire among brain injury populations, and in particular those post-encephalitis, to capture and document their stories: as a way of storing and creating an archive of memory that would otherwise be difficult if not impossible to retrieve at will. On the other hand, however, it could be that memory problems inhibit people's ability to create a coherent narrative or indeed to participate in research in order to understand the role of memory in narratives.

This is in stark contrast to Arthur Frank's (1997b) claims that post-illness memories can be precise and durable. Many authors, like Frank, have created models around narratives in an attempt to understand the reasons why people write them. Masahiro Nochi (1997, 1998 and 2000) considered narratives and narrative models specifically in relation to traumatic brain injury. Both Frank and Nochi's work raises awareness of the importance of narratives, and they present their work in ways that are accessible to a wide audience, from the academic to the lay reader.

Their theories are, however, not without limitations. Models and frameworks, as well as creating a structure in which to understand complex topics, can impose inflexible arrangements (Nettleton, 2006). They have been used infrequently with people affected by neuro-illness and disability and it is not clear how usefully narrative models reflect such populations. Often they emerge from the researcher's interpretation of what people's narratives mean. Few researchers actually ask the people whose narratives they are, what they mean to them as authors and readers. This means it is difficult to know how well these models and their conclusions reflect the experiences of the people they are intended to represent. This 'one size fits all' modelling is problematic and advocates of narrative models need to be clearer about the populations under study and upon whom their work was based, and thus more transparent about the limitations of their models when considering other study populations. In addition, Pickard (2010: p. 474) suggests that their lack of engagement with social factors means they "float in a space of unlimited possibilities"; the implication being that they are somewhat disconnected from key influences. These issues mean we risk losing the experiences of those who do not 'fit the box', in this case for example people with memory problems, along with being able to take account of variables that are less common or that fluctuate.

To illustrate some of these difficulties in more detail, and in particular in relation to memory, Paterson and Scott-Findlay (2002: p. 399) state: "The traditional view that reality is captured only in the subjective accounts of articulate people who can remember events in a precise and reflective manner is challenged". Like other narrative researchers, both Frank (1997b) and Nochi (1997) state that it is by organising our narratives we better understand our present experiences and plan for the future. Inherent in this is, however, the capacity and ability to call upon our autobiographical memory (Schacter and Addis, 2007). Much of Frank's work assumes the existence of an unimpaired memory and in fact he goes as far as stating, "The disruption is not of remembering; people's memories of illness are often remarkable in their precision and duration" (Frank, 1997b: p. 59), and later suggests that memory can be created and restored through narrative (p. 61). However, Rier (2000) describes how a notebook (at his bedside during a critical and acute illness) allowed him to record and retrieve memories that would otherwise have been completely forgotten the next day. Similarly another phenomenon following brain injury and related to memory, albeit rare, is the occurrence of confabulation. Confabulation is the confusion of imagination with memory, and/or the confusion of true memories with false memories. Due to gaps in memory, the individual will unknowingly create events or describe situations that have never actually occurred. They are not lying because they do not *know* they are inventing the information. Confabulators may therefore offer "an unrivalled glimpse at the power of the human impulse to narrative" (Young and Saver, 2001: p. 76). Confabulation should therefore also act as a cautionary tale to authors such as Frank who downplay the role of memory in illness narratives and who suggest that people's memories of their illness experiences are reliable and robust.

So, whilst it may be true for some to state that memory of illness is precise or can be recreated through narrative, it is not true for all, and in particular often not for a group affected by neuro-illness and disability. This assumes a simplistic view of memory, but as Wilson (2009: p. 1) reminds us: "Memory then, is not one skill or function but rather a 'complex combination of memory subsystems' (Baddeley, 1992, p. 5)".

Nochi does acknowledge that the lack of memory for some people affected by brain injury may inhibit their ability to construct narrative (Nochi, 1997); however, his study only included four participants and so it would be difficult to make any robust assertions about memory and narrative with this sample size. A subsequent study by Nochi (1998) is based on that of ten participants: none of the cases were severe, and people with communication problems were excluded. A further study conducted by Nochi (2000) contains a further ten participants; however, seven of them are the same people as in his 1998

study. Publication of multiple reports using the same data sets compli-
cates matters and in particular can skew conclusions particularly where
little is written about a condition as in the case of brain injury and
neuro-disability (Thorne *et al.*, 2002). Nochi describes most of the
study participants as having short-term memory problems; however, he
does not define short-term memory. If we assume he uses a standard
clinical definition of short-term memory – holding memories for a few
seconds, i.e. long enough to dial a telephone number (Wilson, 2009)
then it would be fair to assume that his work does not include those
with more densely amnestic states and/or those who cannot recall autobiographical details, and whose narratives may differ.

It is therefore particularly important to be mindful of the torment
that can be experienced by those people affected by neuro-illness/disa-
bility who are unable to remember or create a narrative. Webb (1998),
when noting memory loss as a sequelae of brain injury, states "being a
competent social agent is further thwarted by the incapacity to generate
a coherent personal narrative or biography" (p. 548). Young and Saver
(2001) call this 'dysnarrativia' (p. 75). Clive Wearing sustained significant temporal and hippocampal damage to his brain following herpes
simplex encephalitis. In her book his wife, Deborah Wearing (2005)
describes his inability to remember large parts of his past (retrograde
amnesia) and the awful realisation when they discover that Clive is
completely incapable of setting down new memories (anterograde
amnesia). Therefore he can only exist in the present, thinking that
every few seconds he is waking from an 'unconsciousness' for the first
time. Young and Saver (2001) remind us that "consciousness needs a
narrative structure to create a sense of self ... like coherence, consequence and consecution" (pp. 78–79). It is interesting to consider
whether, in the early years following Clive's encephalitis, he had this?
A prisoner of his own consciousness, Clive's early diaries were a
record of his constant 're-awakening' (see Wearing, 2005; Wilson *et
al.*, 1995; and Wilson *et al.*, 2008). The writings of Clive in the first
decade or so clearly demonstrated despair and re-awakening so
powerful he was compelled to record them. In a very distressing
excerpt his wife describes a disturbing note he wrote to her that simply
reads: "I am completely incapable of thinking" (Wearing, 2005:
p. 124). Clive's only narrative, repeated almost constantly for the first

few years, was: "I haven't heard anything, seen anything, touched anything, smelled anything ... it's just like being dead..." (Wearing, 2005: p. 128). Some 22 years on from the onset of his encephalitis, Sacks (2007) described Clive as no longer having any 'inner narrative'.[2]

Some authors argue more broadly that identity narratives "are shaped as much by what is left out of the account – whether forgotten or repressed – as by what is actually told" (Kuhn, 1995: p. 2). This along with the concerns raised previously in relation to Frank (1997) makes such concepts difficult to accept in relation to people who experience memory problems following illness. Caution must be urged among authors who explore narratives and memory, and their assertions must be accompanied by appropriate qualifications and limitations.

The implications for the self and therefore our narratives are clear, at least in my mind: lose your memory and you cease to know about your existence except in the present (Mattingly, 1998). Without memories of the past you are unable to reflect upon, or compare yourself today, with yourself of yesterday. With no capacity to reflect, you become unable to project thoughts of yourself in the future: imagining, day-dreaming, wishful-thinking – formulating ambitions and aspirations for the future may be beyond the grasp of the densely memory-impaired (Baddeley and Wilson, 1986).

Memory is directly connected to our narratives and our capacity to not only allow us to organise and understand the past but also in allowing us to look to the future. Memory problems can complicate and in some cases inhibit people's narratives, and should be considered and accounted for in more detail when conducting narrative research with people affected by neurological illness and disability.

Capacity, consent, cognition and communication

Narrative work such as that of Nochi (1998) does not only tend to exclude participants with memory problems, but by his own admission excludes people with more significant brain injury, and those with communication problems. He also says his work is conducted with those interested in the topic under investigation. A broader reluctance to interview people who have complex disabilities such as cognitive problems or speech impairments is documented among researchers

(Lawton, 2003; Paterson and Scott-Findlay 2002; Thorne *et al.*, 2002). Moreover some people (as we saw in Chapter 1) suggest that the contributions of people with neuro-disabilities are not considered reliable, valuable or important (a topic returned to in more detail in Chapter 9). Charles Warlow (2005) warns of the role ethics committees may also play in the exclusion of some populations in research, in particular where there are concerns about capacity and consent. He explains that the complex regulation of research results in delays, and in some cases even prevents research, meaning that in some cases public health is compromised and harm may occur to patients.

Whilst not advocating the use of unwilling study participants, it remains often equally important to capture, and explore, the perspectives of people who do not engage with a topic, and to better understand why. If we resist including patients who may have issues consenting or who have presented in ways that are considered challenging to work with then whole populations of people are being effectively excluded from research. In turn this must mean that this very same population are at risk of being denied treatments, therapies and other interventions or methods of engagement that might improve their health, well-being and quality of life. It might also mean that research purporting to be representative of certain patient populations is in fact biased since those who could not, or were prevented from engaging, are in fact excluded. We risk excluding and under-representing whole sub-sections of populations: those struggling with their recovery; those who don't share a common interest in the topic under study; those less capable of participation.

It should of course not be our intention to burden people who already have difficult lives. My own experience of working for many years with people who have sustained brain injury is that they are only too willing (like many of the authors mentioned earlier in this chapter and the contributors to Chapters 4–7 of this book) to participate in research that might make a difference for those that follow them. Their needs of course must not be disregarded. They should be acknowledged and we should take steps to address them in order to facilitate the sharing of their experience, rather than simply exclude them.

Bias in research

There is a preference in the literature for work with spoken narratives as opposed to written narratives. How much could be said to be the individual's narrative may be confused as their narratives were created in direct response to interview questions. Casting more doubt on the appropriateness of describing these narratives as the patient's own is a literature that suggests interviewees may also tailor their responses according to what they think the interviewer wants to hear (Seidman, 2005). These narratives, it could be argued, may therefore experience a form of Hawthorne effect (Pope and Mays, 2005). It would take very little to challenge them as not being entirely the narrative of the author but more a collaborative narrative between the interviewer and the interviewee. Narratives created as part of a collaborative process are very important in aiding our understanding of people's experiences. However, a greater focus on narratives already in existence and not created as part of a collaborative or research process also provide interesting and often unique insights in people's experiences, as the survivor and family narratives in this book demonstrate.

In a similar vein much work exists on the 'therapeutic' role of narratives for those who write them. Little work has been conducted on their role and impact with those who read them. This is an area where much more research could be conducted. As this chapter demonstrated earlier, narratives have a valuable role for many readers, as well as authors.

Finally, neuro-narratives are less commonly created with the intention of publication in academic journals or books, and indeed they rarely feature in the medical and academic literature, unless written by someone already familiar with publishing in such journals. On the one hand it is true to say that many people do not write with the intention of publication. On the other hand however it is also true (as discussed earlier and in Chapter 1) that in some circles the narrative contributions of people affected by neuro-disability are not considered reliable, valuable or important (Cloute et al., 2008; Lorenz, 2010; Segal, 2010). Perhaps patient narratives produced outside of the often controlled environments associated with research are considered too speculative and subjective. Meisel and Karlawish (2011) describe the narratives of celebrities affected by prostate cancer, as part of a campaign promoting screening, as being 'shunned' by experts, in the 'name of science'. They go on to argue that patient stories need to be included in addition to scientific, evidence-based medicine, and that in doing so, health behaviours of the general population can be improved.

Narratives are therefore not taken as seriously as perhaps they should be: their authenticity is, in effect, in question. Strangely this is a common criticism of patients: that their condition or at least their experience of their condition is not afforded due respect and in turn they are left feeling 'fraudulent' or lacking in validity (Atkin *et al.*, 2010). We should perhaps not underestimate the impact that not being believed may have on a population whose difficulties are already largely invisible, and we should perhaps afford their narratives a little more attention. Shapiro (2011) concludes her paper by reminding us that the patient's story is theirs alone and does not belong "to the physician and not the literary scholar, and needs to be approached with humility, respect and honouring" (p. 71).

Narratives are not for everyone

As alluded to earlier in this chapter, narratives are not useful for everyone. Not all will be drawn to a narrative approach, be they authors or readers. Some people will not be interested in telling their story and of course not every consultation requires a narrative approach (Kalitzkus and Matthiessen, 2009). In those cases people should be allowed and empowered to find their own recovery pathway even if that involves denial or a more distal recognition of their dis/abilities. The choice of how to cope with, and respond to, ill-health and disability remains theirs regardless of what others may think or desire.

In particular for some, reading other people's stories prompts a good deal of worry, with a minority worried that the stories might be indicative or predictive of their future (Easton, 2012). This causes anxieties. What follows are quotes that illustrate these fears and anxieties.

Rachel and Ginny describe how reading stories made them feel and in Ginny's case how reading them influenced the way she viewed and felt about her child who was affected by encephalitis:

I think at the beginning I didn't really want to read it. I could only ever read, like the first two lines of it because, I don't know, I think I was in, slightly in denial as to how ill I'd been.... Um, I probably am still now to a certain extent but reading what someone else had been through and any similarities between their story and my story would kind of, go to make me realise how ill I had been. Or whether I had been worse than them which was sometimes the case and I didn't want to, think of that ... um, so at first I didn't want to read them at all ... 'cos, I just ... it made the whole illness too real for me and bring up too many feelings and emotions that I didn't necessarily want to face at that point.

(Rachel, person affected, age 26)

I was prepared, but I don't know if that's a good thing or a bad thing, in how it makes you feel towards your child. Perhaps that's it, you suddenly look at your child, you know each child and you accept whatever, but you're suddenly looking at your child as like a description of something awful that could happen, not as your child and I think if you haven't understood everything about the illness and what it is you wouldn't view them as that. It's, it's the suddenly it's not a child, it's all this, you know, it's going to be awful, you know she's going to be dreadful, and of course, you don't know and actually even when the behaviour is dreadful you love them to bits.

(Ginny, parent, age 47)

Some people describe feelings of anger and resentment that others have fared better:

...at the beginning you feel slightly angry because why should they be OK from it when I'm not, kind of thing. Um ... I dunno, just confused and thinking you know, what ... why have I done this, why am I more ill than others, why? You know, why have I got these side-effects and they haven't ... there's definitely more wrong with me.

(Rachel, person affected, age 26)

Some family members also described similar effects for their loved ones:

> I think it discourages J when she gets one who's been written by somebody who's been poorly and really come through it and she … 'cos she can't understand why she hasn't.
>
> (Charles, husband, age 67)

For some people of course, their feelings were not always black and white. In Ginny's case, despite causing her distress, she also found herself being 'compelled' to read stories:

> …there's that pull, once you've seen them, there's that pull of 'ooooh, its awful', it's like Pandora's Box, the temptation to open the lid and have another look even though it's really painful, um and the horror of some of the stories.
>
> (Ginny, parent, age 47)

It seems then that for some people there is a point at which it might be too soon to engage with narratives, their own or other peoples. For others, creating narratives and engaging with the narratives of others may remain unappealing, or even harmful. Who these people are, and when this occurs, remains unclear. Therefore it is difficult to predict who they might be and when access to narratives and narrative approaches will be a positive or a negative thing. Nevertheless it is something we can remain mindful of when working with people and utilising narrative approaches, and is a subject we return to in Chapter 9.

Conclusion

Narratives are a useful resource for people's understanding, and making sense of their experiences following illness and disability.

People tend to read and write narratives for both personal and broader more public, or collective reasons.

People write stories to understand and make sense of what has happened to them; to support a process of recovery and in some cases reconstruction; to create perspective, and reduce their sense of isolation by engaging with others similarly affected. In some cases people write narratives to help reframe and put a positive 'spin' on what has happened to them.

More broadly people write their narratives to bridge gaps in communication, not just at a personal level but also in patient-practitioner settings. In some cases people's narratives are borne from frustration in relation to their expectations of healthcare: the reality of that which they actually received, and the unexpected changes that brain injury resulted in for those affected, and the family that surrounds them. In other cases people wrote with the explicit aim of altering practice and behaviour, and to support survivors and families who may follow in their footsteps.

Little research exists on the impact of reading narratives. However, Easton (2012) suggests that, for a majority, reading the narratives of others is a largely positive experience. Like authors, people read them for personal and collective reasons. Examples include understanding and making sense of their experiences, as well as a tool for communication. More broadly people read them to compare and contrast their own experiences with that of others, and people describe gaining a sense of validation, perspective and belonging.

This chapter also considered factors that complicate our understanding and use of narratives: memory; working with people who have communication difficulties; where more than mild cognitive challenges exist; people where capacity and consent may pose a challenge; and a lack of focus upon readers, as opposed to authors of narratives.

Finally consideration was given to the fact that narratives have a positive role in the recovery of many people following ill-health and disability, but that we must be mindful of the small but significant minority for whom they are not helpful, and among whom harm may result.

In the next chapter we look in more detail at narratives in professional practice.

Key messages

- Narrative study includes both authors and readers.
- Narratives are a tool of great importance for many authors and readers, and they play an important part in their recovery.
- Narratives can be a source of distress for a significant minority.
- Memory, communication, cognitive impairment and capacity to consent may all complicate the study of narrative with neuro-populations.
- Research needs to consider the impact of narratives upon readers, as well as focus upon written narratives (in addition to those spoken and delivered as part of qualitative interviewing).

Notes

1 Indented quotes in this chapter are from a doctoral thesis (Easton, 2012) and are used to provide more in-depth empirical evidence for some of the theoretical literature.
2 During the course of preparing this manuscript I had email dialogue with Deborah Wearing, Clive's wife. Deborah pointed out that Clive is a very different, almost unrecognisable man from the Clive written about in the first decade or so post-illness. Deborah describes Clive as having a sunny personality, kindness and a gentle bonhomie (all traits he had prior to his encephalitis) and that he does retain a sense of self, along with some capacity to learn certain types of things, implicitly via procedural non-declarative memory, such as finding his way from one room to another in the specialist brain injury unit where he lives. Deborah and I hope this acts as further inspiration, along with the other survivor narratives contained in this book: no matter how devastating an outcome post-encephalitis, there is still hope and the capacity for progress to be made.

References

Adams, J. 1995. 'I am still here': a life with encephalitis lethargica. *Oral History*, 78–81.

Alheit, P. 2005. Stories and structures: an essay on historical times, narratives and their hidden impact on adult learning. *Studies in the Education of Adults*, 37, 201–212.

Aronson, J. K. 2000. Autopathography: the patient's tale. *British Medical Journal*, 321, 1599–1602.

Atkin, K. 2003. Ethnicity and the politics of the new genetics: principles and engagement. *Ethnicity and Health*, 8, 91–109.

Atkin, K., Stapley, S. and Easton, A. 2010. No one listens to me, nobody believes me: self management and the experience of living with encephalitis. *Social Science and Medicine*, 71, 386–393.

Baddeley, A. D. 1992. Memory theory and memory therapy. *In:* Wilson, B. A. and Moffat, N. (eds) *Clinical Management of Memory Problems* (2nd edn) (pp. 1–31), London, Chapman & Hall.

Baddeley, A. D. and Wilson, B. A. 1986. Amnesia, autobiographical memory and confabulation. *In:* Rubin, D. (ed.) *Autobiographical Memory* (pp. 225–252), Cambridge, UK, Cambridge University Press.

Baikie, K. A. and Wilhelm, K. 2005. Emotional and physical health benefits of expressive writing. *Advances in Psychiatric Treatment*, 11, 338–346.

Bell, S. 2000. Experiencing illness in/and narrative. *In:* Bird, C., Conrad, P., Fremont, A. and Levine, S. (eds) *Handbook of Medical Sociology* (pp. 184–199), Upper Saddle River, NJ, Prentice-Hall.

Biderman, D., Daniels-Zide, E., Reyes, A. and Marks, B. 2006. Ego-identity: can it be reconstituted after a brain injury? *International Journal of Psychology*, 41, 355–361.

Bruner, J. 1990. *Acts of Meaning*, Cambridge, MA, Harvard University Press.

Bruner, J. 1994. The 'remembered' self. *In:* Neisser, U. and Fivush, R. (eds) *The Remembering Self: Construction and Accuracy in the Self-Narrative* (pp. 41–54), New York, Cambridge University Press.

Bruner, J. 2002. *Making Stories: Law, Literature, Life*, Cambridge, MA, Harvard University Press.

Bury, M. 1991. The sociology of chronic illness: a review of research and prospects. *Sociology of Health and Illness*, 13, 451–468.

Carbaugh, D. 2007. Commentary. Six basic principles in the communication of social identities: the special case of discourses and illness. *Communication and Medicine*, 4, 111–115.

Carey, M. 2014. Narrative therapy and trauma. *In:* Weatherhead, S. and Todd, D. (eds) *Narrative Approaches to Brain Injury* (pp. 77–99), London, Karnac Books.

Chamberlain, D. J. 2006. The experience of surviving traumatic brain injury. *Journal of Advanced Nursing*, 54, 407–417.

Charmaz, K. 1994. Discoveries of self in illness. *In:* Dietz, M. L., Prus, R. and Shaffir, W. (eds) *Doing Everyday Life: Ethnography as Human Lived Experience* (pp. 226–242), Mississauga, Ontario, Canada, Copp Clark, Longman.

Charon, R. 2001. Narrative medicine: a model for empathy, reflection, profession, and trust. *Journal of the American Medical Association*, 286, 1897–1902.

Chesson, R., Moir, E. and Tavendale, A. 1999. More than a sympathetic ear? A report on the first year of a writer in residence in a unit for young, physically disabled people. *Clinical Rehabilitation*, 13, 310–321.

Cloute, K., Mitchell, A. and Yates, P. 2008. Traumatic brain injury and the construction of identity: a discursive approach. *Neuropsychological Rehabilitation*, 18, 651–670.

Crow, L. 2006. Extreme measures: a personal story of letting go. *Death Studies*, 30, 177–186.

Dowell, E., Easton, A. and Solomon, T. 2001. *The Consequences of Encephalitis*, London, The Encephalitis Society.

Durham, C. 2005. *Doing up Buttons*, Camberwell, Australia, Penguin Books.

Easton, A. 2012. *The Role of Written Narratives in the Recovery of People Affected by Encephalitis.* PhD, University of York.

Egdell, R., Egdell, D. and Solomon, T. 2012. Herpes simplex virus encephalitis. *The British Medical Journal*, 344.

Foust, R. J. 2008. Poetry and medicine: head injury odyssey. *JAMA: Journal of the American Medical Association*, 299, 142.

Fraas, M. R. and Calvert, M. 2009. The use of narratives to identify characteristics leading to a productive life following acquired brain injury. *American Journal of Speech-Language Pathology*, 18, 315–328.

Frank, A. 1997a. Illness as moral occasion: restoring agency to ill people. *Health*, 1, 131–148.

Frank, A. W. 1997b. *The Wounded Storyteller: Body, Illness and Ethics*, Chicago, University of Chicago Press.

Frank, A. 2000. Illness and autobiographical work: dialogue as narrative destabilization. *Qualitative Sociology*, 23, 135–156.

Galski, T., Tompkins, C. and Johnston, M. V. 1998. Competence in discourse as a measure of social integration and quality of life in persons with traumatic brain injury. *Brain Injury*, 12, 769–782.

Glover, A. 2000. 'Is this what life is going to be like?' The story of a 34 year old man (T) who suffered a severe head injury after a fall. *Disability and Rehabilitation*, 22, 471–477.

Green, M. C., Strange, J. J. and Brock, T. C. 2002. *Narrative Impact: Social and Cognitive Foundations*, Hove, Psychology Press.

Hammond, R. 2007. *On The Edge: My Story*, London, Orion Publishing Group Ltd.

Hare, P. 2005. *'A Light In a Very Dark Place': An Independent Evaluation of the Encephalitis Society's Support Service.* October. Acton Shapiro.

Harrington, A. 2005. The inner lives of disordered brains. *Cerebrum*, 7 (2), 23–36.

Haslam, A., Jetten, J., Postmes, T. and Haslam, C. 2009. Social identity, health and well-being: an emerging agenda for applied psychology. *Applied Psychology*, 58, 1–23.

Hill, H. 1999. Traumatic brain injury: a view from the inside. *Brain Injury*, 13, 839–844.

Hogan, B. A. 1999. Narrative therapy in rehabilitation after brain injury: a case study. *NeuroRehabilitation*, 13, 21–25.

Hyden, L.-C. 1997. Illness and narrative. *Sociology of Health and Illness*, 19, 48–69.

Hyden, L.-C. 2008. Broken and vicarious voices in narratives. *In:* Hyden, L.-C. and Brockmeier, J. (eds) *Health, Illness and Culture: Broken Narratives* (pp. 36–53), Abingdon, Oxon, Routledge.

Johansen, R. K. 2002. *Listening in the Silence, Seeing in the Dark: Reconstructing Life After Brain Injury*, London, University of California Press.

Jones, C. A. and Turkstra, L. S. 2011. Selling the story: narratives and charisma in adults with TBI. *Brain Injury*, 25, 844–857.

Jumisko, E., Lexell, J. and Soderberg, S. 2007. Living with moderate or traumatic brain injury. *Journal of Family Nursing*, 13, 353–369.

Kalitzkus, V. and Matthiessen, P. 2009. Narrative-based medicine: potential, pitfalls, and practice. *The Permanente Journal*, 13, 80–86.

Kemp, M. 2000. *True: The Autobiography of Martin Kemp*, London, Orion Books Ltd.

Kuhn, A. 1995. *Family Secrets: Acts of Memory and Imagination*, London, Verso.

Lanza, M. 2006. Psychological impact of stroke: a recovering nurse's story. *Issues in Mental Health Nursing*, 27, 765–774.

Lawton, J. 2003. Lay experiences of health and illness: past research and future agendas. *Sociology of Health and Illness*, 25, 23–40.

Lillrank, A. 2003. Back pain and the resolution of diagnostic uncertainty in illness narratives. *Social Science & Medicine*, 57, 1045–1054.

Lorenz, L. 2010. *Brain Injury Survivors: Narratives of Rehabilitation and Healing*, London, Lynne Rienner Publishers.

Luria, A. R. 1987. *The Man with a Shattered World: The History of a Brain Wound*, Cambridge, MA, Harvard University Press.

Man, D. W. K. 2002. Family caregivers' reactions and coping for persons with brain injury. *Brain Injury*, 16, 1025–1037.

Markham, K. 2014. *Our Time of Day: My Life with Corin Redgrave*, London, Oberon Books.

Marshall, J. 2011. Gripping yarns. *The New Scientist*, 2799, 47–49.

Mattingly, C. 1994. The concept of therapeutic 'emplotment'. *Social Science & Medicine*, 38, 811–822.

Mattingly, C. 1998. *Healing Dramas and Clinical Plots: The Narrative Structure of Experience*, Cambridge, UK, Cambridge University Press.

McAdams, D. 2001. The psychology of life stories. *Review of General Psychology*, 5, 100–122.

McCann, A. 2006. *Stroke Survivor: A Personal Guide to Recovery*, London, Jessica Kingsley.

McLean, A. M., Jarus, T., Hubley, A. M. and Jonbled, L. 2012. Differences in social participation between individuals who do and do not attend brain injury drop-in centres: a preliminary study. *Brain Injury*, 26, 83–94.

Medved, M. I. 2007. Remembering without a past: individuals with anterograde memory impairment talk about their lives. *Psychology Health & Medicine*, 12, 603–616.

Meisel, Z. and Karlawish, J. 2011. Narrative vs evidence-based medicine – and, not or. *American Medical Association*, 306, 2022–2023.

Morris, P., Graham, Prior, L., Deb, S., Lewis, G., Mayle, W., Burrow, C. E. and Bryant, E. 2005. Patients' views on outcome following head injury: a qualitative study. *BioMed Central Family Practice*, 6, 1–6.

Muenchberger, H., Kendall, E. and Neal, R. 2008. Identity transition following traumatic brain injury: a dynamic process of contraction, expansion and tentative balance. *Brain Injury*, 22, 979–992.

Murray, M. 2000. Levels of narrative analysis in health psychology. *Journal of Health Psychology*, 3, 337–347.

Nettleton, S. 2006. *The Sociology of Health and Illness*, Cambridge, UK, Polity Press.

Noble, I. 2005. *Like a Hole in the Head*, London, Hodder & Stoughton.

Nochi, M. 1997. Dealing with the 'void': traumatic brain injury as a story. *Disability and Society*, 12, 533–555.

Nochi, M. 1998. 'Loss of self' in the narratives of people with traumatic brain injuries: a qualitative analysis. *Social Science & Medicine*, 46, 869–878.

Nochi, M. 2000. Reconstructing self-narratives in coping with traumatic brain injury. *Social Science and Medicine*, 51, 1795–1804.

O'Brien, M. and Clark, D. 2006. Online illness narratives about living with motor neurone disease: a quantitative analysis. *British Journal of Neuroscience Nursing*, 2, 410–414.

Opher, S. and Wills, E. 2004. Workout with words – a poetry project in a GP surgery. *British Journal of General Practice*, 54, 156–157.

Ownsworth, T. 2014. *Self-identity After Brain Injury*, London, Psychology Press.

Pape, S. 2005. *Stepped Off*, Frederick, MD, PublishAmerica.

Paterson, B. and Scott-Findlay, S. 2002. Critical issues in interviewing people with traumatic brain injury. *Qualitative Health Research*, 12, 399–409.

Pennebaker, J. W. and Seagal, J. D. 1999. Forming a story: the health benefits of narrative. *Journal of Clinical Psychology*, 55, 1243–1254.

Phillips, J. 2003. Psychopathology and the narrative self. *Philosophy, Psychiatry, & Psychology*, 10, 313–328.

Pickard, S. 2010. The 'good carer': moral practices in late modernity. *Sociology*, 44, 471–487.

Pinhasi-Vittorio, L. 2008. Poetry and prose in the self-perception of one man who lives with brain injury and aphasia. *Topics in Stroke Rehabilitation*, 15, 288–294.

Polkinghorne, D. 1991. Narrative and self-concept. *Journal of Narrative and Life History*, 1, 135–153.

Ponsford, J., Olver, J., Ponsford, M. and Nelms, R. 2003. Long-term adjustment of families following traumatic brain injury where comprehensive rehabilitation has been provided. *Brain Injury*, 17, 453–468.

Pope, C. and Mays, N. 2005. *Qualitative Research in Healthcare*, London, BMJ Publishing Group.

Price-Lackey, P. and Cashman, J. 1996. Jenny's story: reinventing oneself through occupation and narrative configuration. *American Journal of Occupational Therapy*, 50, 306–314.

Rier, D. A. 2000. The missing voice of the critically ill: a medical sociologist's first-person account. *Sociology of Health and Illness*, 22, 68–93.

Riessman, C. K. 1990. Strategic uses of narrative in the presentation of self and illness: a research note. *Social Science and Medicine*, 30, 1195–2000.

Riessman, C. K. 2004. A thrice-told tale: new readings of an old story. *In:* Hurwitz, B., Greenhalgh, T. and Skultans, V. (eds) *Narrative Research in Health and Illness*, Oxford, Blackwell Publishing.

Robinson, M. 2000. Writing well: health and the power to make images. *Journals of Medical Ethics*, 26, 79–84.

Sacks, O. 1991. *Awakenings*, London, Picador.

Sacks, O. 2007. *The Abyss: Music and Amnesia* [Online], *The New Yorker*. www.newyorker.com/reporting/2007/09/24/070924fa_fact_sacks (accessed 10 July 2007).

Schacter, D. L. and Addis, D. R. 2007. The cognitive neuroscience of constructive memory: remembering the past and imagining the future. *Philosophical Transactions of the Royal Society Biological Sciences*, 362, 773–786.

Segal, D. 2010. Exploring the importance of identity following acquired brain injury: a review of the literature. *International Journal of Child, Youth and Family Studies*, 1, 293–314.

Seidman, I. 2005. *Interviewing as qualitative research*, New York, Teachers College Press.

Shapiro, J. 2011. Illness narratives: reliability, authenticity and the empathic witness. *Medical Humanities*, 37, 68–72.

Skultans, V. 1998. Anthropology and narrative. *In:* Greenhalgh, T. and Hurwitz, B. (eds) *Narrative Based Medicine* (pp. 225–233), London, BMJ Books.

Skultans, V. 2000. Editorial. Narrative illness and the body. *Anthropology and Medicine*, 7, 5–13.

Smith, B. and Sparkes, A. 2006. Men, sport, spinal cord injury, and narratives of hope. *Social Science & Medicine*, 61, 1095–1105.

Smith, C. 2007. Innovative rehabilitation after head injury: examining the use of a creative intervention. *Journal of Social Work Practice*, 21, 297–309.

Smith, C. and Squire, F. 2007. Narrative perspectives: two reflections from a continuum of experience. *Reflective Practice*, 8, 375–386.

Sorum, P. C. 1994. Patient as author, physician as critic. *Archives of Family Medicine*, 3, 549–556.

Sparkes, A. and Smith, B. 2002. Sport, spinal cord injury, embodied masculinities, and the dilemmas of narrative identity. *Men and Masculinities*, 4, 258–285.

Teske, J. A. 2006. Neuromythology: brains and stories. *Zygon*, 41, 169–196.

Thorne, S., Paterson, B., Acorn, S., Canam, C., Joachim, G. and Jillings, C. 2002. Chronic illness experience: insights from a metastudy. *Qualitative Health Research*, 12, 437–452.

Warlow, C. 2005. Over-regulation of clinical research: a threat to public health. *Clinical Medicine*, 5, 33–38.

Wearing, D. 2005. *Forever Today*, London, Doubleday.

Webb, D. 1998. A 'revenge' on modern times: notes on traumatic brain injury. *Sociology*, 32, 541–555.

Whitehead, L. C. 2006. Quest, chaos and restitution: living with chronic fatigue syndrome/myalgic encephalomyelitis. *Social Science & Medicine*, 62, 2236–2245.

Williams, G. 1997. The genesis of chronic illness: narrative reconstruction. *In:* Hinchman, L. P. and Hinchman, S. K. (eds) *Memory, Identity, Community: The Idea of Narrative in the Human Sciences* (pp. 185–212), New York, State University of New York Press.

Wilson, B. A. 2009. *Memory Rehabilitation: Integrating Theory and Practice*, New York, The Guilford Press.

Wilson, B. A., Baddeley, A. D. and Kapur, N. 1995. Dense amnesia in a professional musician following herpes simplex virus encephalitis. *Journal of Experimental and Clinical Psychology*, 17, 668–681.

Wilson, B. A., Gracey, F. and Bainbridge, K. 2001. Cognitive recovery from 'persistent vegetative state': psychological and personal perspectives. *Brain Injury*, 15, 1083–1092.

Wilson, B. A., Kopelman, M. and Kapur, N. 2008. Prominent and persistent loss of self-awareness in amnesia: delusion, impaired consciousness or coping strategy? *Neuropsychological Rehabilitation*, 18, 527–540.

Woody, J. M. 2003. When narrative fails. *Philosophy, Psychiatry, & Psychology*, 10, 329–345.

Yeates, G., Gracey, F. and McGrath, J. C. 2008. A biopsychosocial deconstruction of 'personality change' following acquired brain injury. *Neuropsychological Rehabilitation*, 18, 566–589.

Young, K. and Saver, J. L 2001. The neurology of narrative. *SubStance*, 30 (1&2), 72–84.

Chapter 9

Narratives in professional practice

...there is a positive role for narratives in supporting health professionals to better understand their clients as a whole person rather than an assembly of diseases or dis/abilities...

Introduction

In the last chapter (Chapter 8) we saw how survivor and family members use narratives, and the impact reading and writing narratives has. In this chapter we focus on patient, and family (and touch upon professional) narratives in a range of domains: medical practice and public healthcare; rehabilitation; research; the not-for-profit sector; and in reflexive practice. This chapter concludes with a section which considers when narratives (which, as we have already demonstrated, are an overwhelmingly positive tool for the majority) should be approached with caution.

Professionals are increasingly sympathetic to the patient narrative (Fraas and Calvert, 2009; Prigatano, 2000). People's narratives can provide important understanding and insights for professionals, practitioners and other healthcare staff (Alcauskas and Charon, 2008; Carroll, 1998; Charon, 2001; Chesson *et al.*, 1999; Cox, 2001; Flynn *et al.* 2014; Harrington, 2005; Lawton, 2003; Lorenz, 2010a; Pinhasi-Vittorio, 2008; Price-Lackey and Cashman, 1996; Sorum, 1994), in particular around how people understand their illness experience, how they make sense of it and how they cope over prolonged periods of time (Bennett, 2007; O'Brien and Clark, 2006; Wilson *et al.*, 2014, 2015).

We have already explored the dearth of literature that exists in relation to acquired brain injury, in particular encephalitis. A meta-study of chronic illness experience explicitly stated that people with conditions affecting the brain are rarely included (Thorne *et al.*, 2002). Chapters 1 and 8 also demonstrated how some practitioners remain sceptical of a person's ability to accurately self-report, particularly after neuro-illness and disability. This may contribute to why some medical and psychological reporting reveals little about people's illness or injury experience (Cloute *et al.*, 2008; Nochi, 1997, 1998; Segal, 2010). Such biases may contribute to the ongoing medicalisation of a person's illness experience.

Other things may contribute to a lack of emphasis on the patient narrative. It might be argued that commissioners and service managers place too great an emphasis on services and not on the individual. Or that legal and medical discourses existing within some brain injury and rehabilitation services have led to paternalistic rather than empowering practices (Weatherhead and Todd, 2014), with service users moulded to fit the service rather than the other way around. In Chapter 3 we saw the effects of nineteenth century developments in technology and their impact upon practitioner-patient relationships. Some authors provide more contemporary accounts of similar concern:

> due to increasing sub-specialization, technologization, and managed care restrictions, neurology as a field has taken a giant step back from patients in recent years. Connecting with patients and one another, finding fulfilment in caring for people, in contrast to curing, managing or triaging, is no longer discussed. It is simply deemed unimportant.
>
> (Alcauskas and Charon, 2008: p. 894)

Burn-out among neurologists is apparently becoming more prevalent, resulting in not only a loss of expertise in the sector but also physicians lacking in empathy for their patients, and poorer patient care (Sigsbee and Bernat, 2014). As these changes take place, the need to take account of the patient's perspective becomes more important (Bajo and Fleminger, 2002).

Narratives in medical practice and public healthcare

As well as a reminder of the human condition – and refocusing attention on the individual – people's stories are rich in evidence and information. This can support the diagnosis and management of a patient's condition as well as inform therapeutic and nursing interventions (Bennett, 2007; Chamberlain, 2006; Fraas and Calvert, 2009; Nochi, 2000; Pennebaker, 1997; Robinson, 2000). As Dr Jerry Vannatta advocates, "the diagnosis is in the patient's story" (Ragan *et al.*, 2005: p. 261). Time to hear a patient narrative might be a concern for some practitioners. However, a study looking at 335 patients in an outpatient clinic found that two minutes was long enough for 80 per cent of the patients to describe their concerns, with only seven patients needing more than five minutes. Therefore patient narratives should be considered an important contribution to medical or health-related consultations (Langewitz *et al.*, 2002).

There is a distinction between a consultation history obtained by a doctor and the patient's 'story', however (Frank, 1997), and understanding the subjective experience of illness has not always been a traditional part of the physician or scientist's work (Feinberg, 2005) particularly in modern society. One author-patient suggests that "[narratives] can lend perspective and vitality to issues that are ... written about in a quantitative and analytic fashion" (Mullan, 1999: p. 124) suggesting that our human experiences are more complex and diverse than can be captured in scientific language and hypotheses alone (Harrington, 2005; Hyden, 1997).

Returning to Tom who we met first in Chapter 8 (an encephalitis lethargica patient), Adams (1995) stated the reason for working with him was to capture his story because he felt that the voice of the patient was drowned out by "the intimidating clamour of professional discourse" (p. 78) and that accounts such as Tom's provided a "valuable counterbalance to a discourse dominated by professional imperatives" (p. 81). Therefore, with their narratives patients can not only understand and make sense of what has happened to them, but also distance themselves from perceived limitations by widening the gap between themselves and the medical language that is used to describe their injury and sequelae (Pinhasi-Vittorio, 2008).

Narratives are used as a vehicle to support health professionals in better understanding their clients and seeing beyond their disease. People's stories empower patients, enabling them to be the author of their own interventions as opposed to being someone about whom reports are written, as well as helping professionals acquire a deeper understanding of those they treat (Hogan, 1999). Patient perspectives and knowledge of their condition should be welcomed by the professionals involved in their care, and making space for their narratives "is as important as understanding the functional neuroanatomy and cognitive profile of the injury" (Weatherhead and Todd, 2014: p. xix). Hogan (1999) makes the compelling argument that a narrative approach empowers patients, enabling them to be the author of their own intervention as opposed to being someone about whom reports are written. They do not therefore succumb to disempowering practices such as diagnostic labelling; patient as object; patient exclusion in problem identification. Hogan recognises that people's stories can provide professionals with a deeper understanding of their experiences and feelings. This is a view shared by others (Carroll, 1998) who go on to recommend that the patient's perspective and knowledge of their condition should be welcomed by the professionals involved in their care, broadening their scientific approach beyond medicine, and embracing the social. Moving from theory to practice some authors have demonstrated significant changes in attitude (for the better) of practitioners after listening to patient narratives (Fraas and Calvert, 2009), a finding which must undoubtedly result in improved outcomes for the patient. This concept is considered in more detail later in this chapter when we turn to narratives and reflexive practice.

People's narratives can also be used to support the dissemination of evidence-based research and healthcare campaigns to the public, helping recipients identify with the people included in the stories, resulting in greater credibility, clarity and believability in the eyes of the public. Chapter 8 touched upon this in relation to a prostate cancer campaign, and although some experts in the field may resist, the use of patient narratives in this way can be a useful way to improve patient, as well as public, engagement.

There is no doubt there is a positive role for narratives in supporting health professionals to better understand their clients as a whole person rather than an assembly of diseases or dis/abilities, and to work with the general public when delivering health messages.

Narratives in rehabilitation

In order to be effective in their work, Prigatano (2000) suggests professionals working with brain injury survivors must understand their patients' experiences. Hearing a patient's story is undoubtedly one way of achieving this, especially when this can be used in addition to broader information and approaches.

Narratives are perhaps an extension of that which we do naturally and since our realities are socially constructed and maintained via the stories we tell, then a narrative approach can enable a person to re-tell their story following illness/trauma, reframing themselves (as briefly touched upon in Chapter 8) and their situation in increasingly more positive terms (Hogan, 1999).

There have been several theories suggesting ways in which narratives affect patient therapies and rehabilitation. One suggestion being that they enable patient reflections on progress over time, which may be useful when recovery begins to plateau (Chesson et al., 1999). Currently the emphasis seems to be on narratives as a therapeutic tool and as a result documented cases are often written with predetermined goals in mind, as opposed to professionals finding a value in their patients' stories per se. There is, however, a distinction between stories being written for therapeutic use (a conscious and explicit aim) and stories written which result (unconsciously) in therapeutic outcome (Robinson, 2000). There is a tension here since the use of stories as a therapy or even their use in less explicit ways, for example keeping a diary with a view to encouraging people to cope better with their condition, means that the person's narrative is no longer necessarily their own. Once this occurs, there is a risk that the sense of regaining control over one's experience is diminished or lost, and subsequent failure to achieve predetermined outcomes or goals the patient might not share, may only add to the sense of frustration and failure many people who have had encephalitis or other neuro-illness/disability experience.

One alternative, in assessing and illustrating the progress of a brain injury survivor over time, is to simply listen to their story at varying points in time, noting the subtle changes rather than influencing or becoming heavily involved in the production of *their* story (Frank, 1998; Lorenz, 2010b).

Whether people's narratives written without a therapeutic intention are more revealing, or of equal therapeutic value, is of course an interesting point which requires more attention and research. Either way, given research findings that suggest returning home following neuro-rehabilitation, psychological functioning can deteriorate and return to levels present upon admission (O'Connor *et al.*, 2005), the importance of narrative (and continuing narrative) and its potential for healing and recovery-promotion become even more important.

A person's narrative can, of course, be used in more diverse ways. Simmonds (2014) describes how the narrative of a young person with mental health problems who had completely disengaged with their service, was used not only to re-engage the young person, but also the other members of the team. Simmonds and the young person conducted an interview together, about the values held and hopes of, the young person. They re-staged this interview with the other members of the team and involved third parties, asking them to contribute ways in which they felt they could support those values and hopes. The young person was provided with a narrative record of the meeting which they could edit and, dependent on the professional responses, could choose with whom they wished to share it. Sometimes it helps to reflect upon and consider if we can include people's narratives in ways that sit outside our dominant professional discourses, as this example illustrates.

Narratives in research

As demonstrated in Chapter 8 there is a lack of literature surrounding the psychosocial outcomes and experiences of people following neuro-illness and disability. Several reasons for this have been mooted, among them were: concerns among ethics committees in relation to capacity and consent, and a reluctance among researchers to conduct research with people who have more than mild cognitive and communication problems. These issues are of course complicated by some people in the field resisting the narrative experiences of people affected by neuro-illness and brain injury. The result is that we are excluding whole sub-sections of populations from our research and understanding; populations it is suggested who may already be subject to greater distress and social isolation (Barrow, 2014).

Researchers in the field need to provide stronger evidence for their inclusion and their plans to minimise and mitigate issues around capacity and consent to ethics committees. Research must also work with people who have cognitive and communication problems to facilitate the sharing of their experience and not shy away from it. Simple approaches can be adopted. Taking as one example a population with moderate to severe memory problems, you can adapt your methods of enquiry and data capture: use a non-structured approach to your interviews to allow a free flow of narrative and experience; include the experiences of family members and those around them; capture your meeting on film or by tape and provide participants with a copy to reflect on; allow people to provide their experience in a variety of ways subsequent to any meeting, such as emails or a telephone call as things occur to them. Give them time to prepare and remind them of your visit and the reason. You might also need to think about structuring your research over a longer period of time allowing for multiple opportunities to collect data.

As a minimum their inclusion would begin to demonstrate to what extent cognitive problems, in this case memory, affect and influence people's engagement and experience of narratives, or not. There are information and tools out there which can form part of the research planning and process. See for a further example Rozanne Barrow's suggestions for engaging with populations who have communication difficulties where she explores tools such as attentiveness, timing, pace and arts-based methods in successfully engaging with populations who have communication difficulties (Barrow, 2014).

More research with these populations will hopefully contribute to professionals having a better understanding of people's illness experiences, how best to work with them and include them in their services (Barrow, 2014), as well as opportunities to reflect upon and develop their practice with these communities. Those who have experienced neurological problems will likely feel less isolated and have a greater sense of validation as they encounter more people with similar difficulties, and a professional approach, which is more understanding and accepting of their problems, as well as improved patient pathways and patient outcomes.

Narratives in the voluntary and not-for-profit sector

The voluntary sector is often responsible for promoting and publishing narratives of people affected by a variety of health conditions. As we have already learnt narratives are a positive experience and a key tool in recovery for many people. This is, as we have seen in Chapter 8 and go on to consider in more detail below, not the case for a minority. There are a number of things that voluntary sector organisations might like to consider. First, a mindful approach to the range and balance of narratives they publish. This means newsletters, websites or other media carrying a harrowing story, also featuring a more positive, upbeat story. Second, ensuring that a range of genders, ages and experiences are featured so that readers are more likely to find a story with which they positively connect. Given the lack of minority ethnic and low socio-economic representation in patient/support groups more broadly (Farris Kurtz, 1997), organisations and researchers might want to consider what they can do to more positively engage with and represent in their literature, the stories from these sectors of society. Third, on websites, some consideration given to including a gentle warning, grading or traffic-light system about the possible content of the stories they feature and a reinforcement of how to contact the organisation for support. We are all used, these days, to watching a soap episode on television or a documentary that covers controversial or challenging topics, and for which the programme-makers provide details of where to go for help if you have been affected by the content. These stories are, in many ways, no different. Finally, organisations and professionals could consider publishing and including articles that consider the pros and cons of narrative approaches, thus opening the idea up to those who had not considered it before, and lending some reassurance and validation to the experiences of those for whom narratives are not a source of comfort.

Narratives in reflective practice

Patient (and practitioner) narratives can be particularly useful in reflecting on professional practice and re-energising approaches to patients who sometimes challenge working practices. Their value in offering insight and opportunities for reflection should not be understated. There is no doubt that patient narratives can support practitioners in seeing the person and not the condition (Alcauskas and Charon, 2008; Bennett, 2007; Fraas and Calvert, 2009; Lorenz, 2010b; O'Brien and Clark, 2006; Pinhasi-Vittorio, 2008).

Some authors go further, suggesting that by reading narratives they engender a greater capacity to humanise and empathise, resulting in an increased sense of self-satisfaction in their work (Alcauskas and Charon, 2008; Charon, 2001; Divinsky, 2007; Hogan, 1999; Johansen, 2002) and changes in attitude (for the better) of practitioners (Fraas and Calvert, 2009). This is nowhere better illustrated than if I return to the study mentioned earlier in Chapter 8 about a doctor's practice whose work with patients improved outcomes but who also described an impact upon the treating physicians (Opher and Wills, 2004). The practice was repeatedly attended by a young woman with a brain injury who complained of a range of medically unexplained symptoms. The practice began a writing course for patients and saw her number of visits reduce significantly as she embraced poetry as a way of expressing her feelings and experiences. The doctor reflected that he had to review *his* view of her and acknowledges that through their long association he had "lost sight of her humanity and had become incapable of giving her the respect I owed her" (p. 157).

Simmonds (2014: p. 180) discusses how narratives can be used in peer supervision, to:

- make space to deconstruct taken for granted ideas;
- empower marginalised people and their voices;
- value the diversity of experience and different knowledges;
- place the people we are seeking to help firmly at the centre of the supervision sessions.

Returning to the topic of burn-out amongst neurologists, Sigsbee and Bernat (2014) advocate preventive measures that include mentoring, counselling, the recognition of achievements and a focus upon personal development. All concepts that form part of good reflexive practice and peer supervision, and in which patient narratives could be located.

The steady stream of patients for doctors and other medical professionals may mean that it becomes increasingly difficult to maintain one's interest in the individual. At what point do people and their experiences become a blur of symptoms, disease and treatment? Understandably practitioners can on occasion become jaded or disillusioned, in the same way members of other professions do. The consequences, however, can be severe when dealing with life, death and the human condition more generally.

Of course narratives are not just written by patients. Sometimes doctors, nurses and practitioners record their own narratives, or those of colleagues. Kalitzkus and Matthiessen (2009: p. 81) remind us that "Physicians' stories can also contribute to the rehumanization of medicine in the same way as patient narratives". Compilation examples exist such as Kapur's *Injured Brains of Medical Minds* (1997), and sometimes, although more rarely, we see reflective texts such as those of Smith and Squires (2007) (mentioned earlier in Chapter 1) and senior lecturer, and nurse, Sharon Edwards (2015) examining her personal narrative and its influence on her nursing practice. Tomlinson (2014) suggests that engagement with doctor-patient narratives is an effective way of understanding problems from the patient perspective, yet educators continue to fail in engaging with, and using these narratives, to improve practice. Research that has looked at the impact of a narrative-medicine elective with medical students found they reported improvements in communications skills; their capacity to collaborate; empathise and be patient-centred; and the capacity to reflect (Arntfield *et al.*, 2013). In contrast they reported the concept of narrative-medicine is resisted and misunderstood by others, citing three responses in particular: 'fluffy', 'unnecessary' and 'touchy-feely'. It seems we still have some way to go.

Narratives therefore have the potential to provide understanding and insight for professionals (Alcauskas and Charon, 2008; Lorenz, 2010a; Opher and Wills, 2004), raising awareness of people's conditions and experiences, and enabling professionals involved in their care to see the person and not just the disease. This can result in improved reflection and professional practice, outcomes of which may be better healthcare experiences and improved social support for people affected by neurological illness/disability and other chronic conditions.

Practitioners for whom patient narrative is a new concept or for those who are re-engaged with it might review their use of narratives with their patients and clients. They might want to consider integrating narratives into their consultations in order to better understand their patient and their experiences; consider using patient narratives to reflect on their practice and perhaps reframe their perspectives of certain patients; consider using narratives in their peer supervision; and finally supporters of patient narratives (old and new) could consider alternatives to narratives in patients for whom their use might be detrimental, a concept considered in more detail in the next section.

Approaching narratives with caution

Narratives are however not a tool to be used with, or imposed on, everyone (see Chapter 8 for more detail). There is a general sense that narratives are harmless – they are *only* people's stories, after all. For some, they will of course turn independently to the reading and/or writing of narratives. For others, as Chapter 8 demonstrated in detail, encouragement to do so may be a positive step forward in their recovery or that of a relative. However, for a significant minority they can be a source of distress and their use requires discretion and insight on the part of professionals.

Professionals (doctors, therapists, nurses, for example) should consider carefully, as should researchers, why, how and when they become involved in a person's narrative. There is always the risk of trauma when "playing with another person's life" (Harrison, quoting Plummer, 2008: p. xli; Cloute *et al.*, 2008). For example, Gelech and Desjardins (2010) found survivors pressed into using narrative as a therapeutic tool risked the possibility of suffering and distress (see also Segal, 2010). They go on to warn that inappropriate therapeutic discourses might compromise the patient-practitioner relationships and to consider to what extent therapists' moral evaluations of a person's pre-injury self, plays a role in the way they conduct their narrative interventions. As a researcher, I consider at great length my 'right' to ask about, and become involved in, the deepest experiences of another person, and I generally have a range of 'tools' which I can call upon where I sense or inadvertently cause *any* distress to the people I am working with.

Those responsible for the availability, promotion and use of narratives among neurological populations have a duty of care in ensuring that any risks in their use are minimised and that those using them do not experience harm. In contrast we can also use narratives to counter other narratives that misinform people. Meisel and Karlawish (2011) describe how the maternal narrative of a seriously unwell child too young for the measles vaccine, could be used to add weight and provoke questions around misleading narratives which suggest for example, the MMR vaccine causes autism.

These examples are not intended to suggest that narratives should be discouraged, more that we must remain mindful that narratives are not useful for all people and that a 'duty of care' exists. Professionals should assess their client's capacity to produce narratives. In addition to capacity, consent must also be considered: those not drawn to narratives should be allowed and empowered to find their own recovery pathway even if that involves denial or a more distal recognition of their dis/abilities. The choice of how to cope with, and respond to, ill-health and disability remains theirs regardless of what others may think or desire. Practitioners can of course support people in exploring alternative ways of coping.

Conclusion

We have seen a move away from and, more recently, back to the patient's narrative in more recent times. Despite some scepticism and indeed some resistance, there is evidence to suggest the patient's narrative, and indeed those of professionals, are important in practice. This chapter considered their role and made some initial suggestions about how narratives might be used in a range of domains, and encouraged a mindful approach when working with people for whom narratives might not be useful. It is with the inspiring and wise words of Rita Charon (2012: p. 346) that we draw this chapter to a close:

> Receiving our patients' stories mobilizes material deep within ourselves, transforms us, situates us at the threshold of illness with patients, humbly recognizing the patient and appreciating the magnitude of what must be done by that person, now at least not alone.

> **Key messages**
>
> - Narratives can provide professionals with in-depth insight into how patients experience their illness, and subsequent recovery.
> - Narratives can inform diagnosis, and cast light on the often complex nature of the condition.
> - Sometimes we should look outside of the dominant discourse of our professions, and new ways of using narratives can emerge.
> - We must consider including the narratives of under-represented sub-groups in research in order to be able to truly say our research reflects a population.
> - Not-for-profit organisations can be more mindful in their use of narratives.
> - Narratives can be used in reflective practice and in peer supervision.
> - Narratives are not for all people, all of the time.

References

Adams, J. 1995. 'I am still here': a life with encephalitis lethargica. *Oral History*, 78–81.

Alcauskas, M. and Charon, R. 2008. Right brain: reading, writing, and reflecting: making a case for narrative medicine in neurology. *Neurology*, 70, 891–894.

Arntfield, S., Slesar, K., Dickson, J. and Charon, R. 2013. Narrative medicine as a means of training medical students toward residency competencies. *Patient Education and Counselling*, 91, 280–286.

Bajo, A. and Fleminger, S. 2002. Brain injury rehabilitation: what works for whom and when? *Brain Injury*, 16, 385–395.

Barrow, R. 2014. Narrative practice in the context of communication disability: a question of accessibility. *In:* Weatherhead, S. and Todd, D. (eds) *Narrative Approaches to Brain Injury* (pp. 117–141), London, Karnac Books.

Bennett, B. 2007. Gaining understanding from patients' stories to inform neuroscience nursing practice. *British Journal of Neuroscience Nursing*, 3, 308–312.

Carroll, L. W. 1998. Understanding chronic illness from the patient's perspective. *Radiologic Technology*, 70, 37–41.

Chamberlain, D. J. 2006. The experience of surviving traumatic brain injury. *Journal of Advanced Nursing*, 54, 407–417.

Charon, R. 2001. Narrative medicine: a model for empathy, reflection, profession, and trust. *Journal of the American Medical Association*, 286, 1897–1902.

Charon, R. 2012. At the membranes of care: stories in narrative medicine. *Academic Medicine*, 87, 342–347.

Chesson, R., Moir, E. and Tavendale, A. 1999. More than a sympathetic ear? A report on the first year of a writer in residence in a unit for young, physically disabled people. *Clinical Rehabilitation*, 13, 310–321.

Cloute, K., Mitchell, A. and Yates, P. 2008. Traumatic brain injury and the construction of identity: a discursive approach. *Neuropsychological Rehabilitation*, 18, 651–670.

Cox, K. 2001. Stories as case knowledge: case knowledge as stories. *Medical Education*, 35 (9), 862–866.

Divinsky, M. 2007. Stories for life. *Canadian Family Physician*, 53, 203–205.

Edwards, S. L. 2015. The personal narrative of a nurse: a journey through practice. *Journal of Holistic Nursing*.

Farris Kurtz, L. 1997. *Self-Help and Support Groups: A Handbook for Practitioners*, London, Sage Publications.

Feinberg, T. E. 2005. Four fictional odysseys through life with a disordered brain. *Cerebrum*, 7 (4), 51–64.

Flynn, K., Daiches, A. and Weatherhead, S. 2014. Brain injury narratives: an undercurrent into the rest of your life. *In:* Weatherhead, S. and Todd, D. (eds) *Narrative Approaches to Brain Injury* (pp. 27–50), London, Karnac Books.

Fraas, M. R. and Calvert, M. 2009. The use of narratives to identify characteristics leading to a productive life following acquired brain injury. *American Journal of Speech-Language Pathology*, 18, 315–328.

Frank, A. W. 1997. *The Wounded Storyteller: Body, Illness and Ethics*, Chicago, University of Chicago Press.

Frank, A. W. 1998. Just listening: narrative and deep illness. *Families, Systems and Health*, 16, 197–212.

Gelech, J. M. and Desjardins, M. 2010. I am many: the reconstruction of self following acquired brain injury. *Qualitative Health Research*, 21, 62–74.

Harrington, A. 2005. The inner lives of disordered brains. *Cerebrum*, 7 (2), 23–36.

Harrison, B. 2008. *Editor's Introduction: Researching Lives and the Lived Experience*, London, Sage Publications.

Hogan, B. A. 1999. Narrative therapy in rehabilitation after brain injury: a case study. *NeuroRehabilitation*, 13, 21–25.

Hyden, L.-C. 1997. Illness and narrative. *Sociology of Health and Illness*, 19, 48–69.

Johansen, R. K. 2002. *Listening in the Silence, Seeing in the Dark: Reconstructing Life after Brain injury*, London, University of California Press.

Kalitzkus, V. and Matthiessen, P. 2009. Narrative-based medicine: potential, pitfalls, and practice. *The Permanente Journal*, 13, 80–86.

Kapur, N. 1997. *Injured Brains of Medical Minds*, Oxford, Oxford University Press.

Langewitz, W., Denz, M., Keller, A., Kiss, A., Ruttimann, S. and Wossmer, B. 2002. Spontaneous talking time at start of consultation in outpatient clinic: cohort study. *The British Medical Journal*, 28, 682–683.

Lawton, J. 2003. Lay experiences of health and illness: past research and future agendas. *Sociology of Health and Illness*, 25, 23–40.

Lorenz, L. 2010a. *Brain Injury Survivors: Narratives of Rehabilitation and Healing*, London, Lynne Rienner Publishers.

Lorenz, L. 2010b. Discovering a new identity after brain injury. *Sociology of Health and Illness*, 32, 862–879.

Meisel, Z. and Karlawish, J. 2011. Narrative vs evidence-based medicine – and, not or. *American Medical Association*, 306, 2022–2023.

Mullan, F. 1999. Me and the system: the personal essay and health policy. *Health Affairs*, 18, 118–124.

Nochi, M. 1997. Dealing with the 'void': traumatic brain injury as a story. *Disability and Society*, 12, 533–555.

Nochi, M. 1998. 'Loss of self' in the narratives of people with traumatic brain injuries: a qualitative analysis. *Social Science and Medicine*, 46, 869–878.

Nochi, M. 2000. Reconstructing self-narratives in coping with traumatic brain injury. *Social Science and Medicine*, 51, 1795–1804.

O'Brien, M. and Clark, D. 2006. Online illness narratives about living with motor neurone disease: a quantitative analysis. *British Journal of Neuroscience Nursing*, 2, 410–414.

O'Connor, R. J., Cano, S. J., Thompson, A. J. and Playford, E. D. 2005. The impact of inpatient neurorehabilitation on psychological well-being on discharge and at 3 month follow-up. *Journal of Neurology*, 252 (7), 814–819.

Opher, S. and Wills, E. 2004. Workout with words – a poetry project in a GP surgery. *British Journal of General Practice*, 54, 156–157.

Pennebaker, J. W. 1997. Writing about emotional experiences as a therapeutic process. *Psychological Science*, 8, 162–166.

Pinhasi-Vittorio, L. 2008. Poetry and prose in the self-perception of one man who lives with brain injury and aphasia. *Topics in Stroke Rehabilitation*, 15, 288–294.

Price-Lackey, P. and Cashman, J. 1996. Jenny's story: reinventing oneself through occupation and narrative configuration. *American Journal of Occupational Therapy*, 50, 306–314.

Prigatano, G. 2000. Neuropsychology, the patient's experience, and the political forces within our field. *Archives of Clinical Neuropsychology*, 15, 71–82.

Ragan, S., L., Mindt, T. and Wittenberg-Lyles, E. 2005. Narrative medicine and education in palliative care. *In:* Harter, L. M., Japp, P. M. and Beck, C. S. (eds) *Narratives, Health, and Healing: Communication Theory, Research, and Practice* (pp. 259–276), New Jersey, Lawrence Erlbaum Associates.

Robinson, M. 2000. Writing well: health and the power to make images. *Journals of Medical Ethics*, 26, 79–84.

Segal, D. 2010. Exploring the importance of identity following acquired brain injury: a review of the literature. *International Journal of Child, Youth and Family Studies*, 1, 293–314.

Sigsbee, B. and Bernat, J. L. 2014. Physician burnout: a neurologic crisis. *Neurology*, 83, 2302–2306.

Simmonds, L. 2014. Using narrative ideas and practices in indirect work with services and professionals. *In:* Weatherhead, S. and Todd, D. (eds) *Narrative Approaches in Brain Injury* (pp. 165–183), London, Karnac Books.

Smith, C. and Squire, F. 2007. Narrative perspectives: two reflections from a continuum of experience. *Reflective Practice*, 8, 375–386.

Sorum, P. C. 1994. Patient as author, physician as critic. *Archives of Family Medicine*, 3, 549–556.

Thorne, S., Paterson, B., Acorn, S., Canam, C., Joachim, G. and Jillings, C. 2002. Chronic illness experience: insights from a metastudy. *Qualitative Health Research*, 12, 437–452.

Tomlinson, J. 2014. Lessons from 'the other side': teaching and learning from doctors' illness narratives. *Student BMJ*, 22, 22–23.

Weatherhead, S. and Todd, D. 2014. *Narrative Approaches to Brain Injury*, London, Karnac Books.

Wilson, B. A., Robertson, C. and Mole, J. 2015. *Identity Unknown: How Acute Brain Disease Can Destroy Knowledge of Oneself and Others*, Hove, Psychology Press.

Wilson, B. A., Winegardner, J. and Ashworth, F. 2014. *Life After Brain Injury: Survivors' Stories*, Hove, Psychology Press.

Chapter 10

Concluding remarks

There were several aims when the idea of this book first emerged, and it is hoped that the book has come close to achieving them.

There is so little written about encephalitis it is hoped Chapter 2 provides a neat overview. Encephalitis is a continually changing entity, and what is written there will continue developing. It was only in 2007 that we significantly increased our knowledge and subsequently developed improved diagnostics for certain forms of autoimmune encephalitis. As this book is being completed further indications continue to emerge of the changing nature of the condition with what appears to be evidence of a new borna-virus, spread by captive, rare-breed squirrels, resulting in the deaths of three of their owners from encephalitis. Nevertheless it is hoped Chapter 2 provides a broad overview which, through some simplification, is relatively easy to understand, in what is an often complex condition.

Chapters 4–7 really are the cornerstone of this book. To my knowledge it is the first published compilation of encephalitis-survivor experiences. It is hoped that the book has provided a medium through which people affected – and their families – have a voice and an opportunity to convey their extraordinary stories and wise words to those that will sadly, but undoubtedly, follow them. It has not been possible to include every type of encephalitis nor every type of outcome of course, but it is hoped that the book provides a sufficient range to illustrate the wide variety of experiences and ways that people find to cope.

Chapters 3 and 8 provided much more detail about the role that people's stories have, both in history and in the present day. It is fascinating to realise the long-held status that people's narratives have had, and how much they have, and will continue to, shape our behaviours and other people's perceptions of us. It is extraordinary to think that they might help us reframe and change our future too. As well as looking in some detail at the role and impact of writing stories, the book also took the unique step of looking in detail at the role and influence that reading other people's stories has. It is heartening to learn the very important role that stories play in people's recovery and in helping them find better ways of coping. It is also important to take on board that, for a few, engaging with stories is not a source of comfort and therefore more detailed thinking about alternative ways of supporting these people should be considered.

Finally Chapter 9 considered the role of narratives among professionals, and provided a few thoughts about how narratives might be used in a variety of practice and personal settings. Areas for future focus and research were considered including a greater focus upon the impact of stories on those who read them, and a call to action of sorts, championing more research with people with brain injuries including those whose injuries may not present an easy research pathway. There is no doubt that a more mindful approach to narratives can not only improve the patient experience, but also the enjoyment and practice of people who work in healthcare with those who are often experiencing some of their darkest times.

This book did not set out to provide all the evidence, nor all the answers, and no doubt much more could be written. What is hoped is that it offers a beginning, a catalyst for generating more thought around the experiences of those affected by encephalitis, the use of narratives among this population, and maybe those affected by other forms of neuro-illness and disability.

Index

absence seizures, Sophie's story 44, 45
acceptance 16, 86, 138, 141
Aciclovir 9, 18, 52
acquired brain injury (ABI) 12, 15,
    16; *see also* brain injury
Adams, J. 145–6, 175
Addis, D. R. 156
adjustment process 12
Alcauskas, M. 29, 30, 173, 174, 181,
    182
alcohol use, Roy's story 40, 54
anger 12, 86, 110, 146, 162; Jean and
    Phillip's story 84; management 87,
    111; Roy's story 37, 40, 42
anterograde amnesia 83, 157
anti-fungal treatment 9
anti-inflammatory drugs 52
anti-NMDA receptor encephalitis 8,
    55
antibiotics 9
antibodies 8, 62–3
antiviral drug treatment *see* Aciclovir
anxiety 15, 61; caregivers 14; Jean
    and Phillip's story 68, 82, 84;
    Sophie's story 48
Armangue, T. 62
Arntfield, S. 182
Aronson, J. K. 139, 140
Atkin, K. 10, 13, 25, 26, 27, 28, 31,
    138, 144, 161

autoimmune encephalitis (AE) 5, 6,
    8, 9, 30, 62–4
Awakenings (Sacks) 30

bacterial causes 9
Baddeley, A. D. 156, 158
Baikie, K. A. 139
Bajo, A. 174
Barker, L. 85
Barrow, R. 179
Barthes, R. 25, 31
Bauby, J.-D. 30
behavioural problems 10, 13, 14, 84
Bell, S. 25, 138, 144, 145
belonging, collective 142, 152–3, 164
Bennett, B. 31, 173, 175, 181
Bernat, J. L. 181–2
bias in research 159, 160–1
Biderman, D. 137
biomedical model 18
biopsy, brain tissue 8
Blakeslee, S. 29
blood tests 8
body, and disease 25–6
body–mind separation 18
Booss, J. 82
Boss, P. 112
brain imaging 8, 52
brain injury 16; acquired 12, 15, 16;
    hidden nature of 11–13, 19;

brain injury *continued*
    traumatic 15, 16; *see also* acquired
    brain injury (ABI)
Brain on Fire (Cahalan) 30
brain tissue biopsy 8
British Medical Journal (BMJ) 31
Britton, P. N. 9
Broks, P. 29
Bruner, J. 138, 139
burn-out, neurologist 174, 181–2
Bury, M. 18, 25, 26, 144
Buteri-Prinzi, F. 109, 114, 115
Butler, K. 86

Cahalan, S., *Brain on Fire* 30
Calvert, M. 137, 142, 148, 173, 175,
    176, 181
capacity concerns, and use of
    narratives 159, 164, 178, 179, 184
Carbaugh, D. 145
cardio-vascular accident (stroke) 15,
    16
caregivers: children as 114;
    emotional stages 86; psychological
    difficulties 14; sense of identity 14
Carroll, L. W. 25, 26, 27, 173, 176
case histories 29
Cashman, J. 142, 143, 173
Cassuto, L. 29
cerebro-spinal fluid 8, 51–2, 62
Chamberlain, D. 111, 137, 175
Charmaz, K. 137, 139
Charon, R. 26, 28, 29, 30, 139, 173,
    174, 181, 182, 184
Chaudhuri, A. 7, 18
Chesson, R. 139, 173, 177
children with brain injured parents
    113–14; caregiving role 114;
    support services for 114; *see also*
    Thomas's story
chronic encephalitis 5
Clark, D. 138, 139, 173, 181
Cloute, K. 2, 160, 174, 183

cognitive behaviour therapy (CBT)
    27, 57
cognitive problems, and research
    158–9, 178, 179
collaborative narratives 160
communication: and health
    professionals 145–7; narratives as
    medium for 144, 164; research and
    problems with 158–9, 178, 179
confabulation 156
consent, and use of narratives 159,
    164, 178, 179, 184
consequences of encephalitis 7–8, 10,
    11, 19
Cooper, J. 18
Couser, T. 29, 30
Cox, K. 173
Cracknell, J. 30
Crosson, B. 84
Crow, L. 146, 147
CT (computerised tomography)
    scans 8

Daisley, A. 108–15, 116
David's story 96–103, 111, 116
death from encephalitis *see* mortality
    rates; Tiggy's story
delusions 61, 62, 82
denial 86, 111, 161, 184
depression 12, 15, 61; caregivers 14,
    86; Jean and Phillip's story 68, 69,
    70, 82, 85; Ross's story 57, 60
Desjardins, M. 183
despair 12, 109
Dewar, B.-K. 14, 85
dexamethasone 52
diagnosis 8–9, 63, 82–3
disease, embodiment of 25–6
Divinsky, M. 181
Dowell, E. 154
drug treatment 9, 18, 52, 63
drugs (recreational), Roy's story 40,
    53

Durham, C. 30, 140, 148
dysnarrativia 157

Easton, A. 1, 8, 12, 15, 25, 27, 28,
    31, 87, 139, 142, 148, 161, 164
educative role of neuro-narratives
    148
Edwards, A. R. 114
Edwards, S. 182
Egdell, R. 53, 146
electroencephalograms (EEG) 8
emotional lability 84
emotional problems 10, 84
encephalitis 4–22; anti-NMDA
    receptor 8, 55; autoimmune 5, 6,
    8, 9, 30, 62–4; consequences of
    7–8, 10, 11, 19; diagnosis 8–9, 63,
    82–3; herpes simplex 9, 18, 52,
    53, 81–4; and identity 13–14,
    85–6, 137; incidence of 6–7;
    infectious 5, 6, 9, 64; Japanese 9,
    10; lethargica 146; mortality rates
    7, 18; outcomes 4, 15–16; post-
    infectious (autoimmune) 5;
    prevention of 7, 9–10; primary
    causes 5; and quality of life
    15–16; rabies 10; rates of
    recovery 7, 15; social
    consequences of 13–14; sub-
    acute, chronic and slow 5;
    symptoms 6, 51, 82; tick-borne 9,
    10; treatment 9, 63; what it is 5–6;
    see also drug treatment
Encephalitis Society 17, 43, 51, 53,
    80, 104–6, 127, 131–2, 135, 141,
    145
epilepsy 4, 10, 53; Sophie's story
    44–6
European Brain Injury Questionnaire
    (EBIQ) 15
Evans, J. 10, 13
executive functioning 83–4
externalising feelings 141–2

families 13–14, 86; coping strategies
    112; finding new meaning 112;
    hope narratives 109, 112, 113;
    relations with health professionals
    110–11; resilience 112–13; sense
    of loss 109–10, 112; social support
    networks 87; struggles with health/
    social care system 111; see also
    children with brain injured parents;
    parent stories
Farris Kurtz, L. 31, 180
fatigue 4, 10; Sophie's story 47, 48
Feinberg, T. E. 175
fever 51, 82
Fleminger, S. 11, 174
Flynn, K. 173
Foust, R. J. 147
Fraas, M. R. 137, 142, 148, 173, 175,
    176, 181
Francis, R. 111
Frank, A. W. 17, 112, 140, 142, 143,
    144, 145, 155, 158, 175, 178
frontal lobes 83, 84
fungal causes 9

Galski, T. 144
Gan, C. 113
Gelech, J. M. 183
Glover, A. 142, 147
Godwin, E. 113
Gracey, F. 14, 85
Granerod, J. 7
Green, M. C. 154
Greenhalgh, T. 28
grief 12, 109; Tiggy's story 120, 126,
    127, 129
group membership 142, 152–3
grown self model 143
guilt 83, 110, 112, 115–16

hallucinations 62
Hammond, R. 30, 148
Hare, P. 145

Harrington, A. 28, 138, 173, 175
Harrison, B. 183
Haslam, A. 14, 142
headache 51, 82
health professionals: family relations
    with 110–11; and narratives 144–8,
    173–7, 181–3; peer supervision
    181, 182; reflective practice 181–3
healthcare: patient–physician joint
    management in 27–8; patients
    central role in 18, 26–7
healthcare campaigns 176
herpes simplex encephalitis 9, 18, 52,
    53, 81–4
hidden nature of brain injury 11–13,
    19
Hill, H. 147
HIV 8
Hodgson, J. 80–7
Hogan, B. A. 147, 148, 176, 177, 181
Hogarth, S. 25
hope 109, 112, 113, 142
hopelessness 112
Hoppitt, T. 7
House (TV series) 30
Hurwitz, B. 28, 30
Hyden, L.-C. 137, 138, 139, 142, 175

identity 13–14, 85–6, 137
immune-modulatory therapies 9
immunoglobulin exchange 9
incidence of encephalitis 6–7
infectious encephalitis 5, 6, 9, 64
internet 31
Irani, S. 61–4
isolation, sense of 15, 28, 142, 143,
    144, 152, 153, 164, 179

Jacobson, L. 86
Japanese encephalitis 9, 10
Jean and Phillip's story 67–79;
    neuropsychological perspective of
    81–7 (emotion and behaviour 84;

executive functioning 83–4;
    memory 83; reduced self-awareness
    84–5; sense of self 85–6)
Jenkins, R. 13
Jewson, N. D. 25
Jmor, F. 7
Johansen, R. K. 30, 145, 181
Johnny see Tiggy's story
Jones, C. A. 1, 138, 139, 142
Jumisko, E. 146

Kalitzkus, V. 25, 182
Kapur, N. 29, 182
Karlawish, J. 161, 184
Kay's story 90–6, 115–16
Kelly, E. 85
Kemp, M. 30, 140, 142, 143
Kendall, E. 27
Kennedy, P. G. E. 7, 18
Kilty, S. 115
Kirk, U. 85
Kneen, R. 9
Kreiswirth, M. 1, 28
Kübler-Ross, E. 86
Kuhn, A. 158

Lancet 31
Langewitz, W. 175
Lanza, M. 147
Lapotaire, J. 30
Lawton, J. 137, 142, 159, 173
Lezak, M. D. 14, 82
LGI1 antibodies 62
Lillrank, A. 139, 144, 148
limbic structures 83, 84
Lorenz, L. 1–2, 14, 147, 160, 173,
    178, 181, 182
loss: ambiguous 112; sense of 18,
    109–10, 112, 140
low socio-economic groups 180
lumbar puncture (spinal tap) 8, 51–2
Luria, A. 29, 139; The Man with a
    Shattered World 141

McAdams, D. 138
McCann, A. 148
McLean, A. M. 142
magnetic resonance imaging (MRI)
  8, 52
Man, D. W. K. 14, 146
Man with a Shattered World, The
  (Luria) 141
Markham, K. 148
Marks, L. 25
Marshall, J. 142
Matthiessen, P. 25, 161, 182
Mattingly, C. 145, 158
Mays, N. 160
medicine, and narratives 25–8, 32
Medved, M. I. 139
Meisel, Z. 161, 184
memory problems 4, 10, 12, 13, 14,
  53–4, 83; and narratives 154–8;
  Ross's story 60; short-term 46;
  Sophie's story 44, 46–7, 48–9;
  strategies to help with 54; verbal
  memory 47, 53
Michael, B. D. 10, 51, 53
mind–body separation 18
mindfulness 57
Minnes, P. 110
minority ethnic groups 180
mood 12, 13, 14; see also depression
Moorthi, S. 7, 15
Morris, P. 140
Morris, S. D. 111
mortality rates 7, 18
Morton, N. 85
mosquitoes 10
MRI (magnetic resonance imaging)
  8, 52
Muenchberger, H. 137
Mullan, F. 175
Murray, M. 25, 142

narrative models 155
narratives 1–2, 3; caution in use of

183–4; collaborative 160; and
  health professionals 144–8, 173–7,
  181–3; and healthcare campaigns
  176; historical context of 16,
  17–19, 24–35; and medicine 25–8,
  32; in reflective practice 181–3; in
  rehabilitation 177–8; in research
  178–80, 183–4; restitution 143;
  spoken 160; as therapeutic tool
  177, 183; in voluntary and not-for-
  profit sector 180; see also neuro-
  narratives
Nelson, E. C. 63
Nettleton, S. 18, 26, 155
neuro-narratives 24, 28–31, 32,
  137–72; and academic literature
  160; and authors 139–48;
  collective belonging and sharing of
  142, 152–3, 164; collective reasons
  for reading 150–3; and comparing
  experiences 150–1; creating
  perspective through 152, 164;
  creating positives through 142–3,
  164; educative/guidance role of
  148; and externalisation of feelings
  141–2; and health professionals
  144–8; and loss 140; as medium of
  communication 144, 164; and
  memory problems 154–8; missing
  voices and factors that complicate
  154–64; orderliness and process of
  writing 140–1; personal reasons for
  reading 149–50; personal reasons
  for writing 139–43, 163–4; public
  reasons for writing 143–8; reading,
  impact of 148–53, 160, 164; and
  reconstruction of self 140;
  reliability of 159, 160; and sense of
  validation 142, 151, 164; as source
  of distress 161–3; for
  understanding and making sense
  138, 139, 142–3, 149–50, 153, 163
neurologist burn-out 174, 181–2

neurology 61–2
neuropsychology 53
Nightingale, S. 8
NMDA receptor antibodies 62, 63
Noble, I. 142, 143
Nochi, M. 85, 137, 138, 143, 155, 156–7, 158, 174, 175
not-for-profit sector, narratives in 180

O'Brien, M. 138, 139, 173, 181
obsessive compulsive behaviours 15, 54; Roy's story 39
obstructive sleep apnoea (OSA) 60
occupational therapy 53
O'Connor, R. J. 178
Opher, S. 144, 181, 182
order, sense of 140–1
outcomes 4, 15–16
Ownsworth, T. 85, 137

panic attacks 62; Ross's story 57
Pape, S. 148
parent stories 109–13; fears for the future 116; finding new meaning 112; guilt 115–16; hope 109, 112; relations with health professionals 110–11; resilience 112–13; struggles with health/social care system 111; themes of loss 109–10, 112; see also David's story; Kay's story; Tiggy's story
partial seizures, Sophie's story 45
Paterson, B. 155, 159
patient organisations and support groups 31, 142, 180
patients, central role in healthcare 18, 26–7, 32
peer supervision, health professionals 181, 182, 183
Pennebaker, J. W. 175
Perlesz, A. 114
personality changes 4, 10, 54; Roy's story 39–40

Pewter, S. M. 7, 15
Phillip see Jean and Phillip's story
Phillips, J. 138, 139
physiotherapy 53
Pickard, S. 155
Pinhasi-Vittorio, L. 139, 140, 173, 175, 181
plasma exchange 9, 63
poetry 140, 144
Polkinghorne, D. 137, 138
polymerase chain reaction (PCR) test 52
Ponsford, J. 11, 146
Pope, C. 160
Porter, R. 18, 25, 26
positives, creating 142–3, 164
post-infectious (autoimmune) encephalitis 5
prevention: of encephalitis 9–10; of ill-health 27
Price-Lackey, P. 142, 143, 173
Prigatano, G. 173, 177
psychiatry 61–2
psychological difficulties 12; caregivers 14; see also anger; anxiety; depression; emotional problems; mood
Public Health England 7, 52
public and neuro-narratives 28–31

quality of life 15–16

rabies encephalitis 10
Ragan, S. 175
Ramachandran, V. S. 29
Ramanuj, P. P. 15
Raschilas, F. 7
reconstruction of self 140
recovery rates 7, 15
referrals 16
reflective practice 181–3
rehabilitation 53, 86–7, 111; narratives in 177–8; Sophie's story 44

reliability of narratives 159, 160
research: bias in 159, 160–1;
    capacity concerns and 159, 164,
    178, 179, 184; cognitive problems
    and 158–9, 178, 179;
    communication problems and
    158–9, 178, 179; and consent 159,
    164, 178, 179, 184; exclusion of
    populations in 158–9, 179;
    narratives in 178–80, 183–4
resilience 109, 112–13, 114, 115
restitution narratives 143
retrograde amnesia 83, 157
Richmond, L. 30
Rier, D. A. 12, 142, 156
Riessman, C. K. 138
Robinson, M. 140, 175, 177
Ross's story 55–61; depression 57,
    60; memory problems 60;
    neurological perspective of 61–4;
    panic attacks 57; sleep problems
    56, 57, 59–60
Roy's story 36, 37–42, 64; alcohol and
    drug use 40, 54; anger 37, 40, 42;
    neurological perspective of 50–4;
    obsessive compulsive behaviours
    39; personality change 39–40;
    seizures 38–9, 40–1; violence 40
Rytina, C. 4

Sacks, O. 29, 146, 158; Awakenings
    30
Saver, J. L. 154, 156, 157
Schacter, D. L. 156
Scholz, U. 27
Scott-Findlay, S. 155, 159
Segal, D. 2, 10, 137, 138, 154, 160,
    174, 183
Seidman, I. 160
seizures 51, 53, 62, 82; absence 44,
    45; partial seizures 45; Roy's story
    38–9, 40–1; Sophie's story 43–4,
    45–6; tonic-clonic 43–4, 45, 46

self: reconstruction of 140, 164;
    sense of 18, 85–6, 137, 140
self-awareness problems 84–5
self-care 18, 26
self-management 18, 26–7
Shapiro, J. 2, 161
short-term memory 157; Sophie's
    story 46
Sigsbee, B. 181–2
Simmonds, L. 178, 181
Sköldenberg, B. 52
Skultans, V. 138, 142
sleep problems 62; Ross's story 56,
    57, 59–60
Smith, B. 142
Smith, C. 1, 140, 147, 182
social care services 111
social consequences 13
social support networks/services 87,
    114, 115
Solomon, A. 114–15
Solomon, T. 5, 9, 10, 31, 50–4, 64
Sophie's story 43–9, 50, 64; anxiety
    48; fatigue 47, 48; medication 46;
    memory problems 44, 46–7, 48–9;
    neurological perspective of 50–4;
    rehabilitation 44; seizures 43–4,
    45–6; symptomatic epilepsy 44–6;
    word-finding difficulties 47;
    working life 47–8, 54
Sorum, P. C. 145, 173
Sparkes, A. 142
speech deficits 62
spinal tap (lumbar puncture) 8, 51–2
spoken narratives 160
spouses see Jean and Phillip's story
Squire, F. 1, 147, 182
Stapley, S. 8, 13, 15
steroid treatment 9, 63
Stone, S. D. 11
stroke 15, 16
Stuss, D. T. 85
sub-acute encephalitis 5

sub-acute sclerosing pan-encephalitis (SSPE) 5
symptoms of encephalitis 6, 51, 82

Tattersall, R. 27
Teasdale, T. W. 15
temporal lobes 83, 84
Teske, J. A. 138
Thomas, R. H. and Thomas, N. J. P. 31
Thomas's story 104–9, 113–14
Thorne, S. 157, 159, 174
tick-borne encephalitis 9, 10
Tiggy's story 119–36
Todd, D. 174, 176
Toglia, J. 85
Tomlinson, J. 182
tonic-clonic seizures, Sophie's story 43–4, 45, 46
traumatic brain injury 15, 16
treatment of encephalitis 9, 63; *see also* drug treatment
Tselis, A. 82
tumours 8, 9
Turkstra, L. S. 1, 138, 139, 142
Turner, B. 30

uncertainty 12

vaccination 7, 9–10
validation 142, 151, 164

Vannatta, J. 175
verbal memory 47, 53
violence, Roy's story 40
voluntary sector, narratives in 180

Wade, S. L. 110
Walsh, F. 112
Warlow, C. 159
Wearing, C. 141, 157–8, 165n2
Wearing, D. 157–8, 165n2
Weatherhead, S. 174, 176
Webb, D. 12, 14, 157
Webster, G. 109, 113
Whitehead, L. C. 137, 142
Wilhelm, K. 139
Williams, G. 138
Williams, H. W. 10, 13
Wills, E. 144, 181, 182
Wilson, B. A. 10, 147, 156, 157, 158, 173
Woody, J. M. 138
word-finding difficulties 53; Sophie's story 47
working life 54; Sophie's story 47–8, 54
Wotton, D. 25

Yeates, G. 154
Young, K. 154, 156, 157

Zeman, A. 62

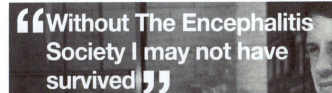

"Without The Encephalitis Society I may not have survived"

Encephalitis is inflammation of the brain caused by infection or when a person's immune system goes wrong. Acquired brain injury, and in some cases death, are outcomes of the condition.

Encephalitis is a thief

It robs people of abilities that most of us take for granted; it can rob families of their loved ones and even in those families where the person affected survives, it often leaves them experiencing a complicated form of bereavement for the person they once knew.

The Encephalitis Society **supports** people in piecing their lives back together following Encephalitis. We also raise **awareness** of the condition and collaborate on **research** trying to recognise and treat the condition and its consequences more effectively.

Find out more
www.encephalitis.info